MESSENGERS

JULIAN SAYARER has made many journeys by bicycle and as a hitchhiker, writing books and articles that give a passing view of the world's roadsides. In 2009, he broke the 18,000-mile world record for a circumnavigation by bicycle, a story told in his first book, *Life Cycles*. He now lives in London.

Arcadia Books Ltd
139 Highlever Road
London W10 6PH

www.arcadiabooks.co.uk

First published in the United Kingdom by Arcadia Books 2016
Copyright © Julian Sayarer 2016
Map illustrations: Jessica Templeton Smith

A catalogue record for this book is available from the British Library.

ISBN 978-1-910050-76-7

Typeset in Garamond by MacGuru Ltd
Printed and bound by CPI Group (UK) Ltd, Croydon CRO 4YY

ARCADIA BOOKS DISTRIBUTORS ARE AS FOLLOWS:

in the UK and elsewhere in Europe:
Grantham Book Services (GBS)
Trent Road
Grantham
Lincolnshire
NG31 7XQ

in the USA and Canada:
Dufour Editions
PO Box 7
Chester Springs
PA 19425

in Australia/New Zealand:
NewSouth Books
University of New South Wales
Sydney NSW 2052

MESSENGERS

JULIAN SAYARER

A

DOCKETS

RIVERTHAMESRIVERTHAMESRIVERTH

#1, 38, 41, 43

#34, 44

#10

#12, 14, 26, 40

#16, 18, 24, 30

#5, 15, 29, 36

#3, 13, 17, 25, 32, 35

#23, 28

#8

#19, 31, 42

#20

#2, 4

THAMESRIVERTHAMESRIVER

THAMESRIVER

THAMESRIVERTHAMESRIVERTHAMESRIVER

#7, 9, 11, 21, 22, 27

#6, 33, 39

AMESRIVER

#37

For the Pigeons

Prologue

It was outside the Harp, Charing Cross station just over the road, that point from which all distances to London are still measured. My bicycle was leaning beside me as always: old track frame, fixed gear, cobbled together from bits and pieces after the last had been stolen. The sun catches the fracture in the frame, the repair of which had prompted so many conversations with those who liked bikes … chrome, welded together with a seam of bronze fillet braze, bicycle scar tissue at the top of the seat tube. The phone rang, summoned me cheerfully from my pocket. It was Hendriks, the agent who would eventually come in for me, voice as reverend as ever. We exchanged hellos, civilities, he cut to the chase.

'They want another one.'

'A manuscript?'

'Yes. A manuscript.'

'About what?'

'About bicycles … about bicycles, and the city.'

'*Bicycles*? … you know I've had enough of writing bicycles.'

'But your first went down so well … everyone who doesn't hate it thinks the thing really rather good.' I aim to interject, but Hendriks keeps on, 'And more's the point … it's what they want.'

'But I'm tired of it … there's so much more to write … I don't want to write any more about punctures and brake pads!'

'But think big, Emre … The City!' Hendriks is getting excited, blowing big time in his words but always with that same twentieth-century patience, ever a tendency to sound like a man speaking sense. 'The capital of the world … on two wheels! Listen. Everyone, so it seems, loves bicycles lately. They're so, so life-affirming! The spirit of the human, a *joie de vivre! Life as it could be!*'

'I know. That's why I ride one.'

'So … write it!'

'Can't we just leave it. Can't we let people think it for themselves?'

'If you don't, then mark my words, they will find a name instead of yours to put on that spine!'

He has a point, and besides, I sense it's foregone … look to the next battle.

'But afterwards, after this one, you promise we'll have something else … another subject. They'll let me write my modern classic, and no bicycles?'

'Yes, Emre, just one more, and then your classic.' Hendriks' tone shifts, 'But enough of books, how are you … how is the return treating you?'

I ponder as wind blows through, tears over the microphone so that I hear myself, my stretched, echoing words: 'It could've been kinder.'

Direct, Hendriks comes back, 'How do you mean?'

'Well … believe it or not, I actually thought that whole cycling around the world protest might have changed a thing or two, made people think differently about banks, big finance … corporate adventure and all the marketing rubbish.'

'Ah! The tenacity of youth. Don't be so hard on yourself, Emre …' the signal breaks to a muted distortion, then resurrects, '… and age … is what ideals are all about, don't you think?'

'I'm sorry, Hendriks, I didn't hear you … the signal.'

He repeats, some agitation, 'I said that if the young don't aspire to change the world, then who will? It strikes me that these days …' a police car pulls from its parking space, 'there seem to be …' sirens flare, screech murder, fire and madness, blue light over white noise, fading back to Hendriks … 'Emre? I mean … surely that's the most important thing in all this?'

'Sorry, Hendriks, there was a police car … I missed the last part.'

I hear an impatience, a sigh. 'It's as if nobody hears a word that anyone says any longer, or even cares to listen.'

'I got that … loud and clear.'

Hendriks softens, tries again, 'So tell me, what's proving so difficult?'

'Well … the couriering … is hard. I mean, I still remember eagles in the dawn over the Steppe, and people wanting to buy me dinner because they loved that I was cycling across America.' A truck passes, refrigerator unit growling loud. I pause. 'And now I'm just in everybody's way and everybody's in mine, and it all feels such a long way off … as if everything is so temporary all of a sudden. I'm just making deliveries that don't mean anything.'

The wind goes panting down the street, but it's been a long time since anybody asked this, good to get it off the chest. 'And my identity … it's like it's been replaced by the number the radio controller calls when there's a job to collect.'

There's a pause on the line. 'I'm sorry, Emre, you're breaking up quite badly now. You said something about a new job?'

Eyes roll. 'Forget it … forget it, Hendriks. Thanks for the call … I'll get on with the story.'

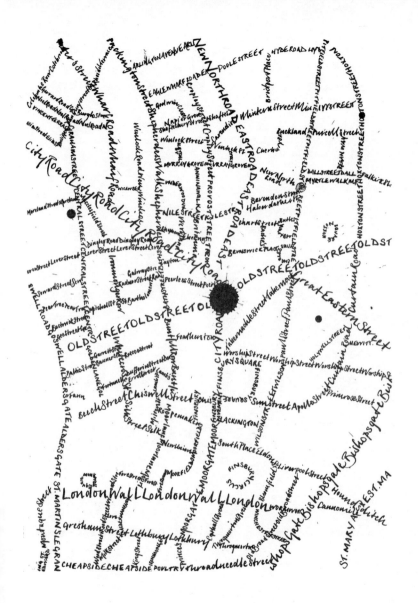

Part I

BACK ON THE ROAD

2 April 2010 – Papillon

One night we took it back, we took it all back, made the city ours again. One of the girls from another firm was leaving, a French rider returning home to Paris, her third attempt at quitting London and the family of riders she'd seen each day for a decade. I was riding home that Friday, and standing at that same corner of Great Eastern and Old Street was Two-Four. We hadn't seen one another in a while: he had shaved off his curls of hair, still kept the purple bags beneath his eyes from all the dope his mother wished he'd stop smoking. He told me he'd found a part-time job making mirror balls at a workshop in Islington, laying shards of glass into large spheres to be hung from ceilings. I laughed, and from bent teeth he gave that grin of his, lifting his shoulders nonchalantly. He tells me there's a race on, looks at me. 'You doing it?'

I think to myself, eyebrows up, it's only been a few months since I got back to the circuit, but whatever, I'm enthusiastic. 'Go on then … I'm out of practice, probably not as good at streets as I was a year ago, but why not?'

Papillon was the name of the race. They hold them every so often in the courier world, the alleycats in which couriers, joined by salaried professionals who had fallen for the courier image, would race the streets of London. Two-Four and I bought cans of beer, stood on the kerb outside the Foundry, closed for the redevelopment awaiting that brick and mortar. Two-Four looked up at the building, shut behind boards painted with a white rabbit, half the letters of the old name pulled down so that instead it read only F-U-R-Y. He shakes his head as he speaks:

'Can't believe they closed it.'

'They're opening a new hotel, aren't they?'

'Yeah … because we need another of those.'

He was still wearing his courier bag, fastened with a seatbelt buckle, the radio still on his chest. He stood with his arms crossed, can of beer held in the fold of his arm, Lycra leggings under jeans cut short.

'I didn't come that often,' I murmured, finding my voice, 'but it was amazing to know that you had something in common with everyone else here. It was always good to drop in and see how people were doing.'

Other riders had started to gather, bicycles pulling onto pavement … more couriers, lenses around their faces, radios on chests. Two-Four grew animated, where normally he so often seemed happy to let life wash over him.

'It was such a great place … that turntable in the basement, where they used to take deliveries of metal back when this was a working building. The turntable used to turn trucks around on the spot,' Two-Four went on. 'I remember watching Seven-One down there one night, taller than everyone else, with his beer can in the air and shouting "*Fucking yeah!*" as they flicked the switch and the turntable started rotating with everyone still standing on it dancing.' Two-Four smiles with dismay. 'There'll never be a place like this again.'

I pause a while, take a swallow of beer, let out some introspection. 'The people who come next, they won't know these places existed to begin with.'

Two-Four looks at me, arms folded, beer can under armpit. His eyes roll up as he cocks his head to one side, purses his lips with a thought, drinks down the beer with a shrug.

The alleycat is to be a French affair, an homage to the outgoing rider, checkpoints set accordingly along a French theme. It's well after dark before we are due to set out, by which time riders have started to arrive from all London's firms. Uniforms of green, blue and pink gather together, anticipation growing as bicycles are leant against one another and riders start to drink, the streetlights slicing frames and spokes into shadows on the pavement. Some riders, those nursing injuries or without the energy for the race after a week of work, would stay at the Foundry and wait on our return. Clean-cut competitors begin to appear as evening deepens, bringing with them expensive road bikes and Lycra jerseys, the employees of the Shoreditch design agencies showing up after leaving their desks. Couriers call them '*fakengers*', resent the appropriation of their aesthetic, shoot disapproving glances obliquely at the newcomers.

Two-Four brings me up to speed with his life and tells me about his last alleycat: the fox hunt. Excited, he talks of how he'd pinned a bushy tail to his jeans, attached a gallon bladder of white paint to the back of his bike, opened a tap and set off into the night ... a two-minute head start before the pack started chasing down his trail. A girl appears out of the crowd, interrupts Two-Four to hand us an entry card in laminated plastic: a butterfly lifting free with a bicycle lock. We slip them into our spokes, pay our fivers, and then, from her bag, she pulls a pile of small papers. She licks a finger, the nail painted with chipped polish. The paper checklist comes towards us, other riders already leaving as we grab the papers from her hands, check the route.

We must ride to Café des Amis, Tottenham Court Road: price of a bacon roll and cup of tea. Madame Tussaud's: the entrance price for a child with one adult. Agent Provocateur, the lingerie shop down by Sloane Square: what colour stockings on the mannequin in the window? Ride to Petty France: get your race slip signed. Ride to French Ordinary Court: get your race slip signed. What's the name of the patisserie on Judd Street? We scarper.

Two-Four and I jump for our bikes, dart into the night, legs turning fast as we roll out. Some way down the road we find two others on our rear wheels: one in a Lycra jersey, the other in a grey top with a sock hat pert on top of his head. We shout at one another: directions, shortcuts. We cut through the traffic, voices snatched at by engines as we head west in a hurry.

'There's only French Ordinary Court in the east, it's off Fenchurch Street. Take the Euston Road for Madame Tussaud's, then into the middle.' A lorry roars past, competes for attention, we ride in its wake, slip back together. 'Petty France is Westminster, turns into Broadway ... round the back of St James's. We'll take the Embankment east to finish, right? Keep it in a circle!'

We ride: the four of us in a pack, close together, enfilade. We take turns to set a lead as the other three hang to the one ahead, sucking on the back wheel until the pace of the leader wanes and another picks up duties on the front. We ride through King's Cross, one after another banking left into that dog leg before filing into a flat line: four abreast down two lanes of the Euston Road, a wind pressing us along at 30mph, eyes starting to water with the speed. The city opens to us, traffic approaching up ahead, cars backed up so that we peel, split in two, ride two to the left and two to the right of the jam. Handlebars, cut narrow for just this purpose, plunge between wing mirrors either side. You hear the flailing straps of your bag tapping the bodywork of cars, the stereo too loud for a driver to notice as life rushes by outside. We roll beneath the wheels of the lorries, tyres above head-height ... we head through the blind spot, the half of the vehicle where the driver has no idea what's there. A swinging hatch, the rear of a cement truck ... you pray the lights don't change while you're still under its flank. Red, amber, green, hold your breath, cheeks fill with air and ... *pop!* ... you rush out ahead of the truck, pull in front and dash through those first fifteen metres to safety, to where you know you've appeared from under the radiator and into his windshield, into his vision where he can see you again. We're back, we're riding, four in a line with the cars waiting behind our pace. We shout possible directions to one another: 'Take Edgware Road south. *NO!* Baker Street ... *got to be Baker Street!*' We pull up outside Tussaud's ... £11.50 and breathing deep. Two-Four and I greet the guys we're riding with, never met, the grey hat speaks, breathless: 'I just got back from working as a messenger in

Wellington, New Zealand. Promised myself I'd never race one of these again … but it's just too good.'

Those alleycats … they gave couriers a bad name, make no mistake about that. We'd ride the wrong way against traffic, weaving through the oncoming cars until the railings in the centre of the road abated and we could get back onto the left. Red lights did not exist, the lights did not exist at all. When you spend your life being shunted around the roads, treated like a street urchin and told what to do without thanks for just £250 a week, after not very long you decide that society was not made with you in mind, and as a consequence neither were its rules. If that was the norm anyway, then alleycats took it to new extremes. Ordinarily you stop when it makes sense to do so, when traffic flows in front of you. For an alleycat there is no chance in the world that you stop for anything. Rules are nothing: just watch the traffic, that's all you care about. Watch the traffic and you'll be fine. There comes a peculiar safety in the knowledge that you're not stopping, that you are obeying the hard laws of moving objects rather than those of a road system that had been designed with only cars in mind and without a thought for bicycles.

We move within the traffic like plankton amongst a pod of whales, all four of us on fixed gear bicycles: regressive technology, no freewheel. If the wheel turns, then so does the cog, chain, pedals, legs. Your legs can't stop turning. Two-Four rode without brakes, I had one on the front: your legs are your rear brake, you move your bodyweight forward and resist the pedals to stop the rear wheel. I remember Trafalgar Square that night, coming onto the loop, a tide of traffic circling the island before us. A fixed gear allows such perfect adjustment of speed: none of the crude power of a lever, cable and brakes clutching at the wheel, you just resist the chain until your speed is perfect. One car passes, two metres until the next, you jump back on the gear and accelerate into the flow, weaving in and out, banking down to the right. The pedals never stop spinning, you hope the pedal at its lowest is above the kerbstone at its highest, a scraping of metal as you get your answer and pedal hits kerb on way down. The bike lurches, pivots and you rock back upright, right and then left, peeling down Whitehall. A row of manholes comes up ... *one, two, three* ... a rail of metal along their edge catches the back wheel as you ride over: the wheel is dragged from underneath, snatches away. You pull the handlebars, back wheel snatches back to line. Down Whitehall, down Whitehall where you pass the memorials to the fallen soldiers, the women of World War II, who took to the factories to preserve a nation that ... *not now, Emre! We're racing* ... all that is for another time.

At Petty France we pull up at the checkpoint. A few riders have beaten us there, or else done the circuit in a different order. There's a tall guy, curly hair, dressed in a London Courier Emergency Fund hooded sweatshirt. That was the fund into which riders pitched their money, so that an injured rider could draw a small allowance when a crash left them unable to work. The fund was the only social security of the courier world. I recognise the guy on the checkpoint, he'd sold me the shoes I'm wearing, the cycling shoes I'd pulled on every day for 18,049 miles around the world. I'd met him in his father's bike shop, he'd agreed to sponsor me the shoes at trade price. Riders are thrusting race tickets at him to sign, but as my mouth opens to say hello, he recognises me, calling at his helper on the checkpoint. I remember his words: '*Somebody sign this man's docket ... he achieved something amazing while we were all getting drunk and staying in bed!*'

He slaps me across the back, the two of us with big smiles as he gives a salute and I wave over my shoulder, cycling back into the night ... fleeing the hive with swarms of riders darting from all angles, the sound of rattled spokes as wheels clash against one another.

At Sloane Square the stockings are pink, just like the lights of Blackfriars Bridge, reflecting on the surface of the dark waters as we race back along the Embankment. All London is alight ... fireflies and glow worms shine through the skyline as into the tunnel we race, our echoes chasing behind as we shout at one another to hold the pace. French Ordinary Court is off Fenchurch Street, a marshal hiding in a corner with her face illuminated by a torch, the light clipping at her bare, pale sternum and the tattoo inked there of a saint with arms spread. We race over the cobbles of Leadenhall Market … the cobbl-es, co-bbles, the cobbles they rattle between one another on a patch not yet laid, one stone popping up from beneath a hard tyre, turning over itself in the air to reveal sand in the city with a whispering *sous, sous* … the cobble falling back to earth and cracking *les pavés la plage!* Faces rattling, cheeks turning liquid, electrified, we bounce over the cobbles and suddenly … suddenly they were not cobbles at all. It was pave … yes, dammit! … we were not in London … we were riding the Paris-Roubaix! The goddamn Paris-Roubaix and the final section of pavé: riding the crown, the crest of the ridge, keeping the power down so that you don't fall into the rut, so that the rut doesn't pinch your wheels from beneath you and yes … one last push and we're through. We flash past the large doorway off Leadenhall Street, where once I'd seen a bankeress, drunk to the gills and steaming on a Friday night. There on the flagstones she'd been squatting in her stilettos to take a piss: wobbling, a face full of crotch for all the street to see as the heels toppled like skittles. Lying on her side she burst with laughter but all the time unable to stop herself pissing, laughing on her side, spewing like a dropped bottle of lemonade that's sprung a hole: piss dribbling over one step at a time, bubbling up in white cascade. I shake my head, the memory flies free to join all the others.

You can sense us tiring, the pace must have slackened, though endorphins make up for the slowing speed. We shout less at one another, heads down, all the focus is going into the pedals, pedals, pedals. The night's almost up, coming to an end, race winding down … slipping away as we come into the final mile with a final push. Energy gone and only adrenaline left, heads moving faster than bodies. We make mistakes. We miss a turn. Lights up ahead are changing too soon: lights green, to amber, to red. Four lots of RED are right before our eyes ... no way we're going to make it and no way we can consider stopping either, the finish is all but in sight. After five. Six. Seven red seconds we burst on through, me and Two-Four at the front, a police car at the head of the traffic, ready to pull out as we appear. I see the officers from the corner of my eye: one head, two heads, back and forth, turning with we four cyclists. *Boom-boom-boom-boom.* We're gone. A shake of disbelief flails, receding into the distance. Their mouths open as they look at us, pause a second and then realise they've no time for anything but fist to steering wheel and firing off the horn. We win!

We speed into the traffic, diving through the aisles, cut down Liverpool Street, the Broadgate Octagon: privately owned public space in the centre of London. '*No bikes allowed*' shouts from plaques on walls, private security goons stand yawning in fake police uniforms. We bank high up the curved walls of the Octagon, ride the luge, the snake, plunge back down, race through the gates. We hammer at the pedals as the lights of the Foundry grow slowly. The rider from Wellington is barely rolling, is suffering, head lolling back and forward over his wheels. He goes for his bidon, takes it from the bottle cage but squirts only air and spray into a pleading mouth. Two-Four clocks the empty bottle, reaches for his own and hands it over. From a backstreet a car emerges, I watch as headlights cast them both in black and white, the bottle clasped momentarily by both of their hands and suddenly, suddenly we're 1952 ... we're Coppi and a struggling Bartali on Tormalet.

The Foundry crowd ahead are waiting on the road for signs of life, cheers already going up for two riders vaulting the kerb onto the pavement, arms aloft. A rider jumps from his bike, throws it down like some rock star with a guitar. Feedback: wires spring. Two-Four and I pull to a halt, we hug, our companions arriving just behind as the crowd begins to chant the name of the winning rider. Beers are thrust into our hands, other competitors are rolling slowly to a halt, smiles across faces as chaos peaks and then a calm jubilation flows out to the streets.

Riders continue trickling in, the race at a close as speeches begin. The crowd applauds each name, because we're all heroes tonight, even those arriving last, to stand hands on knees and under heaving chests. I look round flush, sanguine faces, smiles brighter than any streetlight, a flesh-and-blood tribe united in a pool of automobiles. Suddenly everything's all right again, the only thing I need is for this moment to last. For right there, amongst all the vast city, in which we were only ever the messenger boys and girls, in that moment there was no community more united, and no triumph or belonging more complete. Without anyone else even needing to know about it ... London was ours.

Sevenoaks – TN13

In the plains of northern Hungary, riding for Shanghai, I had met a German man, Karsten: a banker from Kent, cycling the Danube to Budapest for his holiday. No matter what they've done, the way they hoodwinked us, I'd still take a straight-talking banker over a self-satisfied charity worker. Karsten was as honest as they come. Fair hair and big smile, a German humour so that, to Karsten, almost everything was worth making a joke out of. We spent a day together on the road: he'd hit me with excitement, right on the shoulder, at the end of every sentence. I'd told him I was riding for Shanghai, headed towards the Gobi. I remember his words. *'My God … you'll never be able to go back!'* I laughed at the time, never expected him to turn out so right. I visited him once … after my return I headed down to his place in Sevenoaks. It transpired Karsten was richer than God. He was ex-Goldman Sachs, had outgrown the squid and yet when I arrived he was standing proud beside an old cement mixer in his garden. He gave the drum a slap. It boomed hello. Karsten shouted: *'Emre! This is my favourite possession, because with it I can build a wall, and a wall is something that actually exists!'*

He shopped at German discount supermarkets, repaired his own punctures, and sewed patches on to old clothes. With a cup of tea we sat eating his wife's chocolate cake, which he referred to as the greatest pleasure in his life.

Despite all that, Karsten still lived for the markets … couldn't help himself. I watched him wring his face despairingly into his kitchen table. *'I wish I didn't know so much,'* he said. *'Money is just a faith, a social lie.'* He sloped off upstairs, went to check his algorithms before bedtime. Don't worry if things seem unfair sometimes – we're all victims at the end of the day.

11 December 2009 – E10

Let me explain what happened, bring these threads together and say straight out that not all of this was written quite within my right mind. Most of this tale happened the wrong side of social mobility and, as with most things, it only makes sense at the end. Social mobility, whatever the precise definition, only really boils down to the bargain whereby those with rights and brains enough to experience injustice, and who are smart enough to articulate that injustice, are given wellbeing enough to shut them up and accept that the system works because it worked for them. At the same time, it is silently accepted that a far greater number will not perceive or articulate their injustice, and so can be anticipated to settle for far less.

For those years as a courier I watched myself flatlining, saw myself preparing for life on the wrong side of the divide in a society where you could bet your last I was going to be forced to settle for less, despite some belief, instilled by education and a sense of what it is to be human, that I deserved something more. I can explain the phenomenon in sophisticated terms, but none of it is much more complicated than ... well ... you shit yourself. Every day, you shit yourself. You fume, you fright, you hate and you panic because you have nothing in this world but the body that you stand in, the ability to use that body in performing manual labour, and nothing in the present to suggest a better future. I'm not disowning all of what's coming in these pages ... it's not all lunacy, some of it falls spot-on and all the more for its perspective from the outside. The thing is, when you have faith in something, whether it's politics or some other belief, that faith guides you through the very many ways and moments in which things just don't quite stack up. When you lose that faith, when the life you're left gives no cause for any sense of fairness, all you can see are inconsistencies. The result is that you come to see people as Others: other races, genders, creeds … those with different stories and those belonging to different wealths. Your own scarcity and frustration bores down on you, as if the world has made you its enemy, with everything and everyone else on an opposing side in a conflict where you are the victim. I'm not suggesting this is universal, I know people far better than me, who would never have found their way to some of the ugly thoughts I reached. But there again, I warn you, some minds will be taken by ideas far worse, more extreme, than any I ever entertained.

All told, that's how you wind up seething, your future mortgaged as you watch men in suits stand around calmly arguing the toss as if everything were under control. Set upon by anxiety you stop thinking rationally … you make poor decisions and cruel judgements. I read academic papers that verified as much … observed similar behaviour in rats subjected to conditions of scarcity. That anybody would liken the behaviour of poor humans and rats is still something that strikes me as altogether quite impolite.

༄

Christmas was hardly the best time to have returned. Fairy lights promised magic through half of London, twinkling at darkness around streets dressed with a nativity cheer far from my own mood. Cycling across continents you contract a case of perspective hard to come by through any other means. When you crawl across the face of the world like that, blessed each day by its beauty and the generosity of the strangers you happen upon, a tender kind of insignificance takes hold. I remember early mornings, back on benches in London's parks, where I would sit alone and see the sun land cold on my chest, see my shadow behind me on the bench, and finally imagine both my shadow and body disappearing, so that it was all the same whether the sun landed on the fabric of my clothes or to thaw the frosted blades of grass beneath. Cycling 110 miles a day had been a cinch next to just one month of life in your mid-twenties in London. Whether the groups in down jackets at café tables, or else couples walking arm-round-shoulder on winter streets, everywhere was an appearance of wellbeing to which I could not relate. I suppose that the solitude of a city explained a lot of it, and mark my words there is no loneliness quite like the one waiting at the centre of a crowd. In comparison, without another soul to be found and 200 miles of Kazakh National Highway 32 to the next village, I'd never been more content.

Sleeplessness didn't much help either. So many hours I must have spent in dark rooms, wide awake but staring at the backs of my eyelids. In those first weeks after the return, there was nothing more terrifying than that moment when head hit pillow and so began the long hours I knew would have to be endured until sleep took me. Then, unconscious, began the countdown to some slight noise of dawn that would disturb and set my brain in motion so that once more I'd be awake, listening as the flight paths reopened for a new day. Lavender became one particularly surprising friend in my attempts to calm myself, and in the front gardens of Islington, green-grey leaves hanging through black railings, riding by I would grab with an outstretched hand and feel it pull free as my bicycle moved on. I'd put the fragrant leaves inside a glove and place a palm across nose and mouth to gulp happy, soothing breaths.

The introspection could only last so long, and my bank balance, rock bottom from the last six months' touring, gave me a maximum two weeks before work became an absolute necessity. In those moments, and to this day, couriering is what would always be waiting for me … like a destructive relationship that you always go back to, despite knowing it's no good for you. In the time apart, you allow yourself to forget how bad it can get, recall only the good bits. Each time you stop you promise yourself it's the last, celebrate the final delivery, relieved to have moved on to better things. You break away and then begin backsliding. Eventually it comes. You're flat broke again, you need the cash, never realised you'd made yourself unemployable. Your CV reads like a Bermuda Triangle, gaps big enough to lose a Cunard but you can't bear the prospect of stacking a shelf or topping a pizza. And so you're back … *'Back on the road'*, as those American riders like to call it. Say what you will about them, Americans have a knack for making any crummy situation sound positive. Sixty daily miles … Monday to Friday, three hundred plus and the worst part being that I'll end up cycling further when there's less work. I'll be too exhausted to put the old politics degree to good use, and even if I can write a few job applications in the evenings, I'll be hard pressed to afford the time off work for the interview. If I'm honest … that's no real problem with the year I've got up ahead … they don't invite me in for interviews so much anymore.

21 December – E10 – Docket #1

The red post bag falls back across my shoulders, collected from a friend's flat near Cable Street and ready to allow for my return to work. The thing has already spent at least a circumnavigation hanging at my back, carried like a toddler along London's endless street. The fabric on one side is loaded with road dirt and dust, while the other looks perfectly clean, but is actually full of my sweat and the dead skin from my back. To be honest, the bag's had it. It leaks. When it rains, my deliveries get wet. I've received severe dressing-downs for showing up with damp paper wearing away and ink smudged on an engineer's technical drawings. There was nothing I could say in my defence. I should fork out the £200 and buy myself a new bag, I know, but that would be to make an investment in my future as a courier, something I tend to avoid at all costs, lest it lead to a situation where I find myself with a future as a courier.

I don't mind admitting I've grown afraid. Circumnavigation, world record, courier – whatever your pedigree it doesn't take so many sweet nothings from a passing skip truck for you to realise you've lost your nerve. I pedal hesitantly. A few crucial years of early twenties separate now from that time when I used to love nothing more than diving for a two-foot gap between a pair of double-deckers, when I'd banter with the cabbie beside me, window down as he revved an engine and promised to shove me off the road. Now though, now I've got the fear in me, the roads scare me. I know that the roads aren't statistically dangerous, they just *feel* dangerous, with the only comfort that old, morbid adage that in couriering the cause of death is less often traffic than suicide. Now and then a courier dies in a road accident, but for the number of hours we put in, the millions of miles we clock up, proportionately we must come out safer than just about anyone else on two wheels.

My own two terms as a rider bore that out: no road fatalities and one suicide. It had been back at the start of my first stint, and you felt it on the circuit, rippling out like a sinking stone, a Chinese whisper through a few hundred radios and nobody naming the actual thing, because everyone had couriering in common and so the very idea of it felt uncomfortably close. I mention it now, only for a moment and only to try and make you appreciate how difficult these lives are, the lives of millions in jobs like it, with little respect from the society they serve and wages suitably low. It's a hard story to tell: if things work out OK then folk will say you've no cause for complaint … and if things don't work out, there's rarely anyone around to listen anyway.

Innards

As a courier I recorded everything, found myself sniffing out a collage of the city, a patchwork of London assembled and stuck together from the leather saddle of my bicycle. The olfactory bulb is large, sits proud and immediate at the front of the brain, so that, for the same reason people snort cocaine through the nose, smell leaves some of the most vivid imprints on a mind.

At Primrose Hill, in summer months, the engine overheating so that bubbling steam rises from the coolant cap in the radiator, a bus struggles up the climb of the road. The smell of hot iron oxide trails out behind, you can taste it in the top of the throat and smell it in the back of your sinus. It lodges there, like eating earth, like sucking on a beetroot, like blood in your mouth. Further south, you smell the hot sugar and margarine cooking on Waterloo Bridge, where a Romanian man caramelises peanuts with a scent that leads the police right to him. They find his pedlar's licence has expired, and with head hanging low, he pushes his cart away. The worst smell in the city comes from the flowers, emptied into the gutters outside offices. A man struggles from the buildings with fifteen kilos of vase, water and dead foliage under each arm, dark orange lily pollen smudged across cheeks. With an outstretched pinkie he pulls down on the door handle so that stagnant water, green from rotting leaves, warmed by the spot lamps and the heat of the office, goes spilling into a drain, rushing with a stench of swamp along the kerbstones.

Trafalgar Square, first thing in the morning, to stop algae from growing in the fountains, you see whole bottles of bleach tipped into the water. When the air is still, before the fumes and noise of traffic arise to disturb all other senses, you smell it hanging all around the forecourt of the National Gallery. If you are there on a Monday, if you start work early enough, you'll see a man with a leather gauntlet and a hawk on his arm, releasing the thing to swoop through the architraves of the gallery. He works in pest control, the hawk a predator to make the pigeons think twice about nesting. The bird watches you over the curve of a yellow beak, and from the corner of its skull, the eye flicks back and forth between you and the handler. A shred of meat waits on the perch, primed to encourage its flight home to the glove.

There are plenty like this, I know ... any number of accounts promising the stories of a *real* London and its characters. There was the old, mutilated alcoholic who'd taken a blade to his leg in an effort to increase begging revenues. He wears three-quarter-length trousers all year round, rolls them up quickly to show off his wounds, and people give money in either pity or disgust, anything to make him disappear. The drug addicts go checking the change trays of parking metres, of phone boxes, ever in search of forgotten coins to help them on their way back to a life with meaning again. I don't pity the drug addicts, not like I used to ... those guys have a clearer purpose in life than the rest of us. It's not only the deadbeats that have it rough. I spent days at the bike shop around the corner from Great Ormond Street and its hospital, where mothers would occasionally come in from their bedside vigil, sad eyes and slow voices as they ask the price of bicycles their child might not get to ride. The comfortable are adept at composing eulogies to this city, as if the suffering of others were life's greatest muse. It isn't very long before you've had enough of suffering ... an awful lot of someone else's misery goes into the safe romanticism that glorifies London.

Down on the streets, life in the city kicks as hard as the death. In the back of a truck on Whitechapel High Street, surrounded by string bags full of onions, a Muslim grocer drops to his knees, facing eternally east and praying to Mecca. On one delivery I found myself holed up in a goods lift, escorted thirty floors up and thirty floors down by a Nigerian evangelical named Innocence. He told me to smile, told me over and over that that night he would pray for me. I still wonder if he got round to it. I once told a homeless man, a Pole begging money, that I'd buy him a sandwich. We walked towards the kiosk on the South Bank, where I kicked myself to see £5 the cheapest sliced bread on offer, but not about to go back on my word. He coughed … *preposterous!* … into his fist, shook his head in sad disgust and apologised gruffly. 'Five pounds! Forget it, my friend! I can't have you pay that for a sandwich!'

Even as the experience slipped away, it was proving a tall order not to be defined by that 18,000-mile circumnavigation, retaking a world record from banks, investment funds and the cycling prop they'd made an ambassador. The courier life I found on London's streets in 2010 had less of that romance I'd known cycling the bayou of Louisiana, or else that corridor between the Gobi and Taklamakan deserts of Uygur, but in its own way, still the bicycle went on quietly saving me from myself on a daily basis. I came to see its turning pedals as some bizarre contraption of the mind … a thought machine with which I would always crank out new ideas and imaginations, visions that injected a life into London's streets as I found them across a year passing.

Riding the city gave a certain continuity to me, a common feature in precarious times, and though it pained me to admit it, the publishers weren't wrong about bicycles. The rest of the city had joined me on two wheels: bankers, lawyers – even the politicians were up for a cycle the day they took on a new brief or were forced to resign. There was something effortlessly down-to-earth, something so human about the whole thing. The fair-weather cyclists had swelled in number, and more than ever before they started persisting into the drizzle and winter, so that at traffic lights where once I'd have waited alone on grey, December evenings, suddenly there'd be a half-dozen of us. Once spring got warm and then summer hit, cycle paths turned bike trains … a line of two wheels and up-down legs that didn't end for a full hour each morning and evening as streams of human capital went rolling to and from work. Despite Londoners being more colourful, less regimented than the northern Europeans, the whole thing had started turning positively Dutch. In the space of a few years, cyclists shifted from unconventional minority to toast of the city, so that a bicycle, coffee and smartphone became the essential ingredients of the modern, aspirational metropolitan.

The die-hard of the cycling community went blue-in-the-face, convinced that this heralded some glorious new age, a new beginning for the downtrodden people of the UK. For myself, I was more sceptical, and I'd watch the impatient cyclist rushing from work, tutting and head-shaking at the child who – in playing on a quiet street one evening – had dared interrupt his record-time journey from the office. The truth, at least it seemed to me, was that we were always going to have arseholes ... but I had rather more hope for a world where the arseholes also rode bicycles. It was an invention that forced us to be that little more in touch with our surroundings and selves – or even better, with one another. In cycling, I still found that same opportunity for independence it had once given me as a teenager riding out of a nowhere town in the Midlands, and as our new economy sought to order every human behaviour for search engine optimisation and algorithms, something about the bicycle defied that logic. In lives of finished products, where we consumed meals, destinations, entertainments and information as it was presented and made ready for us, cycling was a journey the rider had to produce for themselves, confronted by the unremitting calamity of all the life that still existed between A and B. In billboards and window displays, big finance and boutique department stores alike kept chipping away at the humble spirit of the machine, aimed to bend it to commercial ends ... and yet the bicycle seemed able to persist, stay sacred and reproduce its own magic once again.

4 January – E14 – Docket #2

Out along the Highway I rode, made for that left turn that leads into the Isle of Dogs, Canary Wharf and all its glass glowing gold in sun. They say Tower Hamlets is the richest borough in all of Europe during the day, with those banks at work and money coursing through them. Each night, when the suits go home, it goes back to being one of the poorest. The courier office had always been there, down at the tip of Westferry, a small brick building next to a metal hangar full of old vans. From the roof flies the Union Jack, and in front of the building are signs telling staff to stand further away when they're smoking.

I walk back in, first time in six months, immediately faced by the guy who'd given me my first navigational test two years back, assessed how weak or strong my knowledge of London was at the time: which postcodes were linked by which bridges, which road you'd take to which attraction. I remember the ponytail, pulled back tight over his scalp, and with small eyes he stares right through me. I'm new to him, but I'm good with faces, can place him no problem. Two years ago he'd sat me down at that desk in the room behind us now, asked what I'd been doing before couriering. I told him Istanbul, teaching English ... and he told me he'd done the same, in Colombia. Couriering and English teaching are kindred vocations, like clearing houses for the world's souls ... those convinced the world offers something more yet never able to attain it. That day, two years earlier, I remember he'd wiped the back of a short-fingered hand across his nose, gave a great, nostalgic snort: *'Colombia! Ahhh I miss it. Best cocaine I've ever had ... only a tenner a gram.'*

I walk into the kit office. Tony's still there, Tony will always be there. I can never figure out if Tony's small or if the desk they sat him at is huge: covered in maps and clutter, stretching out in front of him as if Tony were working on Barbarossa. He's a good sort: orange hair and wiry frame, pale skin, smiles a lot, which is his disposition rather than a result of having much more than the rest of us to be cheerful about. Tony manages kit. You need to stay the right side of Tony or else end up with dud equipment that leaves you riding back to base for replacements. He steps towards me, hand coming forwards:

'I can't believe you did it! A world-record holder delivering our dockets. We should put it on the website!'

He slaps me on a shoulder, it shrugs and I smile back as Tony goes on looking expectantly at me, waiting for some words befitting the deed. Nothing happens. Tony nods to himself, 'You must still be shell-shocked.' He regathers. 'Greg'll want to see you.'

Few of us have ever seen Greg ... we've only heard his name, and never in good circumstances either. To a courier in that firm, 'Greg' is like the spirit invoked to intimidate children into doing as they're told. Sometimes we'd question whether Greg existed at all, but whether he did or not was immaterial, people had been threatened with *Greg* and then fired without ever having to see him in the flesh. Those who were known to have seen him were never seen again, and so his existence was not firmly established. Tony sits behind his desk, looking across at me with expectancy. 'Who's gone?' I ask, and on his computer he pulls up the fleet, the photos that are on our ID cards.

'No more Three-Two ... One-Six, he's gone too. Did you ever meet Four-One?'

'Yeah, I met Four-One.'

'Four-One must've left just after you ... shame ... good rider.' Tony points to a face I don't recognise, purple bags under bloodshot eyes and straggly hair, 'You ever meet Nineteen?'

I shake my head.

'He was here from Poland.' A tone of gossip is in Tony's voice. 'Turned out he was on the run, nice guy ... only some sort of tax bill he'd missed. When he found out the police had caught up with him …' Tony pulls a noose above his head, slides out his tongue. 'They found him at his flat … he hanged himself.'

I stare straight through the news as Tony keeps on. 'We had a bad run of it to be honest,' Tony points at a younger photo, a baseball cap. 'Six-Two was only here a few months … got himself killed riding the wrong way down Marylebone High Street one night.'

I give half a grimace, because I sense Tony wants the reaction. 'I didn't hear about that.'

'Course you didn't, Two-Two …' He gives a laugh, dark but more serious than normal. 'He weren't no lawyer or accountant … it's only the posh ones the papers make a fuss about getting squashed!' Tony resumes, brighter, 'Remember Five-Five?'

I nod.

'We had to let him go … he head-butted Eight outside a client's office.'

This takes me. 'Eight was such a nice guy.' Then I recall, 'So was Five-Five.'

Tony tips his head knowingly, 'Five-Five and Eight started living together, and then Five-Five kept saying Eight was trying to poison him … in his food.'

I shake my head, a sense of disbelief that at the same time, in this office, isn't so far from normalcy.

'Five-Five smoked a lot of pot, didn't he?'

Tony nods slowly, 'Yep … *a lot* … he was convinced the last guy he lived with was trying to poison his food as well.'

I've no more appetite for this, the news of the sanatorium I return to. Enough stories. 'You kept Two-Two open for me?'

Tony looks at me, solemn, tilts his head. 'You think we'd do that to you?'

He pushes his monitor by way of answer, shows me my photo, my old mug shot: no hair and a big smile. He looks at me on the screen, looks up at my face: no smile, lots of hair.

'Blimey. You look different, mate … we'll take a new one.'

He lifts a Polaroid camera, tells me to smile. Captures. There I am: the new me appears, loads bottom to top, chin first onto the screen. Over his shoulder, a bicycle is leaning on a filing cabinet. I know what that means … means Tony's been cycling to work. Ordinarily that'd be quite a wholesome thing, but in this context I know it means Tony's lost his licence again, will have been caught drunk on his motorbike. In most offices that'd be a point of some shame, but here the embarrassment is attached more to getting caught.

A man appears: tall and thin, cheekbones like coat pegs, neat hair and dark eyes. He wears a pink shirt and nicely cut jeans. Greg. Tony gestures. '*Two-Two … this is Greg.*' Greg sticks out an arm, hair on his knuckles, olive skin. He probably doesn't know it, but down in Docklands, I'd say Greg's got Mediterranean somewhere in his bloodline.

'Nice to meet you, mate … well done on what you've done. You should've told us, we could've arranged some sort of sponsorship.'

'Or a delivery to China!' Tony puts in with a laugh.

'It's a pity,' Greg comes over all thoughtful on us. 'I never meet any of you pushbike couriers … only when one of you fucks up. We only ever see each other when everyone's shouting and angry.'

That's as profound as it gets in this office. I suck in my cheeks, express regret. Greg turns to leave and, in the style of a forgotten grandparent, tells me to come and say hi more often. We shake hands again, and I tell him I will, realise I'm becoming one more of the city's habitual liars, those who agree to ideas only so as to ease the awkward moments when they're first suggested.

From across the room is a ringing of metal: Tony unlocks a cupboard, the door swinging out to crash like a gong, struck to reveal rows of wires and hardened black plastic. This is the most important moment of my visit – the kit. Tony goes through the drill that we both know I know … he can say it in a single breath. He reads me my rights. 'We'll take £25 a week for the first eight weeks, £200 deposit refunded when you leave …' He fills his lungs, sighs, 'Just don't break anything.'

I nod, I smile, 'Never did.'

Tony nods, 'I know you didn't, Two-Two … but you know what some of the guys are like … and I always get it in the neck.' Tony flicks the side of his scrawny neck as he says it, the same way a Chinaman once did when demanding I drink rice wine with him.

Tony starts through the boxes, turning dials that set lights blinking. Hissing noises rise, burst, then settle to the sound of instructions coming from upstairs in the control room. Everything else at the base is formality, but this is important, because if Tony gives me bad kit, if he doesn't take the time to make sure it's working, I'll spend the next days cycling back out to the Docklands and away from the work. There are a number of potential calamities. He can give me a battery that isn't charged, he can give me a battery that is charged but is terminal dead and will run empty in half an hour. He can give me a charger with a bad connection. Most important of all is the radio … that's the key to my work. I want one that's old and heavy. The worst that can happen now is Tony telling me he'll give me a new, lightweight model, because we all know the new, lightweight models don't work. The sound will crackle, you can't hear the controller, underneath buildings the signal breaks. First sign of rain, of drizzle, and the sound goes haywire … you can't hear instructions through the plastic bag you have to put the thing inside. I watch Tony's hands filing through the hardware. He stops on a small radio pack, new and lightweight. I wince. His hand keeps going, moves on to an old model, pulls it out. Relief. Turns out Tony does genuinely like me, it's not just a front he puts on. All through university, Heidegger and Hegel and Kant – all those wonderful words – and it turns out East End geezers like Tony are the ones who will determine my destiny.

'Look after it,' he says, handing the radio pack my way. And I smile. We understand one another. For the most part, courier folk are like Tony: as warm-hearted as they are straightforward. He makes to fetch my papers, leaves me with a colleague I don't recognise, sitting at a desk next to a large jar of instant coffee. He looks round at me, red-eyed, stands to invite conversation. He tells me he's finishing the night shift. I look over, a little surprised, 'What happens at night?'

Glad of the question, he goes to the trouble of breathing in his gut and tucking in his shirt, smoothing it over the belly, ready to present the answer.

'San Francisco, Los Angeles … West Coast only starts happening about 6 p.m. our time. Tokyo comes on stream at midnight.' He wears blue-tinted lenses in his glasses, stuffs his hands in his pockets and rocks on to his heels, pauses for effect. 'It never sleeps, and we've got to be ready … whatever happens.'

After cycling around the world I'd developed a new sense, found myself with the ability to see people as they had been as children. With that sense, when you're listening to a man like that, you realise how all anyone wants is to believe they're a part of something bigger, believe they make things happen and once in a while get the chance to use a turn of phrase like '*Tokyo comes on stream*'. I watched that man, standing opposite, and I saw his child. He had more weight on the face, stubble, a larger belly and more height. But there it was, there in his eyes as he took off the tinted lenses to give them a polish. Still a child in there, a child who grew up with an atlas or a globe next to his bed. Tony returns with clipboard and pen, hands it over for a signature. He smiles, speaks with warmth, 'Two-Two … nice to have you back.'

And somewhere, buried beneath a slight sense of impending failure, a part of me feels it is nice to be back, that all true families are dysfunctional.

I was sitting on my *A–Z*. You have to sit on something, to stop the cold slipping straight into your spine, all your warmth passing the other way and disappearing onto the pavement. I was on Bond Street, just up from the Cartier shop. The radio crackles. *'Kilo Three-Seven ... two on Queen Street for you.'* Not me. I remember the first time I lost a *London A–Z*, knew exactly what had happened. I'd been sitting on it as a collection was called for my number: I listened to the job, got on my bike, cycled away. When the next delivery came in, I realised I had no map to find it, but I could visualise the book in my mind, still there – without me – on the pavement from an hour earlier. That was a landmark moment, almost an achievement: the first time I'd ever known an address without having to check and see where it was. Today, I'm sitting on my third *A–Z*. Eighteen months I've had this one ... we're close, well attached, but it's nearing the end of its life with me and my— Radio crackles: *'Nine-Six ... there's one more on Wardour Street.'* Not me. My *A–Z* is dog-eared, a scrapper, a well-loved stray. The most frequently used pages are missing now. The City, the West End ... they've both gone, but that's okay, because I committed them to my brain instead. Some pages I've covered in Sellotape, a kind of makeshift laminating that buys you a few extra months before the inevitable. Radio crackles. *'Kilo Eight ... there's a couple waiting for you at DDB.'* Not me.

I've spent plenty of time sitting on the pavement of Bond Street. Condé Nast work here. Condé Nast is the name behind half of the magazines you read, which means they also positioned themselves to be the name behind half the websites you view, too. They get a lot of post. I also bring shoes to Bond Street sometimes, those wealthy ladies with a foot big enough to break Pushkin's heart. When they need a size 8 that's only in stock at the Sloane Square store, I'll ride down to put the box in my bag and cycle it back to Mayfair.

Today I'm wearing my favourite jeans: torn at the bottom of the leg, bitten open where they flapped and caught in the fixed and ever-turning teeth of my cog and chain. They're frayed at the front pocket, where the fabric has worn thin, they're torn at the knee and one of the back pockets has fallen away on account of having my lock stuffed into it. I love these jeans, the denim has been worn as soft as cashmere, the things feel like skin to me. It was a two-year investment that got them this way and now it's hard to bring myself to throw them out. Underneath, out of sight of the Bond Street public, the hair on my legs follows a pattern from the jeans: perfect hair removal has been performed on the very tops of my thighs, on the insides of my legs. The fronts of my shins are totally bald and smooth, turning to stubble and then back to hair where denim brushes skin a million times a day. In most of the physical ways I've adapted to this courier life, but in other ways, up in my head, I never will. Radio crackles. *Nine-Six – one on the Strand to help you along, it'll be on your screen in a minute.* Nine-Six gets all the work.

A Bond Street dame marches by: plastic bags sticking at right angles to her forearms, purchases sprouting like some sort of boutique chemical structure below a frown morose enough to stop the sun from rising. Down at me she looks, a face empty of life … and I wonder if she is pitying me my poverty, just as up I stare with pity for her wealth. For a moment we meet, eyes lock, and then the gravity of the endless street pulls her on. Beside us is a sandwich shop, tucked away on a back street, run by Italians who must've come to London and bought property before prices became prohibitive. In the mornings, in their window I see enormous mixing bowls piled two foot high with margarine. The staff have a rubber spatula that bends and hugs the contours of the bowl, allows them to scrape the margarine into a lump again, make use of every last bit that is smeared to the sides. Come the afternoon the bowls will have emptied, and I'll see them being refilled with new bricks of fat. Radio crackles. '*Two* …' he pauses, this could be me, '*Two-Nine…*' Dammit, still not me, I just sit here losing money … '*one to start you off on City Road.*'

Opposite me is a jewellery store, a sturdy-looking Slav with an earpiece stands on the door. I see the customer going in. She's dressed all in black, loose fitting trousers, a jacket. A wide-brim black hat casts a shadow over part of her face, has a short, thin net hanging from it. Her mouth is painted crimson-red, collagen-filled plump inside her lips. Even in this morning's low light, her eyes are shut behind large, black boxes of sunglass, wide and deep enough to conceal the claws of skin gouging the edges of her eyes, where age scratches slowly at her face. Her skin is painted white, a pale shade of ghostly dust, and around the cheeks and jaw you see skin stretched to a burns-victim tight where the Botox was injected. Inside the store I see her, fussed over by some glowing young girl in a cocktail dress. She smiles, beams and shines, sprinkles a little youth on the old woman brushing up against it. I watch them, together holding ornaments of silver and platinum to dangle from the hanging ear lobe that just won't stop growing, the two of them deciding which will best restore a little of the simple youth that she craves far more than beauty. Radio crackles. '*Two-Two,*' that's me… up at last. '*One for you … at the Japanese Cultural Centre, Piccadilly.*'

I stand, swing my leg over the handlebars of my bike, set back to work. Clipping into my pedals, the bicycle rolls back into the flow of traffic as I shiver at the breeze. The city is cold.

12 January – E14 – Docket #4

Before we go further, I should tell you about couriering, tell you how it works. They say that it's the best job in the world … It's not – that much is for certain. But without doubt it's the best of all the worst jobs in the world. Riders will tell you how amazing it feels to be paid money for riding a bike, and they've got a point, the problem is only when you're not getting paid money and not riding your bike. A third of couriering is being paid to cycle, the other two-thirds is not being paid to stand around the street. The numbers are small. People are always aghast when I tell them: 2.50. Two-fifty was the mainstay of my income. On paper, a courier is what is known as a *self-employed contractor*. That was the caveat by which a firm gives you work when there's work and has no responsibility for you when there isn't. There is no sick pay, no holiday pay, no national insurance paid on your behalf. Pension contributions? For a courier, life insurance goes little further than carrying a new inner tube in case of punctures. They don't have to fire you, and there's no notice period because they never employed you to begin with, you were only ever that self-employed contractor. As such your taxes are your own responsibility, not that many couriers would or have ever bothered with as much. At the end of the financial year, if you'd earned enough to get into a taxpaying threshold, once you'd deducted the cost of a bike and your bag, your frame repairs and your tyres, tubes and brake pads, you'd probably be out of it again.

Back at base your invoices pile up in long lines of £2.50. I never collected invoices, the only reason to check my wages at all was because I didn't always trust the company to pay me my correct dues to begin with. Now and then you'll show up at a door you've cycled a mile out of your way to get to: '*Sorry, mate … it's been cancelled,*' comes over the radio. You roll eyes, you calm yourself, radio in: *'I'll be paid a cancellation, right?'* You listen to the gruff reply, *'Course you will, mate … I'll put it down, no worries.'*

Those are the weeks you check your invoices.

As a courier I was paid £2.50 per delivery. That increased to £3.75 if it was an express job – a rush – but because you aren't technically allowed to stop for any other pickups with rushes, it can be better to get two standard jobs than one rush. Sometimes, with banking runs and the signing of documents, you might go to one address for a pickup, take it to another address, and then return to the original. That bagged £3.50, but depending on the location of the addresses, it could set you out of joint on your runs and kick against the natural tide of work. You get paid waiting time, but only after ten minutes, and at a rate of approximately minimum wage. Being made to wait for ten minutes isn't so bad, it earns a quid. Being made to wait nine minutes feels horrendous – your world is ending. Nine minutes is just waiting. Sometimes you got lucky, crossed the Edgware Road and left the conventional circuit, so that your delivery was classed as a long-distance drop. The process of crossing the thirty metres of Edgware Road was worth an extra £1.25 on top of the £2.50 you got for staying inside of it.

While I'd been away, the biggest clients, the banks and the lawyers, those who sent thousands of dockets a year, had realised they could squeeze the courier firms lower on prices. The firms had agreed … why wouldn't they? The savings were made from the riders anyway – were offset in our wages – and so the number 2 was creeping steadily into invoices come that winter. Earning a living as a courier is like that old saying about sausages: you can enjoy a sausage, but it's better not knowing how it was made.

The key to bagging better numbers was politics, an ongoing diplomacy whereby you kept on the right side of everybody at the same time as looking after your own interests. The idea is never to cross London, east to west, for only £2.50. The aim is to start in the east and pick up two more dockets on the way through to the west, so that ultimately your traversal of the city is worth at least a fiver, ordinarily £7.50, and if you're lucky, a tenner. On those rare occasions when you're travelling with five or more dockets on board – when you truly are being paid to ride your bike – in those moments you feel like the richest man in all London.

Managing your estate requires constant vigilance, knowing when to bite your tongue and when to speak out. Loyally picking up the dog's work will get you recognition up to a point, but do it too often and they'll just start to treat you like a dog. Complain too much, act like you're above being made to stretch your legs once in a while, and then too you'll find yourself brought down a peg. The best tactic is remaining upbeat: likeable without sycophancy, an air of good energy. You're resigned rather than furious when you get a raw deal, grateful when luck smiles on you, and most importantly, you always have to be opportunistic, ever asking … the worst thing that can happen is to be forgotten. Couriering refines all manner of personability, the sort of evolutionary talents you only ever need as a poor person, when life is hard and such intuition has yet to be bred away by salary. Any office worker who thinks they've got interpersonal skills should try a month on the circuit: poverty snapping at your ass and amiability the key to the £60 that will make all the difference between breadline and maybe buying a pint if your bag or a tyre doesn't need replacing. It's humiliating, down at that end of things, the sort of amounts that make all the difference to our lives.

One man alone determines a courier's wage, and it's not the courier … it's the man on the box, the man with the radio: the controller. He either likes you, or is ambivalent. Only in rare cases might he dislike you, but that's no worse than ambivalence anyway. *Your* wages need to be in *his* thoughts. He sits in the office, back at base, headphones on ears and a microphone over his mouth, a foot pedal to operate the radio … *in and out, in and out*. Jobs arrive one by one, the position of his riders held in his mind and overlaid against the new work coming in. All day long his voice is in your ear. I've heard a controller's voice echoing from afar onto my pillow as I've fallen asleep at night. It's easy to hate him, to blame him for everything that's going wrong in your life because he's to blame for everything that's going wrong in your wages. He has power over you, and that alone is sometimes enough to get you pissed off before you've ridden anywhere.

When you start on the circuit you're a nobody … you get no work because the controller's giving it to guys he's been saying '*hello*' to each morning for long years past … the guys who've bought him a pint when he's shown up at the pub, the guys who – to be fair – aren't going to quit when it gets cold, or when they've had enough of the bohemian because they were only couriers for the giggles anyway. Those guys had no prospects away from the road, had earned what small favouritism they were afforded within the circuit, and it was only right that you earned stripes before you started eating into their wages. One night I saw Nine-Six outside a cinema, asked how his day had been, even though I already knew from the radio that Nine-Six was always being plied with work, can't ever have been left longer than ten minutes without. Nine-Six grinned, '*Every day's a good day! Top of the food chain … fed scum me.*' At least he was honest about it. It bugged me when guys made out they were just plain quick.

In our company we had two main controllers, though sometimes an unfamiliar voice would come over the radio waves to cover a lunch break. Best of all was Robbie, a gentle bodybuilder with his head disappearing into his shoulders, neck like a coat hanger. Robbie was a genius, a maestro, saw all London perfectly … he knew it was fine to send you out to Belgravia in the mid-afternoon because the regular Hoare & Co. banking run would bring you back to the centre afterwards. He remembered your favours, and when you helped him out or put in miles in the morning, he'd reward you with a good run in the afternoon. He remembered where you lived, made sure the eastern riders among us finished the day in the east, the westerners in the west. We trusted him, that was the main thing: with Robbie you listened and did as you were told because you knew you'd be looked after.

Then came Eduardo … Eduardo was different. Couriering belongs to that breed of capitalism in which it is perceived that if your workers aren't miserable then your workers aren't working. Eduardo liked that approach to business … wanted you to know who was boss, wanted you to know you worked for him, which meant nobody wanted to work for Eduardo. In general, London's couriers are Polish, Brazilian or British: Eduardo was a Brazilian engaged to a Polish woman. He came on the mic each morning with *'djin dobra, djin dobra… jagshamesch! Good morning, everybody … it's Latino time!'* He was always happier than the rest of us to hear his voice, and when Eduardo was up it was easy to wish the firm would follow the example of one London rival who had passed the job of controlling to a wage-free robot. The riders at that outfit were forever complaining that the programme, erratically sending work to their phones, was largely clueless who was closest to a job and left no room for constructive feedback when it got it wrong. They may have been right, but the same set of criticisms would have been no further from the mark in describing the human being that was Eduardo. Waiting in a future too remote for any of us to conceive of, all the capital's businesses would one day book deliveries through a single, giant courier service in the sky – each individual rider apportioned and paid work according to who was closest and rated most favourably. The old company fiefdoms would be removed from the equation, middlemen would lose their share of the profit, and the couriers would instead find themselves laid directly at the mercy of the open market and whoever had developed the software.

Until that day arrived, however, the controllers enjoyed having a certain style to their time on the airwaves, saw the job as a bit of a radio show. They all preferred the pushbike circuit to the motorbikes or vans, said that couriers without the engines were always the most cheerful and agreeable to work with. Now and then a guy called Mark would cover a shift: nihilist was Mark's style, fun to work with, '*All right boys and girls … I've got nobody empty and work on the screen … we're all over it like a cheap suit.*' If there's any thrill in couriering, it's the idea that you're part of a team moving faster than London itself, that each of your journeys has a purpose someone else relies upon without even knowing you exist. We were the us and everyone else part of the them. I remember the day a rider radioed-in to report Oxford Street closed, a woman down under a bus with a touch of death in her pallor. Mark crackled through. '*Don't worry about it, mate … one less idiot in the gene pool.*' For all their good nature, the couriers were not a sentimental lot. They led hard lives and always would … had little compassion for the people of a city with such little compassion for them.

Motley

It was the world and family of work that soon came to seem most familiar to me, and I started to like some of my colleagues more than the people I knew away from the circuit. Within the firm you were never far from a certain sense of camaraderie. We were a team, and would lend a spare inner tube or radio battery if someone needed it, would come over the radio to sound a warning if we saw the police had staked out a junction known for cyclists jumping lights. If the police were on London Wall and Moorgate, we'd take Old Street. If they'd taken Ludgate Circus we went Holborn Viaduct, pleased with ourselves for getting one up on the law, looking down from the bridge at the fluorescent gathering that leapt from doorways to pounce on errant cyclists who burst the red. There was colour amongst us, everyone had a story, and gradually I put faces to the numbers and voices I spent my days with on the radio.

Eight-Seven was south London … or rather, *sarf* London, pure and proud. He was a giant of a man, always radioing through with a mechanical problem, and in the time I'd known him he had snapped at least three bicycle frames with his weight. He put his size to good use at the weekends, when he told us he could steadily turn out £150 of commission as a debt collector. Throughout the week, Eight-Seven would ask for jobs that took him up to Camden, where he augmented his courier and bailiff wages with small-time drug deals. He laughed that a bicycle was by far the best vehicle for the job, added that London's big dealers had abandoned their BMWs and were opting for hybrid cars, engines with hydrogen back-up that gained them an exemption from the city's congestion charge.

More sinister was Four: a youthful-looking South African who would ogle secretaries by day and then joke over the radio about lending himself to men at night. Wide-eyed, he'd told me one night outside the Foundry how he'd come to that persuasion: how back in South Africa he'd shot dead a man – three bullets for good measure, in the face – as he attempted to steal Four's car at knifepoint. Four reported, with a confusion I never myself understood, that the judge had deemed three bullets in the face an excessive use of force, and so sent him to jail for murder. Four delighted in letting people know that it was there, a white man in a South African prison, that he had discovered his sexuality via a series of encounters that, over time, obviously wound-up consenting.

Two-Nine was the first girl on the team. I'd listened adoringly to Two-Nine's radio voice for weeks before finally meeting her. Cheerful. French. Feminine. I imagined her like the girls in the Loire *boulangerie*, or some Parisian with a little beret, Gambetta sort of style, cosmopolitan-chic. In my head I drew up great pictures of elaborate, perfect detail ... profiles in which Two-Nine had turned her back on the snobbery of Sciences Po and made a break for London instead, her leather satchel switched for a courier bag. Finally I met Two-Nine ... found she didn't look much like that. Two-Nine was Macedonian-French, used to taunt me with blame for what the Ottoman Empire had done to her Macedonian ancestry, diplomatically compromising that at least I wasn't a Greek. She was short, incredibly short, always rolling a cigarette, or with one hanging from her mouth, the roots of her teeth stained with tobacco. Her lank hair fell either side of her face, lips protruding, eyes half shut, lids a shade of purple, her face ever dispassionate in that fashion uniquely French.

The nearest thing to me was Two-Four. A literature graduate, Two-Four was always high as a kite ... an artisan of rolling joints and an authority on which public spaces were most suited to smoking without interference from the police. Mayfair was his safe bet while Soho Square the most pointless place to even consider attempting it. His eyes were always that bit shot with blood, which was accentuated by a huge head of floppy curls that flowed down either side of a baseball cap he perennially wore. He was a photographer by calling, always planning to be off to New York '*in a few months*' that never seemed to pass. When Two-Four arrived on the circuit, he became the only courier ever to admonish the other riders for not knowing John Milton and *Paradise Lost*.

Another our age was Four-Six. A wisp of Caribbean beard on his jet black chin … we were the same age, only Four-Six had gotten a girl pregnant a couple of years back, was determined to do the decent thing for the rest of his life. He'd left the mother – '*too much hassle, man!*' – but was staying put in the city so that she wouldn't be able to turn his daughter against him. Four-Six was frustrated by life: '*Just give me the work … just give me the work … I feel better when I'm riding!*', was how he spoke about it with me once. He had no problem with distance, covering miles, just said he needed the money to pay for his daughter. Four-Six amazed me … he felt the world owed him nothing beyond life as a poor man prepared to work hard for the company's profit. He had a silent, unthought-of honour, somewhere close to but still a million miles from stupidity.

14 January – EC2 – Docket #5

Apart from financial necessity, a January return would have always made sense. Fronting up when the weather's bleak is the easiest way to get accepted back into things, and once the festive lull is over, it's also the most lucrative time of the year. Any number of students and fair-weathers come out of the courier woodwork each April, ready to ride their bicycle in the sunshine and under the illusion that they'll make an even half-decent wage. By taking up your position in January, you can hope to earn some respect and a passable income.

Winter 2010 was tough. That winter was so … perilously … cold. That's it … say it like that … with tiny pants of air between the words. Each day the wind would come in from the north, blowing down from the Arctic so that I imagined it having crossed white wastes with dusts of snow barrelling against the ice, over the dark green forests of Scandinavia, the black waters of the North Sea, funnelling between the peaks of the Lake District and down into the concrete of London. At first it soothed me, put me back in my rightful place, conscious of an outside world I missed so much.

Come February the poetry had worn off … I was just plain cold. Sure I'd been cold on my way around the world, suffered rough temperatures, but in those days there'd always been the glow of some humanity to stir you when you least expected it, the embers of adventure always rekindling in a breeze. London was pretty short on both those things. As a courier, winter was impossible. If I wore enough clothes to stay warm when sitting on a kerbside awaiting work, that was the same amount of clothing in which I'd overheat and sweat when riding. The clothes that kept me cooler when riding would have me freeze when waiting … the perfect balance was one that left me always a little cold, but meant I did not overheat too much when in a hurry. I carried only a thin, waterproof jacket: warm clothes were too bulky, took up space in a bag when unworn, and so limited the room for carrying paying work. If a day turned out quiet, with few jobs, then eventually you wound up shivering. Sometimes I would escape the cold in the shadow of a double-decker bus, diesel fumes chugging out at the rear, so that on a winter's day it could be disappointing to find myself coming up behind a hybrid bus with no exhaust. When traffic was backed up, when I wasn't in a rush … quite instinctively, entirely subconsciously …. I would find myself huddling beside the vent above a bus engine, feeling the fumes warm the surface of my skin. I would hold out gloved fingers, spread open towards the automotive hearth and that sound of crashing, spinning metal fast in front of me. Moments like that it can be hard not to dwell on what has happened to your life.

Mornings were my favourite time, when the city was quiet, the comfort of my last cup of tea not yet forgotten. I'd sit and watch the steam rising out of the manhole covers that lidded London's bowels. In the shafts of sunlight you can see frosts lifting, as the rays warm the pavement and the crystals evaporate skywards. I loved the tiny galaxies of ice that would grow beneath a dripping gutter or drainpipe: one big, black pool where the drip had fallen consistently through the night … surrounded by a tiny orbit of droplets, sparkling spheres formed as the drip splashed up and outwards from the centre, the whole thing trapped like a frozen solar system glistening on the pavement.

The best part would come crossing the Thames on one of those crisp, clear days when I'd see London, slow and silent, as if a city beneath frozen waters, cut with sunlight and shining over and across the ornamental skyline. A lantern, chandelier: the city sparkles, the river in silver as I burst out of the concrete and out of the stone, diving into the open space above the Thames, where the world had not yet been taken by metropolis … where wind flooded and where I'd watch my legs churn below with the waters of the river. My heart would throb in my chest as I ploughed onto the bridge, watching great plumes of steam pouring out of my mouth to disappear over my shoulder, so that I would pretend to be some human locomotive, remnants of life receding in my wake.

When there was no work, many of the couriers used to sit against the ventilation ducts of the J.P. Morgan offices, down in Aldermanbury, where warm, waste air was pumped out of the building and would heat a thin stretch of pavement before being swallowed by cold. Once or twice I tried it amongst that crowd, though from the outset I knew I was never really going to fit in. Couriers tend to talk couriering, nothing but deliveries and close shaves and postcodes. One day I joined a small group in the warmth of vents outside a pub kitchen off Gresham Street, sitting down on a wall within the shrubs and the woodchip.

The pub must have had a pest control problem, another of the homes to those rodents you're apparently never more than five metres from in London – the precise distance shrinking according to the storyteller and number of pints. Around our feet were turquoise traps, pellets through woodchip, and a row of plastic cases full of poison. As the courier beside me went on talking, I looked down and saw a mouse: a tiny, grey mouse with a thin, conical nose ending in a cute point of pink. A sad little eye, shining like a button, looked up at me as the creature lay on its side, shoots of white hair amongst its grey down. Four of the tiniest claws imaginable were up in the air, each on delicate limbs the size of toothpicks. The little creature was breathing heavily, a pounding from its underbelly, and I watched the thing gallop away the last of its life, warfarin in the blood, thinning away so that the poor heart pumped after blood no longer there, then pumped at air inside arteries, until five minutes later there was no blood left to catch the pump, and no oxygen in that small, furry body.

Legs upwards, racing headlong to its final heart attack, I sat with those couriers and a dying mouse on that street corner, watching the creature hurry off with the last of its life, just as it felt that mine too went careering by with all too little control. The jobs people suggested I apply for were uninteresting, while those I liked the sound of I couldn't get. After an interview, but three months from my return, a member of the selection board would call to pass on the bad news, say I should make more of my record-breaking ... be proud and show it off. They didn't understand that perhaps I *was* a little proud of, if not the record, then at least my ride ... and for that very reason couldn't bring myself to trot it out, five minutes at a time, just to impress a panel of strangers assembled only to judge me. In no time at all, and low on self-esteem, couriering had taken me back, no longer so sure I'd ever been good for any better.

20 January – SE1 – Docket #6

Darkness on the edge of town at three, no work over the radio come five. Quiet. I was somewhere around Upper Ground, beside the South Bank, sitting on a stone step on top of my *A-Z*. I was empty, hadn't heard my number for three-quarters of an hour, hadn't heard anybody else's for five minutes, no work for any of us. The radio stays silent on my chest. A couple of riders call through, confirming their deliveries complete – now empty. In the trees beside the river are trails of blue lights, sticking out of the night as people walk beneath bare stripped branches. I watch the silhouettes go hand-in-hand, children on scooters, women pulling suitcases that rattle behind, parents with babies strapped to harnesses on their chests, four limbs sticking out like starfish.

Beside me is a restaurant: bottles on the tables, candles stuck inside the neck and glowing on the windows, brightening either side of the black glass where my reflection waits. Beard across face, forearms propped on knees, hands hanging. I see couples arriving at the restaurant, an attendant taking coats and leading them to tables in the window. A candle gutters in the neck of the bottle, a waitress walks over and lights a new wick from it, pushes new candle down on old, which drops into the bottle with a tail of smoke lifting up through the glass. I watch wine poured, watch glasses chink, watch a businessman arrive: balding, arm lifting as a waitress steps to him, slips the long coat from his shoulders. He takes a seat in the window, sits alone and crosses his leg, unfolds a newspaper. All twenty-five of us couriers are sitting similarly around the square miles of central London, locked out of a city that continues all around.

Moments like that, all you want is to go home, but you can't, because everyone else feels the same way, and all our weekly wages are made slightly more worthwhile by an attendance bonus for covering a full week. Five days, nine 'til six, puts ten per cent onto your take-home. There's no such thing as overtime … it doesn't matter if your deliveries last until after seven on Monday and Tuesday, and if you're not home until gone eight. Come Wednesday you're still required to stay until six. I know there are other jobs with similarly demanding schedules, but they pay more than £50 a day, and it's easier to work hard when you're rewarded for it. That it's not fair goes without saying, and so nobody ever said it. The controllers didn't really think it was fair either … controllers were only couriers who had scrambled through to the safety of a salary, they saw our point of view even though they could rarely afford to take our side. It wasn't fair … it was just the way it was.

Radio crackles. The voice of Eight-Seven comes through, gruff, 'Any work going, Robbie?'

'Dead, mate … absolutely dead.'

I watched my reflection in the glass, a phantom diner between tables, making myself at home as diners snapped grissini. Another voice came through, higher pitched, sounded like Six.

'End of January's not normally this quiet, is it, Robbie?'

Crackling. 'No … it does seem particularly bad.'

Eight-Seven came back, 'My rent's already overd—', the word cut out as he released the button early. I remember Robbie's reply, as all of us sat empty, waiting for work, justifying our time on the streets of London.

Radio crackles. 'There'll always be something keeping us poor … don't worry about that, Eight-Seven.'

Poor people don't normally talk about the fact that they are poor, don't like to draw attention to as much: the word 'poor' is only mentioned by those who are not. Given that the poor tend to have been born poor and will most likely die poor, knowing mostly poor people in the meantime, it's easy for them to forget they're poor at all: having no money is as natural and inevitable as breathing. You don't want to talk about how hard your life is, to talk about how you're done-for and how hard you're treading water … you just get on with doing so, leave it to those with money and a bit of comfort to hopefully make some productive noise about the problem. In the years that I rode on the circuit, that evening was the only time I heard the word 'poor' in one of our mouths.

31 January – SW1 – Docket #7

They leave me waiting. The urgent collection, more significant than news from the fall of Verdun, the Maginot breach, siege of Stalingrad, 1815 at Waterloo. The delivery for which the courier really needed to have arrived ten minutes ago, for which controller and I had in turn had our earholes scorched, blazed, for which we had both reorganised our deliveries, was – so it transpired – still being prepared in the office upstairs. I wait. I lean my back against the high desk with the concierge behind it, elbows up. I look around, try to keep my impatience to myself – the courier is never allowed to get annoyed.

They tell you to sweat, to hurry for all you're worth, and then they tell you to wait patiently, all in the same five-minute period. That's the way it goes: beck and call. My time is the most expendable thing in the city. Moments like that are when you feel it ... the in-between parts, the times when you're left with nothing to do but ponder. I stare straight ahead, stare at something the other side of a wall, listen to the sound of the brush as someone sweeps, clears out a nook for me at the wayside. I'm nearing tipping point, where one day you realise the pile of life lived and accumulated has grown bigger, complete with all its baggage, while the life in front of you is starting to grow smaller, and the light of your eyes has faded from what it once was.

I occupy myself, I look around. A television screen in front of me: the market is up, up 0.07 points from its position of that morning. I wonder if one day this sort of news will make for a good day. The banner scrolls through the bottom of the screen. White faces with wrinkles on them are looking at me, looking at me all solemn, like old children sorry for what they've done. They sit, peer out from in front of a hoarding: '*Iraq Inquiry*' it blares proudly (a lovely font too). Politicians don't have to learn from mistakes, there's no injustice that can't be undone by an inquiry: some protocol to make it all upstanding before Westminster calls it quits. I watch a line of white faces, palms flat on the table before them, *Iraq Inquiry* on the hoarding over their heads. One by one, the faces declare solemnly, *cross my heart and hope to die* that … at the time … they felt they'd done the right thing, were sorry for any errors of judgement. Best of all was the hoarding itself. After a million dead Iraqis, the loss of billions of taxpayers' hard-earned, and some Baghdad father crying all over the bloodied face of his dead son, some whizz in a design agency had noticed that the words *Iraq* and *Inquiry* both contained the letter *Q*. The coincidence demanded to be honoured, each *Q* warranted greater attention, and so over their shoulders they danced, the tail of each *Q* floating together, elegantly waving goodbye to one and all as I went on thinking what it—

'Excuse me … excuse me, sir?'

I turn. A receptionist is leaning forwards at me. My eyes widen, lips lethargic, my face asks silently what he wants. I wait for the important business.

'Please don't lean on the desk.'

I pick up my elbows, turn round. He gives a nod of thanks, settles back to his chair. I look at him. He's slight, awkward-looking: his eyes look too big for his head, they glare as if by accident, a shaving cut is high on his cheek. I look at the words on his own hoarding.

Innovation, Inspiration, Excellence

On the desk in front of him is a packet of crisps, crumbs of fried potato on the metallic surface. The lights shine on the oily skin of his fingertips. A half-finished cup of tea is in a mug with the ceramic stained tannin brown, beside a foil wrapper from a chocolate bar. His large, padded shoulders slalom in their ill-fitting jacket. A tie is pulled into too tight a knot around his neck, sticking scrawny from the collar, as if the man is exhausted, buckling under the weight of the words it has been demanded he should uphold. I look up again:

Innovation, Inspiration, Excellence

I don't understand anymore, can't fathom why people lend such grand words to such banal places. The man shuffles in his chair, uncomfortable at my lack of communication. He gives a smile, hand reaches back to the crisp packet, it rings with the sound of plastic as he takes out a slice of fried potato, burnt brown. I listen to it crack between his lips. Deafening, it starts to crunch between teeth. It must take a lot of calories to uphold *innovation, inspiration* and *excellence* all the day through. I look up at the words, searching for direction in this modern chapel of a third-sector think tank. Why struggle for a better reality when we had a utopia of hyperbole just waiting to be believed in. A tax on words, that'd do it ... the only answer was to audit the vocabulary, so that when we communicated we had to actually mean what we said, so that excellence couldn't be slapped on a wall as readily as plaster, so that *community*, *hope* and *change* might not be daubed about until they were only regular platitudes to put people at ease.

A secretary comes down the stairs, totters over, red-painted fingernails hand me an envelope. The courier reboots, is reset from *wait* to *hurry*. Like a robot with a soul ... she tells me to be quick. The envelope has only an hour and a half to make it halfway across London: SW1 to EC4. She doesn't know it'll take perhaps only fifteen minutes. I look at the panic in the eyes, sense her peering at me from inside a tube map: she sees two changes of line between points A and B, possible delays, is only faintly sure of where it is she's standing to begin with. Another of this city, shepherded distanceless and without direction at each day's beginning and close. I nod in earnest ... *of course, of course* ... let her believe I'm headed right there, when really I'm to first ride five minutes the opposite direction to pick up another docket. It's the sense of importance that people really need to feel ... there's time to spare, just so long as it's listening to her riff about the critical nature of the delivery, significance means more to them than punctuality. '*It's SO important!*' she calls once more as I nod my understanding, heading for the door.

Back outside the rain is falling, drips from a guttering as I pull on waterproof trousers, hop back to the bike. On a quiet street in Westminster I see red pools in the wet, black road: a stopped traffic light and deserted pedestrian crossing. I near the lights, watch cyclists as they wait for red to change amber, rain running down their hair and on to noses, the pedestrian crossing without any pedestrians on it. I cycle straight through, glancing back their way: still stationary. And my heart sank to see them, dripping wet and waiting for the lights to change over an empty street. Compared to life on the road, the control of it all was hard not to notice ... it was as if we'd been made unquestioningly obedient, had been domesticated. The suits, I felt, always seemed to be London's most diligent at waiting for the lights: tell a man to unemploy a thousand workers, bankrupt the Greek state, or cut funding to a school and he'll do it without a second thought. The same man will ride home on his bicycle, see a red light over an empty road and pull hard on his brakes ... tut loudly that he's a good citizen as you ride through next to him. Those guys around Westminster, and to a lesser extent the Square Mile, they believed in the importance of rules, believed in systems. As much was hardly surprising, I suppose ... more than anyone else, they enjoyed the benefits of our own.

4 February – WC2 – Docket #8

In my head I went back around the world, thought about Cross Plains in Texas, remembered old James telling his story about the Tennessee miners, the red scarves they'd tied around their necks as a sign of willingness to form a union and defend their rights. They became rednecks so they knew who to aim their rifles at when the mine owners brought in soldiers to disband the protests.

One evening I took an old red shirt from the bag of clothes under my bed. I took out my penknife, cut a length of material away from its hem, ragged threads hanging at each end. Next morning I would wear it, and the day after I would wear it too. I would tie it round my throat so that I could feel its slight press each time I swallowed, so that the blood and oxygen of my every breath would have to travel under that symbol of my convictions. I resolved to wear the neck scarf every day until others were wearing it too, and even if that could never be so, I would at the very least explain the principles of the neck scarf to those who asked, in order that the ideals of unions and the dignity of workers could not be allowed to slip wholly into history. It was a sense of meaning and purpose that I really needed right then. My politics were beginning to feel more and more out of touch with reality … mere remnants from that previous world in which my parents had raised me. Meaning was now to be found in identity and image before politics or people, and I desperately needed something to believe in … an idea to stand for, something that would lift me from my certainty that everything was settled. There is nothing so exhausting as hopelessness, the thought that – one way or another – it all winds up the same. As a symbol of my defiance, I started working with that band of red cloth tied around my neck.

⤫

'*You fucking homo!*' It was Conduit Street, Mayfair, a slight uphill on my first morning as a redneck. I suppose I must have been in his way, the first of many workers who didn't quite realise I was drawing attention to our shared struggle against injustice. I went about my redneck work, brain meditating on whether I believed in unionism anyway, whether the collective could ever work in an age of the individual, whether I was bothered about the broken, angry people around me or only my own sorry lot. Walking into offices, past the wide reception mirrors, I saw it there around my neck: sometimes quite proud, a bold and striking shade of red, a daring statement precisely because nobody else in London was wearing one. Other times my little emblem had come unfastened, was hanging bedraggled downwards, confused and forlorn, so that it just looked as though someone had tied the rag of an old shirt around his neck.

One afternoon I came across Ben. Ben was a former courier, we'd never worked together, which was why Ben had a name and not a number. Ben had done the sensible thing and left the trade for a catering job as soon as the roads started getting to him. The two of us met a handful of times across three London years: on the first occasion he'd got in touch with me, asking for bike advice as he set about planning a ride to Syria, back in the days before the civil war there. By the time he was home from Syria and I'd returned from the world, we'd both lost the other's phone number, and yet on each occasion that we met by chance, we made a point of not taking them, but instead just trusted that we'd bump into each other at a different junction sometime.

Ben was a good-looking boy. I say *boy* because he was baby-faced, pale blue eyes and a wide, straight gap between his two front teeth. He smiled a lot too, especially for a courier, but nonetheless had a six-foot stature, a shaved head and the same slave body as most of the young guys on the circuit. The first time we'd met, he told me with humble pride that he'd been pulled up by the police for speeding on Whitechapel High Street. They told him he'd been doing 37mph … and all he could do was grin. Ben was lucky, Ben was charming too, Ben was the rider responsible for the fact that most of the couriers were absolute pests where female receptionists were concerned. Ben owned a tale of the one day that ended with an evening delivery to a West End media agency, the secretary asking where his next job was taking him. When he'd responded that he was done for the day, she'd suggested he … *perhaps* … stay a little while in the office. Ben had left the building at 5 a.m. next morning, that one-in-a-million delivery that all the other couriers were forever ogling secretaries in hope of. For a rider in London, a story like that would tide you over for the rest of your life as far as being respected was concerned, but you could tell Ben had more going for him. Another scribbler, he'd eventually disappeared to live the dream in Montmartre for a while, and I saw him only once in my weeks as a redneck. We were at the top of Endell Street, St Giles' Circus swarming behind us. He chatted Syria. I chatted World. We both sounded flat. He pointed at my neck.

'Nice neck scarf … looks really cool, quite French.'

I squirmed, it made me uncomfortable to have the scarf reduced to fashion. My convictions came over all shy, self-conscious.

'Yeah?' I murmured. 'It's political actually, an idea I got in Texas.'

'Cool. What's it mean?'

I shrugged, still figuring out the answer to that one myself, gave half a smile with a bewildered shake of the head, 'My willingness to form a union … I suppose.'

Soon after, I took the thing off.

Bandstand.1

It's thick with mist, one of those London mornings when you can touch the sky. The clouds fall right down flat upon us, droplets in hair and beard, everything wet-through without the damp having even been noticed. I climb the steps, I push the sky away. I was east, Arnold Circus, a bandstand at the top of a small hill of earth, red-brick buildings high on each side. I was sitting, waiting for work, the whole world white with mist, London at the bottom of a glass of milk. A dark silhouette appears, makes its way to the top of the steps, looks across at me. He's wearing a long coat, fastened round the front with a buckle, walking my way: smart, respectable, a large leather case in one hand. He comes closer, he's got a moustache, a flat cap, an elder gent, pretty dapper. His arm reaches my way, makes parley.

'Excuse me, sir.' Refined accent, not posh, refined. 'I've lost my phone and my wallet ... and I need to call my wife.'

His voice didn't make apologies for itself ... that voice was proud, the long jacket too, a smart number, the material rich navy in colour, large buttons on the cuffs, its own belt fastened round the middle. I start going into my bag.

'Sure ... you can borrow my phone.'

'Well ... actually ... it's quite a long call. If you could just give me some money for a phone box.'

I pause, my eyes twitch, twitch slowly with a London suspicion, consulting the part of my brain that governs trust. I look him in the face: pale face, the moustache cut neat. That man wasn't begging, that much was certain. He approached me as one of his own, a citizen, a civilian ... not one of *them*, of those in need of charity. In him was all the confidence of a respectable person who's found himself rough luck, the sort of situation that could befall any one of us. I didn't normally give anything to anyone, I've still scarcely enough for myself, and round London, coughing up every time you're asked would get to be a real expense. That one though, that one was different. I went for my wallet instead of my phone, took out a nugget, dropped a pound into a palm outstretched inside a leather glove. He doffed his cap, nodded, as if I'd done the right thing, as if I'd done the only decent thing and no more. He put the pound in his pocket. He strode away, back into the mist.

8 February – SW1 – Docket #9

After a few weeks, it turned out I'd got better at the politics of couriering. The controllers and office staff had a newfound respect for me, thought my round-the-world pretty monumental, the most impressive thing ever to have happened to anyone at the office. As time went by, I started to earn occasional weeks nudging the once-unthinkable threshold of £300. My information-gathering improved, and I suppose I must have been playing the circuit more effectively as a result. They gave me better work, but still I kept on lying … you had to.

What I realised then was that I'd been lied to from the start, all along – from my first enquiries – the whole profession of couriering had been based on porkies and tall tales. You speak to a courier on the street, ask what you can expect to earn and, embarrassed at the pittance they have come to settle for taking home, the courier tells you the amount he earns on the best weeks as if it were some sort of average. You go to the base, the headquarters of the courier firm, and there you collect your radio and pocket computer with a friendly chap telling you to expect low wages for the first weeks, while you're learning the ropes of couriering and the streets of the city. That much is true, but it's a lie in that it leaves an impression that things stand to improve: the wages will stay low, you simply lose the comforting explanation for why. Wages are low because there is no work. Wages are low because there is work, but other riders are getting it. Sometimes there's no work because it's half-term and the kids are home, other times there's no work because the kids are back at school. Sometimes there's no work because it's raining and everyone has apparently decided not to go to the office. Other times there's no work because the sun's out and everyone's on holiday.

There's no work because The Sales are on and then there's no work because The Sales have finished. I've heard American riders speculate that, long-term, there was no work because late-nineties anthrax scares reduced the circulation of letters ... apparently terrorism had killed the scene. You had to hand it to them, they didn't want for imagination. One way or another, whatever the explanation, the fact remains: there's no work. The wages stay low.

Sometimes you visit base, head office, ask after business. You are told the firm has lost one contract but gained two, has employed more riders to cover the workload – but only three. They assure you that you can still count on twenty deliveries a day and a comfortable two hundred and fifty pounds a week. That was a lie. What they meant was that they'd lost two contracts and gained only one, that they'd employed three new riders anyway, there was no longer enough work to go round, and I could count on fifteen deliveries a day and worrying about two hundred and fifty pounds a week. Out on the roads I'd encounter riders from other firms, and there we'd lie to one another about our wages, rather than confess the god's honest truth that we were all being taken for mugs. Out on the roads I'd encounter riders from the same firm, and we'd lie to one another about the number of deliveries we'd done – play coy – reducing the figure so as not to give the impression that any sort of favouritism was being bestowed on us by the controllers. Using a few formulae of arithmetic it became possible to pull the truth from most lies ... you divided numbers that suggested optimism, multiplied those belonging to reservation.

At the end of each week, we received invoices for our work, and that long list of traversals across the capital would culminate with the final lie, barefaced and straight: '*Grand Total*'. There was never anything grand about it. Exhausted once by the toll of worrying all week long about wages, exhausted a second time by the cycling itself, I myself would propagate the first lie that set me on my way as a courier. I would save face, answer enquiries after my wages with the sums of the more favourable weeks, rather than admitting to myself and others that I too had been had.

Out on the road it was the same, lies everywhere, the circuit based on an artificially managed time that all the riders were in on. Mostly it was sustainable, not so very different to the banking sector: the couriers' lies corresponded so perfectly to one another that they might as well have been true. We all knew the limits to keep within to stop ourselves getting caught, and for their part, the controllers had no real interest in pressing too hard. Riders who lived inside the circuit would tell control they were ready for work, when really they were still in bed with a cup of tea ... comfortably the best place in which to pass the half-hour before the first job is sent your way. Cycling in over the marshes, as soon as I crossed the River Lea, I'd radio through that I was coming on to the Hackney Road, which seemed like only the slightest of exaggerations anyway. By the time I really was on Hackney Road, then the radio would be crackling for me, and the first of the morning's work in the City would've come through. Only rarely were any of us caught out, forced to sweat because the controller responded to fictitious locations with a non-fiction job. When that happened you had to ride ten minutes in a time resembling the thirty seconds the journey should've taken from the position of your lie, then you had to lie again ... fabricate difficulties with your pocket computer, with the collection: the secretary wasn't ready, a loading bay hold-up. It didn't really matter ... it was good to have work sent your way, a few malleable truths didn't trouble anyone.

Come that time, however, technology was clamping down on us ... fiction was under threat. GPS in phones was starting to go from advanced to everyday: satellites in our pockets, customers knew where we were better than we knew ourselves. The first firm to offer it had set a benchmark, so that clients soon came to expect it as the norm. None of the courier firms, always racing so fast to the bottom, realised the clients didn't give a hoot about the GPS or where the courier actually was – they only liked the idea of a further bit of evidence when looking for grounds not to pay for a delivery, or else to pay less. Eventually it was figured out that, by turning the phone to stand-by, in the minutes before a delivery was due, the clock would freeze and we could claim late deliveries had actually scraped through on time. In such ways as this we stretched the seconds, eked time from ether. The fiction went upheld … but who knew for how much longer?

One afternoon the dominoes really failed to stack up. It was midday … an unfamiliar voice on the radio, covering the lunch shift. He's low on panache, you hear his hesitation … hear him searching through notes, papers, pen tapping. *Erm, ermmmm* hollers between every breath, each *erm* longer than the one before it. He's out of his depth, doesn't inspire confidence. It had been a wet morning, a downpour starting around 7 a.m. had convinced most of the less reliable riders to figure out an excuse for staying home … never anything quite like heavy rain in the early morning to bring to the fore a whole host of injuries, ailments, mechanical issues and family problems that never surfaced in the sun. The riders who have turned up are all overstretched and pedalling too many dead miles between too little work. Everybody is pissed off, everybody is poor and sweating inside raincoats and increasingly wet shoes. The controllers are getting it in the neck from the clients, the couriers are getting it in the neck from the controllers, everyone's tempers have turned to touch paper.

Radio crackles, *'Two-Seven … job off Parliament Square to go with that City run… urgent pickup, needed lifting out the door five minutes ago … get there now!'*

PAUSE. PAUSE.

'Two-Seven-Two-Seven?' There's a crackle, a crackle that breaks to Two-Seven, 'I'm already Blackfriars.'

PAUSE.

'What?' …

PAUSE.

Two-Seven comes back, '*Blackfriars going through…*'

A spark. '*Well what are you doing in Blackfriars? I told you to wait for work in Westminster.*'

PAUSE. '*That was ten minutes ago. I didn't expect any to come up … I rolled on.*'

The silence turns to a high pitch, a shriek that turns roar … like a window pane's been smashed right in all of our ears. A dog comes barking out from through the shards:

'*I don't give a fuck, Two-Seven. When you say you're waiting I expect you to be fucking waiting … Four-Six … Four-Six … where are you?*'

PAUSE.

Crackles. '*Four-Six here …*' PAUSE … '*just by Temple.*'

The pauses are getting longer. A crackle, Three-Four comes through in earnest,

'Not fucking now, Three-Four, some fucker is shouting at me to get this docket picked up and none of you pricks are where you're supposed to be. Four-Six … I told you to hold for work at Waterloo!'

Don't worry about place names, geography has long gone out the window, none of it means a thing anymore. In short, succinct terms: nobody's where they said they were, where they're supposed to be. It's anarchy, we're like a pack of beagles ignoring the horn. Four-Six comes through, sounding sheepish.

Crackles. 'You know most work comes in on the north … sorry, fella … I made my way back over.' *Silence.*

There's a crackle, Three-Four's been trying to break-in for a while, keeps being shouted down. Radio shouts out: 'Not now, Three-Four … carry on for Clerkenwell.'

Three-Four keeps trying, controller keeps shouting her down. Finally she makes it in, 'Send me the job … I'm close to it … I'm in St James's.'

PAUSE.

'St James's?' … *PAUSE* … 'But you told me ten minutes ago you were on your way with the Park Lane job?'

'Well … I am, but I was just finishing a coffee here first.'

The controller heaves a sigh of angry relief. 'Thank you, Three-Four … you're all fucking useless … but thank you, docket coming down now.'

The best bit comes in last. A long PAUSE … all of us silent and meditating on what's going to be said next, how long it'll be before we kiss and make up and everything's forgotten. Calm returns and then it comes, only two words … two words but the effect is instant. They drop out of the air.

'*Chupa hola.*'

A slow gasp rises up over the steeples and spires of the city, reverberates inside the cloud. *Surely not … did someone just say?* The radio on my shoulder gives its own personal sigh of disbelief, like it can't bear to listen to what's about to happen, the fury waiting to be tipped into it and hammered on the buttons. As I mentioned, the courier circuit is full of Brazilians, and they – as is traditional in any meeting of the international proletariat – had taught us only and all of the crassest expressions of their Portuguese tongue. '*Chupa hola*' meant cocksucker. We all knew it … British, Polish and Brazilian alike, every monocultural, Dagenham-born, East End, passport-less rider on the circuit still knows how to call someone a cocksucker in Portuguese. Likewise the Poles from Gdansk, who scarcely speak a word of English, those guys too have got those two words of Portuguese categorically nailed. This stopgap controller, he's gone and insulted us all, every one of us, but nobody knows who's called him a *chupa hola* for doing so. Two-Seven would have to be prime suspect, he's been given the sternest dressing-down, but it isn't his style. Then Four-Six, though it isn't really in his nature either. All told, the culprit is well and truly anonymous, could be any disgruntled one of us, breaking our backs even worse than usual and only to be called fuckers in return. The radio crackles. The silence breaks and out it comes again. Even clearer: singing, laughing, '*Chupa hola-chupa hola!*'

There's a pause. I'm rolling through Somerstown, just behind the

Euston Road. I wince. The drama is perfect. PAUSE. Radio crackles. Softly, slow and dangerous comes the question: '*Who's calling me a chupa hola?*' PAUSE-PAUSE-PAUSE. The rage builds in the silence, then breaks, cataclysm tumbles, hisses with distortion, an inferno burns.

'*Who's calling me a chupa hola? ... Who's calling me a fucking chupa hola?*'

So furious he can only repeat himself, raging at the insolence of the courier scum who's barefaced calling him a cocksucker. You can see him, thrashing in his chair. Some geezer with a perfect East End accent is bellowing the only words of Portuguese he knows like it was his mother tongue ... all we can hear is '*chupa hola*' being screamed, and the invisible voice that did it first has fallen right silent. I'm there with laughter all over my face, laughed so hard I almost got warm again ... could vouch that the rest of the riders were doing exactly the same all across London. The passing pedestrians walk by, clueless as to why the courier can't stop himself from laughing. It doesn't stop, a full five minutes the fire goes on raging. The banks, lawyers and the politicians ... all of them can go to hell right now ... the controller doesn't give a fig about controlling, about work or late deliveries, he just keeps right on burning. The words dissolve slowly to distortion, hissing out violently until, entertainment over, I turn down the volume. I ride on, can still hear a tiny midget, whispering faint but angry:

'*You pussy! Calling me a chupa hola behind the radio ... come down to the office and say it again, why don't you?!*'

18 February – N1 – Docket #10

For a while I retained a social life away from the circuit, still saw people from my previous life at university. Even if the couriers weren't so smart, even if they were laddish and crass and loud, still, at least they were honest, and with them you got exactly what you saw … raw humans, faults and all. I came to prefer them to the graduate schemers, interns paid by parents, and the politics students who'd had hastily constructed idealisms dismantle into the first pay packet that came knocking.

Dinner parties were worst of all … when I'd turn up beneath the red door of a house dressed in ivy, the fruits of a father's banking salary, a daily reminder to the child with his name on the deeds that – whatever happened – things would turn out right in the end. Shuddering at the winter cold, I stood with my bottle of wine under one arm, looked up and down the street at identical houses: large front windows revealing perfect front rooms, straight on to large rear windows and then perfect back gardens. Hinges glide, door opens … my mouth smiles … and we're delighted to see one another.

I tried my hardest. I promise I participated, conversed amongst candlelight and ripples of safe laughter. I complimented the tagine, the flaked almonds and sultanas in the couscous. I trotted out a tired spiel about politics and society, words that even I didn't care about come that time. My mind was elsewhere, tuning in and out of snippets of conversations that shouldn't have been real. Six months in touch with the actual world and you land back into '*the Kenyan massacres sound really fascinating*' … and, '*I work for a small organisation, we have a broad remit: human rights violations, trafficked women, rape survivors … that sort of thing. It's been three years now … I'm starting to get a bit bored with it.*'

More crazy than the career talk was the way people spoke about relationships… as if the things were cancers, people always so eager to stress just how fast they were growing serious. All anyone wanted was to say they'd fallen in love with someone they were about to grow old with, and half the loves so wafer-thin you got the impression it wouldn't have been inconvenient if the aging had started sooner rather than later … the dying together bit was almost the most important thing. In my chair I sat, bemused, looking at an opposite wall and the photos of my hosts with: great pyramids, Angkor Wat, Taj Mahal, Eiffel Tower in black and white. I suppose we were at an age where, if you were doing all right, it was exciting to find yourself fulfilling the role of an adult social animal. For me, pedalling all week at the furrows of an endless road, the excitement felt a long way off.

In my distracted state it became unfathomable that all I'd seen still existed out there. Islington was under the same moon as the Steppe, as bayou, and across those miles I'd allowed myself to completely forget the social norms that had once driven me so spare. I listened, blinking slowly, tired of all life and London. I listened to the scrutiny and deliberation of other people's misfortune, eloquent discussion of the wretched of the earth, before the table would turn instead to testing each other. I could sense my sigh extending each time I was asked those insidious, metropolitan questions.

That evening saw one guest in particular, lifted from an estate and into Cambridge on a scholarship, positively giddy, falling over himself with meritocracy. Across the table he sat, shirt unbuttoned and black hair spilling up as he … albatross-like … perched with arms spread between the back of his own chair and the one next to it. He smiled with a soft, false modesty as he explained his success compared to those he'd grown up with: 'They didn't apply themselves …' he mustered, 'and I suppose I did.'

No teachers, parents, community: just him and a neoliberal dream had got him where he was. I must have given a deep breath of sorts, a sound not as quiet as it should have been. Shuffling in my chair, the wind shunted a sash window back-forth in its box. He sensed my ill adjustment, seized on it with the tenacity of a state school boy who'd been thrown to private school kids and taught quickly how to be self-conscious ... learning the hard way about how to make others feel uncomfortable instead of him.

He turned a teaspoon in his hand as he cleared his throat and I shifted in my shirt. Straight my way, a chill, silent air whispers it at me ... '*You're up, boy, it's your turn to talk.*' He traced the back of the spoon across the table, metal dusting oak with the crunch of sugar granules beneath it. He interrogated on behalf of the room, attacked from behind a guise of civility.

'What was your university, Emre?'

I answer, and he rattles the remaining questions as if straight from a list learned by rote: *subject, final grades, address in London* ... he stops short of asking my postcode. Then, from the bottom of a diaphragm he gathers up, drops that atom bomb of a question.

'*What do you do?*'

Everybody loved that gem as much as ever. And by it he did not mean what was it I enjoyed, my passions as a human ... the odd idiosyncrasies that made an individual. Nobody gave two hoots about that mumbo jumbo. *What do you do?* meant what I did forty hours a week, what job fetched or didn't fetch the money to pay for me to be the human I wanted to be in the remaining leisure hours. But even that was not quite it ... most of the time the *what do you do?* actually meant '*how much do you earn?*' ... '*what are you worth?*' and ... overall ... '*how much respect do I owe you?*' As a messenger boy that was not an awful lot. That night the word simply plopped – vulnerable as you could imagine – like a piece of metal to be smashed on a blacksmith's anvil. Up it came, quietly from my mouth ...

'A courier.'

As if that wasn't bad enough, the damn table hear '*career*' ... they seize on it, think I've misunderstood. 'Yes ... but what *career?*' and they wait for the glorious profession I refer to, the title of which they hadn't quite caught.

I gather myself, laugh in pain, repeat: 'Courier ... a *career* as a *courier* ... delivering things.'

A pause settles ... then an 'oh' – like some sort of bereavement has just been reported – and then finally an awkward silence as they wait for me to offer up news of the accident ... how it happened that I'd wound up that way. They stop short of responding with 'I'm sorry to hear that', but it makes the exchange no better. I don't want to talk about why I'd chosen couriering, don't want to give some speech about not wasting my life in an office ... and they don't want to hear it. Conversation in freefall, dessert halfway ruined ... the host intervenes, puts everyone at ease and explains why I've been let in. From down the table, fulsome, on my behalf it is said: '*Emre has cycled around the world.*'

My eyes arc a high east to west. I grimace, uncomfortable, pull eyebrows up and then hide beneath them as people demand a story. I stumble into one sentence: 'Well ... another guy did it ...' then, 'and I didn't really like the way he did it.' I trail off, audience watching. Rows of heads pointed my way ... all of them so confused at the sad, sombre person who only a moment ago was supposed to have been interesting, who was supposed to have done something larger than life.

25 February – SW1 – Docket #11

Department for Environment, Food and Rural Affairs. Delivery complete. Waiting. Sitting on the white stone step of Smith Square, beside me a procession of ants trail busily up a small tree trunk, the line disappearing into a hollow in the bark. I look at the old church above, through green leaves onto blue sky as an opaque, black eye emerges on the balustrade above, cocks a tiny head. The eye is followed by a beak, and then the red breast of a robin, clear and proud against sky and tree. Its wings beat the sky, breast fills and a shadow of movement ripples through feathers as down it flies to my step, taking a kernel of grain in its beak. The robin hops towards me, and I smile and wonder— Radio crackles, scorches the silence. In frantic haste the robin hops, hops twice, flies away.

'*Two-Two … work coming down. International jobs for the depot.*'

✌

Nose to my computer I walk in. The screen waits for information to arrive. Three men stand in the post room, joking with one another in high spirits surrounded by brown envelopes and rolls of Sellotape. On a table is a large hole punch, a laminator, a machine that presses documents into plastic wrapping. They turn to me, wait with a good-natured expectation: faces smiling above smart collars. The information starts appearing on the screen, they look at me as I put a finger in the air for patience:

'OK … I'm picking up,' more loading as – box-by-box – the text appears, 'picking up for New York.'

They explode, as if the years in this basement of logistics has left each of them the exact same sense of humour. The short man standing in the centre spreads wide his arms, his face of tanned wrinkles glows, spectacles gleaming with light and his mouth opening, palms turning to summon the limits of his lungs:

> *'Start spreading the news, I'm leaving today.*
> *I want to be a part of it, New York, New York,*
> *These vagabond shoes ...'*

An envelope is hit across his chest, they all return to laughing:

'All right, all right ... you'll break a window ... the poor lad only wants to pick up the delivery.'

I give a laugh, glad at finding them all so stubbornly determined to enjoy life and one another down in their franking bunker. A set of fingers, squeezed into broad silver rings, goes drumming on the counter in front of me, moving through envelopes. I look up at tattooed forearms, at a face, at the fat gathered between the hem of a collar and rolls of a head – shaved close to hide balding just as trees are cleared to stop a forest fire. Sinatra laughs.

'You're not actually going to New York with it, are you ... on a pushbike?'

They all laugh as I shrug, 'Not this time ...' and in my mind I retreat, remember it all: flashing back to Hudson, remember Mary's dress dancing that night on the Lower East Side, and then Hudson again ... always Hudson.

'You'd have to get pedalling soon for that one,' he keeps laughing.

A single envelope is pushed over to me ... 'There you go, fella' ... I give a nod of thanks, slide the envelope into my bag as the third man – silent until now – standing tall in the corner, opens and straightens with importance.

'I'll tell you what though, if you ever get the chance ... if you ever go there, make sure you walk over the Brooklyn Bridge.'

I stop fidgeting the envelope into my bag, turn and listen to the man, speaking with conviction, the others all with a new patience.

'Danny … you remember Danny Matts, who used to work here. He told me to go there when I went on holiday, and I went, and I tell you, I tell you … some of the views! They are the most marvellous views you'll ever see. I didn't pay him much notice when he started getting excited about it, but I went, and straight away I knew what he was talking about. You wouldn't believe it unless you've seen it. It's like nothing else … the skyscrapers in Manhattan, the water, the subway trains rattling over the bridges.'

I watch him talking, as youth and excitement for the world moves back through his face. The eyes open, shining for one of those precious instances when you see a person in the full glory of the moments that define them, the moments that keep a soul smiling, even as a face ages and everything but memories begins to grow old.

6 March – EC1 – Docket #12

Eating on the circuit caused all manner of problems: ever a choice between something I wanted to eat that was impossibly expensive, or something I didn't want that was affordable. Your health or your wallet, and a daily decision to make between either taste or robbery. As with riding around the world, there are few limits to the amount of food a courier can put away. I'd generally take a large jar full of rice and stew or pasta and sauce, two Eccles cakes, and two or three pieces of fruit. In the mornings, I'd leave the house after a breakfast of two poached eggs on toast, coffee and a thick slice of bread, smothered once with butter and a second time with chocolate spread, so that you could see your teeth marks after they'd bitten through the cross-section of fats.

On the whole I tried to make it through a day with only that, so as to save a little money, but generally I succumbed to the need for more. Cookies were my most regular buy, sold by one of the supermarket chains. Large, soft and buttery: a pack of five had once been £1, with enough calories inside that paper bag to get me through the rest of the day. Even as the cost of everything else went steadily up, the supermarket eventually managed to drop the price to only 50 pence, safe in the knowledge that sugar was what the city wanted most of all. I'd eat my way through all five of the things inside half an hour, all hydrogenated fats and enough sugar to make your teeth chatter. I put them straight down the hatch, guiltily, disgusted to force such junk on my body.

Sometimes I indulged my real desires, those moments where I was overcome with the need for nourishment: a sort of 'you deserve it' euphoria, facing down a chalkboard with an assured entitlement to my own serving from the leg of *jamon*, held in its wooden rack, two bow-headed steel bolts that wound down to clutch it either end of the bone. Something like that would set me back about £6, and mostly I went without, for it was too much. I couldn't come to terms with the idea that 10 per cent of my wages would disappear on just lunch. I'd cycle by the bakeries, drinking down the warm, golden smell of cooked butter and flour, wondering if there'd come a day in my life when the prospect of a coffee and a pastry didn't feel like extravagance.

If I had it bad, at least it seemed that everybody else was suffering something worse still. Food in Britain had turned peculiar, the whole country was in the midst of one giant, torturous, eating disorder. You saw as much in the way people and newspapers talked of 'foodies' ... made a fetish of eating, as if there were some other type of anthropoid who didn't need to eat and survived out of only thin air. Pornographic rashers of bacon and images of buttered toast were slapped up on billboards – no different to the women in hot pants. On the side of bus stops you'd find fruit slipping between great, lipsticked mouths, as if the woman had met Mister Strawberry for a night of passion, and he'd sworn his wife would never find out about the blowjob on the Holloway Road. From above the tarmac, the appointed kitchen gods looked down, grave-faced upon us ... famous chefs who'd been elevated to some mythical status on the basis that they were possessed of the magical power to combine ingredients with heat and create something a person could actually enjoy eating. Two-Nine used to laugh about it all, rolled her eyes in laconic exclamations: '*You British are crazy. In France it would be unthinkable for anyone to be so famous ... just because they can cook!*'

Motivated by the sorry state of affairs, one husband and wife team had left the banking sector, set out to start a café business instead with the goal to provide original food, with personality, to the workers of London. The plan worked a treat, and within a year of the first outlet, they'd opened another fifty ... started providing original food, with personality ... on every second street in central London. A supermarket had come out calling a spade a spade, released a luxury range entitled '*Taste the Difference* ...' they didn't finish the sentence, there was no '... *between this and the shit we normally sell you*,' but credit to them, they'd done a good job of establishing the idea that food tasting good was something beyond what could ordinarily be expected.

Midday in a supermarket was the best time to watch the neurosis in action. In the minutes after one o'clock, the throng on the pavement outside would swell, aisles inside would turn fit to bursting, with sachets of bakery aroma tipped into supermarket ventilation systems in order to stimulate the appetite and encourage the midday rush. The staff had been drilled, as diligent as sappers, waiting at their posts for customers never quite sure what to do with all the choice and promise. I watched them standing there, poring over refrigerators of potted salads and triangular sandwiches, perusing the many combinations of discount that had been put before them. You could see the sorry creatures as they agonised with not an impulse left: the calories, the cost, how many of the government's five fruit or vegetables they had consumed so far that day, quite apart from what they actually even wanted to eat. I watched them lifting an item, replacing it, lifting it again. All around the store would be articles from other aisles: a pot of hummus among the biscuits, where a new year's resolution had buckled, a red pepper with the Cornish pasties, flapjacks in the banana box. All of it discarded in a hurry, just as it had been picked up on a whim, by a maverick impulse that after ninety seconds the customer just hadn't been sure they were comfortable with.

When I was riding even plausibly close to the area, my own favourite meal came from Leather Lane, where I found the King of Felafel. Ever since I first arrived in London, those guys had been making a not-bad wrap for £3.75. Then, one day, there'd been trouble in the Kingdom ... an Iraqi Kurd had fallen foul of the King, left with all

77

the trade secrets plus his own conviction that the wraps should have shredded red cabbage in them, that the cucumber would taste better with a little mint. He took up two doors down the road, resolving to charge just £2.50 for his wraps, and every time he or his brothers made those things it was with such love ... a slither of butter along the outside of the wrap before laying it under the hot press and toasting it off. The lunchtime rush there was always a full hour in length, a slog through which it really showed that all of the staff had served in an army and done their military service. The order of things is perfect: abject regimentation, a system nothing less than immaculate. A queue of twenty people forms, and still nobody left waiting longer than five minutes. Each cousin has his job, either wrapping wraps, grilling chicken or bagging up and taking cash. From across the tables, I'd always watch as they dispatched quiet smiles for each lunchtime saint going to great contortions of limbs and overfilled pockets so as to avoid taking a plastic bag. Corporate lawyers, banksters and marketeers all manoeuvred awkwardly, determined not to put one single carrier bag into circulation before returning to work. Devising ad campaigns for munitions companies, contorting corporates out of their tax dues, PR-ing on another oil spill in the Niger Delta. With that lot for a workload, the last thing they wanted on their conscience was a suffocated turtle and their plastic bag.

15 March – W1 – Docket #13

One day I saw it coming, saw what was in store, another of my pre-
monitions of the future. It was on Davies Street, Mayfair: road rising
slightly, the sort of slope you don't notice in a car … long enough
inside a car and very soon the whole world seems flat. I was going
slow, tired, late in an afternoon … the circuit quiet and no reason
to hurry. It came from nowhere, unannounced, not a sound to be
heard, except perhaps a little hum at the last. A light breeze, a reaper
and the whisper of hydrogen power. A flash of black. It's punched
me, punched me hard, like I've been thumped by a god. *Flying. Air.
What the—?* Tarmac. You pick yourself up to your knees, you look
at your hands, the blood peers through the grazes, waves hello but
doesn't start stinging for fifteen minutes, waits for the adrenaline
to wear off before it lets you hurt. The aches are for next morning.
The battering ram doesn't even know it's toppled me. A dark jeep.
Up there in the armchair is the would-be killer: music playing, air
conditioned, the metal hull of the beast disappears. Like a rock from
a catapult, sailing over the city wall, it recedes into the distance, the
purr of an electric engine glides away.

Do I laugh or cry? At least there's humour in this one. Carbon
neutral bastards, sustainable pricks … cunts into eternity, figuring
out ways to be swines to one another forevermore. I watch it floating away up the road. I shake my head in bewilderment, I could
sob a little, but really … why bother? Part-rage, part-resignation …
it's just not fair. In truth, there's not so much more to say … pretty
straightforward, your life flashes before your eyes, and that's it.

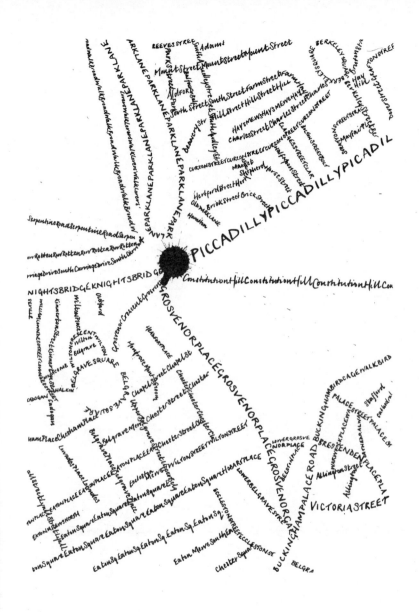

Part II

ASPHALT

Anarchy

Different as the couriers were, at work we experienced the same things, the same encounters and worries of money, the same reactions from the city that kept us on its breadline. Most of the time it felt as though all London was looking down at couriers: people bristled, their noses contorting like concertinas, their spines straightening and lips stuck out. I was shot some priceless glances, and to be honest, you don't know a sneer until you've been a courier or in a similarly low-ranking job.

Harder to stand than the snobbery at each destination were the roads between them: a parallel universe to the society around. Frequently hostile, the roads were like a network of shallow, asphalt trenches, each crammed with alien species unable to get along and locked in a constant state of war. The way of the roads left you glad to cling to those with whom you had the slightest thing in common, even if that was only the vehicle you used to navigate the metropolis. For starters, the air was foul: you'd see two separate articulated lorries, each delivering half-empty loads to separate supermarkets on the same street, fumes spewing out from their exhaust stacks as they pulled away. The buses were worse: walls of red that queued bumper-to-bumper, breathing diesel along some of the most congested stretches of all London. Most of the cabbies rented their Hackney carriages from hire companies – £400 a week – but those who didn't would hang on until the bitter end before having parts in their engine repaired or upgraded. Clouds of black and sulphur would explode from the back end whenever a cabbie nudged at the accelerator. Most thought transport pretty dull, boring, just a question of roads and vehicles, and so without to-do it was ignored when results showed a Lewisham kid was twice as likely to be hit by a car than one growing up in Chelsea. Likewise, when the developers were forced to put in a dozen social housing units amongst two thousand luxury flats … you knew that dozen would be sitting square beside the Old Kent Road: children locked inside with nowhere to play, their developing lungs breathing in the fumes. It wasn't a fashionable cause but transport showed which lives were precious and which were less so.

When the weather was warm, riding in over the marshes, I'd see London below a haze of yellow smog … a visualisation of that constant need to cough-clear my throat, of newspaper headlines announcing ever-rising numbers of asthmatics. On particularly bad days, the heavy morning mist showed what waited: particles of pollution trapped inside a humid net, so that the sky goes crawling down your throat, refuses to budge and sets the mouth with an unslakable need to swallow the diesel ball hanging at a tonsil. The government had the answer, had multiple answers even … the answer, strangely, was monitoring stations. Take out air pollution monitoring and *hey presto* … problem solved … no more air pollution. Local politics offered little more by way of help, the city halfway through its first term with a mayor who would go on to oversee a decade of stagnation. Politicians may all have a fancy for a gimmick, but in that guy it was his very substance, the PR skeleton on which his whole body hung. Even as the pollution deaths mounted, nothing would shake his attention from one vanity project after the next, a whole herd of white elephants roaming London's streets. He threw up cable cars between parts of the city nobody visited, blew the bus budget on a new design that proved not to work, each failure batted away in a buffoonery by which the man dreamed of one day charming his way to the top of Westminster.

Amongst all the traffic, the hard metal and the rock, we cyclists were small fry. Some of us rode fast and confident enough to sit in the slipstream of buses or lorries. Like lamprey feeding off a shark, we'd trail from a fin, bowing out as the driver hit brakes and lunged unindicated into a left turn. Quickly you duck out, scram as a set of eight wheels bumps up pavement, pulled over kerbstones disintegrating to rubble from countless similar strikes. The year after I returned to the courier circuit, sixteen cyclists went down on London's roads: three-quarters of them hit by left-turning lorries and women three-quarters of that number. The consensus was that women didn't ride assertively enough … left drivers the space in which they were prepared to take liberties with the lives of others. Outcry followed carnage, and so a few haulage firms made great to-do about fitting their fleet with alarms and loud speakers, designed to go berserk whenever the steering wheel moved left. It looked good on paper, with suits shaking hands for photos, but in the real world I saw myself in the wake of a cement mixer, driver on his telephone as he swerved at the last, and '*this vehicle is turning left*' to be the final, disappointing words of all the sweet lines I'd heard in my life.

Out there was anarchy, was politics by other means, and you saw the results spread all across the city, with bollards toppled and kerbs upended. I'd listen to the clanking chains of skip trucks … *link-smashing-skip-smashing-link* … a tocsin raising the alarm as I braked to avoid the cement splatter which spilled from the swinging arm of a mixer leaving a construction site, droppings to be left on the tarmac for the next half-decade. There were potholes, too: potholes from disrepair, from falling debris, from the thousand-tonne crane that showed up to lift the air conditioning unit, crushing the tarmac as its hydraulic supports pressed down. The warfare dehumanised, transformed the road users into no more than agents of their vehicles. When an eight-year-old on his way home from school was killed under a black cab, it was not the driver that had killed the child, it was the taxi. If a human being was killed on a bicycle, she soon became only a cyclist, and it was hard to feel too sad for the loss of anyone who'd only ever been an *ist* to begin with. I once rounded Hyde Park Corner with a taxi at my side, don't even know what it was I'd done to enrage him so, but as he passed me, window down, he snarled, '*One day you'll die … and you'll deserve it.*'

There was no trace of decency that the roads would leave intact, no norm of law or behaviour that could not be undone. They were carnal: an eternity of stop-start, halting your rhythm for the changing colour of a light, for the queues, orderly channels and finite space shared with a thousand foes who also wished to drive their cars into central London, all constantly aware that they commanded a vehicle with the potential to go faster than the city permitted.

The motorbike couriers were some of the worst. Cheeks bunched inside helmets and pinching around the eyes … a visor up and soot smeared at their faces like colliers of the road. They were constantly furious, always paying for motorbike repairs and never earning enough money: '*You fucking cunt!*' as he tore past me on his way from the lights. It was a warzone, hellfire … the Enlightenment had never happened, this was not civilisation. One afternoon I arrived to a stopped bus and a diesel spillage trickling over the road. Police arrive, blowing whistles, wailing blood-curdling cries for the extinguishing of cigarettes. The fire brigade came next and opened a hydrant, hosed down the entire street then threw sand all about to calm the bedlam.

One day on the Walworth Road I saw my first injury, my first fistfight: a man punched in the face by a speeding van. He stepped out from behind a bus. *Thwack!* Unorthodox. The body panel slugged him with a southpaw across nose and cheek, took the two of them at once. As that flank of white van burst him open, the blood went flying like a geyser, spewed upwards as he span round frothing like a rescue flare going over a mountainside. He dropped, blood beating him to the ground … falling fast, it landed with the sweetest and most innocent pitter-patter before his head followed down. And you should've heard the … *crrr-aaa-ckkk*.

At the same time, he was one of the fortunate ones, for I watched him pick himself groggily back up, first to his knees and then his feet. Once I came across a motorcyclist less lucky, by Bishopsgate, four police over him, one each corner of a plastic tarpaulin to keep the drizzle off. Underneath, a blanket covered his torso, the street closed as paramedics tried to lift him onto a stretcher ... but a leg that didn't want to budge. I watched a foot, hovering, paralysed in space as if the joints were porcelain and not set for moving. Tiny flickers of brittle pain flashed in the human, the motorbike all but unscathed beside him.

That, however, was only the frantic chaos of central London. Outside of the middle – on asphalt stretches that we couriers feared to pedal for the dead miles it would create in getting there and back – the outer boroughs of London told different stories. Through streets bleached by parked vehicles, and despite an obesity epidemic never far from political mention, the statistics still said around half all London journeys under two miles were driven by car. Stationary cars ran for miles and miles on either side of each street, occupying billions of pounds of real estate and creating narrow corridors of metal through which drivers would shoot. Parked wheels squeezed up on pavements free of children, pedestrians or most signs of life beyond the angry suburbanite behind the wheel of a car, with seemingly never enough time to get where they were going.

School runs were best of all: a million pounds and hundred thousand kilos of machined metal set about moving one child at a time, but twenty kilos in weight and tiny feet dangling in the air above the foot well ... a global industrial complex attached to what might've been ten minutes' walk and some useful exercise. The authorities defended the status quo ... said there were few cyclists or pedestrians to consider in those areas, and though this perhaps was true, it was only because the environment had been made so hostile to any forms of life that were not petrol-driven to begin with. Those authorities would not concede to reducing speed limits because the police would not commit to enforcing them because the authorities would not concede to reducing them. Meanwhile, Transport for London were harangued for not improving roads, only to justify the inaction with the excuse that only major roads were their responsibility while the rest, quite truthfully, went under the semi-feudal jurisdiction of individual boroughs. Even as hundreds of pedestrians were knocked to their roads each year, with dozens hospitalised or killed, still Westminster councillors fought tooth and nail against any change that might affect the journey of a millionaire in a limousine. Around the time of an election, a campaign poster emerged with a photo of a car: '*This runs on money and makes you fat*' and a bicycle: '*This runs on fat and saves you money*' … and yet the powers that be saw sense so slowly.

10 April – EC1 – Docket #14

Cabbies were one of the biggest populations on the streets ... drove like the city was theirs alone. Most cycle couriers despised them for the way they pulled U-turns in the middle of a road, the way they swung directly to the kerbside when a fare presented itself, never a regard for who they might have crushed on their way there. I once saw a cabbie swerve to ram his taxi against a courier in retribution for the courier having collided with his wing mirror. The other couriers, on motorbikes or with vans to pay for, resented the cabbies no less ... mainly because of the wages they were rumoured to earn, because they were permitted to park more freely, and – quaintly – because they had their own tea stands. None of this unpopularity bothered the cabbies much. They took pride in their role as professionals of the road, relished not taking orders from anybody, and enjoyed knowing they had a trade of their own, a knowledge of the city that set them apart from the greater mass. It was no surprise there was such animosity between the couriers and the cabbies ... neither group would have guessed how much they had in common, not that they were ever likely to find out. The cabbies and couriers didn't integrate with one another, they didn't have to, there were enough of each group for them to keep to themselves, extend courtesy inside the group while the rest of the city could go to hell.

My feelings on cabbies were more sympathetic than most: you could sense that, trapped timeless inside their cabs, they felt the world outside was changing for the worse. They were always listening to radio shows, discussions crafted for people already angry at life, and with presenters paid to make the audience angrier. The cabbies spent lives locked wilfully inside an emotional diet of benefits cheats, disability fraud, industrial disputes, bankers' bonuses, and the relentless desire of government to take over our lives. They indoctrinated themselves with simplified versions of all that was wrong in the world, became drip-fed curmudgeons who earned far too much to get on with a simple life like the couriers, but not nearly enough to set themselves free from jobs as gerbils, frustrated at their wheels.

Nine-to-five and their quality of life wasn't up to much either. We all knew the cabbies would take toilet breaks inside their own carriages … now and then you caught a glimpse of them empty-ing an opaque receptacle of yellow liquid into a gutter. Some odd by-law still allowed them to piss in parkland, but only so long as they remained in contact with their vehicle. The residents of Hyde Park Square had pinned complaints about this on their notice board … millionaires powerless to stop a cabbie pissing in the private garden while a nonchalant, all-powerful hand rested on the bonnet. In addition, behind the purring of the engine, a good many of them had grown sex-obsessed. Like some couriers, testosterone seeped from eye sockets, stubble growing by the second as knuckles whit-ened over the wheel. Stuck fast in their jobs and surrounded by the metropolitan catwalk, they took it out on the women, as if lust were the only way they could remember they were humans at all. I once cycled up Rosebery Avenue beside a girl on a bike, bum raised as she lifted from the saddle to take the hill. At the lights a taxi pulled alongside us: window down with an old face leaning out, nothing but ears and a large nose. From flaring nostrils and puckered eyes he leant out, asphalt feral, a beast who'd learned to talk. He panted after the girl, a thick voice rattling through smoker's lungs, a yellow film, dry between cracked lips: '*You look delightfully naughty, you do!*'

Life by automobile slowly captured their souls, dragged them down and took them. The human inside was bent to the will of the machine without, until eventually he was only a pilot for the beast in its black hood: the probing, headlamp eyes, the delighted grimace of a radiator grill. Sometimes I'd look over my shoulder at one of those beetle-like creatures, alerted by the firing of a horn that it was coming for me. I would see the thing nearing, rocking wildly from side to side upon its axles, and there in the cockpit the pilot, caged and silent behind the glass, swaying with slow fury to the rhythm of the car, his nose and mouth contorting in rage ... teeth bared, strands of spittle stretching at the corner of the lips as his mouth opened slowly to let out his voice. From inside his glass-steel box, exhibited like some strange animal of the highways, I watch as he shouts, roars into the mute windshield that I am ... a cunt. My eyebrows lift, '*What was that?*' It comes again. Clarification. *CUNT!*

After five or so encounters that went like that, I'd meet a cabbie whistling as he drove, dressed in bow tie and cardigan, window down as he wished me a good day and forced me to remember that old lesson ... generalisations only get you so far.

14 April – EC2 – Docket #15

One day spelt it out better than all the rest, summed up my relationship with the law back then. As with the cabbies, those encounters were so frequently hostile it could make sweeping judgement impossibly hard to abstain from. It was Gresham Street: heart of the Square Mile, City Police rather than Metropolitan, who cover incidents outside the City and are meaner and more grizzly in the way they go about it. With a Met Police officer you'll see a packet of Marlboro lights in the breast pocket of his shirt. City Police boil down similarly, but they're cleaner cut in the way they go about shafting you.

I had one drop before empty: 4 Gresham Street, a regular delivery, the door right at the near end that I'm riding on to. I pull off the road before the corner, scoot up the dropped kerb and on to the empty pavement where I know number 4 is waiting a matter of metres away. I appear from round the corner, gliding to a halt. Police. Strolling ominously my way. I see his face profile me: bag, radio, bicycle, courier. *Courier.* And his mind is made up. My insides heave, my eyes increase their frames per second, life slows down. I watch the officer as footfall gets heavier, shadow darker. I watch face shift from patrol to pounce: action stirs, nose twitches, eyes snap.

The first seconds when I see police, and my bicycle is on a pavement, last approximately five times their normal length. Time takes on a weight of deep loss … of anger, frustration and helplessness. In my head I see thirty-five pounds leave my wallet … notes unfolded, slipping away. What's happening here is worse than police though, it is *Police Community Support Officers, PCSOs* … 'plastic coppers' as they were known on the street. Police Community Support Officers were police with no real authority, with no power of arrest, and a general toothlessness to them that meant polite, law-abiding citizens who momentarily rode a bicycle on a pavement were their ideal criminal: safe and respectful felons. All of the thrill and none of the risk. Strangely enough it was the original coppers that most disliked PCSOs, perceived them a threat. 'Cheap police' was how one officer once put it to me: coppers without the same training, salaries or pensions.

This one comes to me as I pull to a halt: head falls backwards, rolling up to sky as the officer goes for the Velcro pouch where he keeps his ticket book. Once he's made that move, it's all over, like a motor neurone law. The hand will only return to that pouch after the ticket has been written. There will be no benefit of doubt.

He grins, 'Were you riding your bicycle on the pavement?'

Good cop – bad cop has left good cop at home … brought obvious question cop along for the outing. I point, can't help my voice from pleading, as I stand seconds from the door and my delivery.

'I'm just going to that door there … I don't cycle on pavements,' I point again. 'I just came up that kerb there, it was only five metres.'

He just repeats. 'Were you riding your bicycle on the pavement?'

'I was going slowly, and I don't like riding on the pavement … it slows me down.' I point again, harder, 'I was arriving at *that* door.'

Third time. 'Were you cycling on the pavement?'

They break it right down … put it so elementally that you have to give the answer by which they'll incriminate you, hang yourself. Context does not exist, discretion a dirty word, circumstance make-believe. My voice is rising.

'There wasn't anyone on the pavement! It's empty apart from us!'

'But you were cycling on it?'

'*For five metres!*' He takes that as confession. Ticket book starts journey from utility belt to front.

When you're someone who believes in all the ideals of society and community on which we're brought up, there is something horrendously painful about being told you're breaking the law. It's like being hit with your favourite stick, being told you don't care about the things you know you care about. We're raised with such thorough respect for the law that it's painful to be told you're outside of it, even where that law becomes desperately unfair and horribly, inappropriately enforced. I look at the officer watching me: consider his face, perhaps south Asian, not dissimilar to faces I chatted with at Malaysian roadsides, but the accent says he's been in London a couple of generations at least. He stands back, makes ready my fine as I turn ... turn away with a sigh, put my bicycle against the wall and listen as it falls to land with a clatter. The officer puts a hand to my shoulder and pulls me back ... '*Stay there!*' he snaps. I look at him with my eyes full of rights, full of deaths in police custody, full of cages and railings and how in all hell this man might abuse his power over me. His vision levels at mine, flashes authority my way ... a *do-as-you're-told* sort of glare, his finest, especially for me. '*Stay there,*' he repeats, softer this time, half-menacing.

From his utility jacket, cuffs and canisters latched to it, a small karabiner dangles above his breast with an alcohol-based solution hanging, patiently awaiting post-physical contact. He takes it in one hand, sprays it into palm, turns hands over one another, looking at me as he sanitises his paws, sterilises himself of me. That was rich, a pretty irony. Would you believe it but police scum thinks I'm scum, too ... the bastard's worried about hepatitis. We look at one another, a *feeling's mutual* sort of a look. I sneer. I hate. In another life I'll get my revenge for slights like this ... not this time ... but down the line I'll have the cosmos give them all a fine thrashing, have their pants down and put them over its knee. For now I just laugh a painful laugh. I try one last plea ... just for the hell of it.

'I wasn't cycling on the pavement, I was only cycling to that door there ... the pavement was *empty*! I wasn't endangering anyone. I wouldn't want to endanger anyone, why would I!?'

He steps up to the plate, ready to smack me down with rationality and due diligence. 'The pavement looked empty ... but what if it hadn't been? *What if ...*' Oh I know what's coming now, his mouth opens and ... '*What if there had been a pregnant woman?*'

Always the damn pregnant woman. And if not, then a disabled child, or an elderly woman lying sprawled across the pavement, grasping for her walking stick and prosthetic limb. Clairvoyants of doom ... police are real geniuses where it comes to figuring out calamity at multiple points of abstraction.

'What if there had been a child running towards you?' he goes on ... and the problem is he believes it. He really does think he's keeping the world safe, *Star Wars* right here on the Gresham Street pavement. He's in an alternative reality, doesn't realise there are no children, that we're in the Square Mile and there's not a whipper-snapper in sight. Only suits, spivs, career-driven marketeers and financial freaks ... take one of that lot down and I'd be doing the children of the world a favour, one less mercenary to mortgage their future. I exasperate. I throw up my hands.

'If there had been a child, then I was going slowly enough to stop ... you know I was!'

He scribbles hesitantly at the ticket, looks up at me. Flatly.

'It's against the law.'

'I know the law.'

This is a mistake. In general, you should never suggest to a copper that you know the law ... but this time it's all too far gone and I might as well get it off my chest, get value for money from my thirty-five quid. It's not a question of the law ... it's a question of them, of them and their role. The police are not on the streets to enforce laws, they're on the streets to enforce a dynamic of power. I'm not about to tell him that, but still, I start up: 'I know that when they passed the law about cycling on pavements ... in 1999 ... the Home Office said it was to be enforced *with discretion* ... and not to punish people cycling carefully.'

He looks at me. Flat. Right in my face, I can see he's made this one personal. He speaks. 'We've been told not to use discretion.'

I shake my head. Disgust at the notion of law without discretion, criminalised misdemeanour in a world of oligarchy and mass fraud. I crank up, spring, wounded, all ready to vituperate: 'Do you like your job? Are you new to this?'

He goes on, writes location. He scribbles, doesn't look up, murmurs, 'Some things are harder than others.'

I look at him: a little overweight, unflattering, unsure of himself. Slow eyes, shallow eyes, eyes that just look out at the world, that never asked questions, wouldn't even know where to start. He looks at me, those eyes like a telescope on the promenade of a seaside town, eyes switched off until called to use ... pointed at the exact same view for an entire lifetime, switched off again until the next coin drops. I feel for the guy, only wish he felt the same for me. I start back up.

'I'm going to earn fifty pounds for working today, and you're going to take most of that ... for less than five metres on the pavement.' I'm starting to whine, against my wishes, but the injustice is too much.

'What's your name?'

'Do you feel good about that?' I challenge. '*Do you think that's fair?*'

'What's your name?'

Inside, I hit back on the part of me that's angry. Voice raises.

'Do you think that's fair?'

The officer steps up, 'We're only following our orders.'

We look at one another, the guy so far gone he doesn't even realise he's just uttered the most incriminating, blood-stained words in all history, in the entire English language. I look into him ... the child within is long gone but he's got a human in there, I can see it, he knows I'm right, just isn't too concerned about my thirty-five pounds. It isn't such a big deal to him, no idea how hard I'll work for it and besides, he's seen worse, greater injustices than mine. He knows this won't end any other way. That face sinks into my brain.

Logged. Above-average height, lips a shade purple, dark eyes, cheeks high and full, jet-black hair growing square around the forehead. Indelible. I'll remember him forever, committed to memory. He takes my money. Twenty-eight days to cough up, or else the prompt-paying justice discount, law at bargain prices – 25 per cent off if you empty your pockets inside a fortnight – is gone. Half of my day's wages just went. Today I'll work for the police.

After it's over I cycle away, pedal off through the streets, below the offices in white stone. The streets are silent: just me under the glass and steel where they laundered the money of the Mexican drug cartels, where they manipulate interest rates and mis-sell risky investments as safe bets, speculate on the destruction of a nation's economy, where they use the money of other people to smooth out their failures, to pay bonuses higher than any of us would earn in ten lifetimes. I know that none of this is news to anyone … we've all accepted it as just the way things go.

The police fined my sorry ass … probably got me once every two months, on average, in my time as a courier. They were only ever following orders and following orders and following orders … the same each time. I was always riding slowly, carefully to or from a door, never going fast enough to hit anybody … never fast enough to escape.

&

The more life brings you into contact with the police … I'm sorry … the less you like 'em. Sure, they seem heroic when they show up fearless after you've been burgled, but anyone who's forced to live in the greyer areas of society, anyone who's been to a protest born out of a belief that our system is wrong, not to mention anyone who's ever been young, male and black: they're the ones to ask for an opinion of the police … not the mild-mannered, system-works chap with a respectable wage, the insurance company set to pay out and plod showing up in his *Starsky & Hutch* finest. Each time, down on the streets, I'd talk myself into trouble, without fail, and each time they would obediently only follow their orders and follow their orders.

I knew the statistics for deaths in police custody. I dearly loved a friend who'd been hit across the face at a protest, eyebrow split plum purple and then the girl kissed goodbye with the foulest of words from the officer: '*I'd fuck you if you weren't so dirty.*' I remembered a girl I'd known in London, burgled one night … police showed up dutifully, took her details, told her not to worry. An hour later and one officer called to see if she wanted to … maybe, *perhaps* … go for a drink sometime? Then there was that motorcycle cop – all his social power and that engine so close to his cock had gone directly to his head. I shouted that he'd jumped a red light, wasn't indicating either … not that I cared, but he'd rolled over the solid white line that coppers were always reminding me meant I was supposed to stop. His response came straight, uncomplicated. '*I can do what I want … I'm a police officer …*' and with that, he roared away.

For years I'd made the mistake of carrying that lot into every interaction I ever had with the police, couldn't help talking myself into trouble, and it took time to learn how to show the deference that is actually the single thing a copper needs to feel. The police have a keen sense of smell where two things are concerned: intelligence and rights. Go into a conversation with a copper showing a sense of either, and they'll screw you, especially if you're a young male … they delight in busting you down a few stations and chuckle to themselves after you've moved on. If you're ever dealing with the police from a position of vulnerability, where you need the outcome to work in your favour, my advice is to approach them in the same manner you would a plumber. Keep it simple, pretend you're friends and act like your radiators need balancing. It took hundreds of pounds in fines before I learned that the hard way.

I wasn't the only one on the circuit they'd given cause for a grudge. Five-Two kept having run-ins with them as he went from squat to squat. They didn't care if he couldn't afford the rent the landlords were asking, didn't care that the property had been left empty and abandoned anyway: all the police cared about was the opportunity to flex some authority and throw people out on their ear in the name of justice. Situations like that get pretty simple when you don't bother considering where people go once they're homeless. The squat had been raided, for some reason the perverts had strip-searched every one of them … rubber gloves, the lot, no orifice left unopened. Five-Two had jumped straight out of bed when an armed stranger burst into his room at 5:30 a.m., the police interpreted that as suspicious behaviour: an act of aggression, provocative. They beat him up … not that you'd have known it. They train the cops how to do it without leaving visible marks: backs of the knees, thighs, no cuts or bruises, only the best and most professional thuggery from that gang.

Five-Two was limping for the next seventy-two hours. They ransacked the place, alleged they'd found a stolen handbag, made that the justification to impound the lot of it. Food and belongings were thrown into black liners, driven away to a lockup somewhere. A week later the guys were told they could collect it … the police hadn't found anything, no drugs, no contraband. Five-Two and his friends went to the lockup, unpeeled their books and family photos from between slices of bread, curdling milk. He left the city a month later: a sculptor by training, a gentle spirit by instinct … they'd shaken him up, put him on edge. After the raid he clutched his fists as he spoke to you, he bit his nails, shuffled constantly, scared every moment that someone was about to burst in and rough him up again.

Don't get me wrong, of course there were exceptions amongst those coppers … they weren't all hooligans, there's talent and spirit in any institution. I was well aware there were police officers with great humility and restraint, others with philosophy degrees and doctorates. The thing was, those kind of qualities stuck out like sore thumbs, were conspicuous in their sense of civic duty. In double-quick fashion, the best coppers had all been given promotions, an office and a desk, were never to be seen on the streets of London again.

20 April – WC1 – Docket #16

If all this seems pretty male, well, what you're getting there is a feel for life as a courier. The bus drivers are male, the taxi drivers are male, the couriers are male, most of the police are male: in short, the roads are male. They are impatient, aggressive and angry, so that where a woman does appear on the road, she does a Thatcher and starts behaving like a male to fit in. There were a few females amongst the couriers, though in the main they chose to reject most of what made the fairer sex at all fair in the first place. Swathes of hair were shaved away. One had the map of her home state of Ohio large in Indian ink across her bicep … another had a spider's web tattooed breast to breast and full across the sternum. They had skulls on shoulders, teeth crooked from crashes or fights. They scuttled their faces … sabotaged quaint. I remember the controversy over the radio when a client phoned to complain about a sticker on one of the girl's bikes. '*Obscene!*' was the allegation, the instruction simple: have the stickers removed, or else we find new couriers. I listened in.

PAUSE. Radio crackles. 'But it only says "*Fuck Taxis!*"'

Radio crackles, controller comes back, 'That one wasn't the problem.'

Pause. 'Oh … you mean … "*Suck my cunt*"?'

Their muscles bulged, and on the roads I watched girl couriers shout down drivers with more venom than any man I ever met. They were not, by conventional norms, in the least desirable … but tribalism and scarcity being what they are, the men were attracted to the women, and the women, with ratios stacked so overwhelmingly in their favour, would always remain sought after. Amongst many, egos swelled, and they could easily come to interpret any attention as an advance. There was one: pale-skinned and scowling, body like a boulder and topped in a tangle of lank, red hair. I saw her regularly on the roads, one day ventured *hello*, she looked round:

'Do I know you?'

'No,' I replied, a bit affronted, 'but I see you most days.'

We were cycling away from traffic lights at the time, she looked at me, dropped it my way, might as well have spat:

'*I have a boyfriend.*'

I swallowed. As if I cared, as if – even with the depths of isolation I was plumbing – I might have been interested. I laughed.

'I only said hello.'

Stern-faced, she replied, '*Sorry.* A lot of guys ask me out.'

As a courier, your main encounter with women is the secretaries: at least one in every office, and generally trussed up like Christmas crackers. Couriers and secretaries had a fairly tense relationship. Whereas the bankers, politicians, lawyers and so on were comfortably above our rank, because we were nowhere near them in the pecking order, and because our jobs didn't affect them, we generally flew well below their social radar. The secretaries were a different matter, we were like neighbouring castes of Untouchables, down at the bottom, in the margins and blurred boundaries where difference becomes most pronounced.

It went beyond that too, because the secretaries spent their days being patronised and talked-down to by bigwigs and high-flyers, and as a result they'd gotten the art of disdain down to a tee, knew how to look down at us as if they were genuine aristocrats ... disgusted by our dishabille, the impertinence of our even showing up. What you learn down there as a courier is that, at the bottom, everybody needs somebody else to look down on ... the only reason the upper classes aren't quite so vicious is because they know they're nobody else's scum. Once you've accepted you're bottom of the pile people begin drawing up subsections in the shit. Added to that, society had grown post-work, post-labour: in the modern age the noblest vocation was that which took least exertion. More money for less effort was the balance to strike: sweat was undignified, physical work a sign of stupidity, so that even if the secretaries weren't that much better off than we, they didn't have to do much more than sit, greet or usher for their pay.

Sometimes I'd encounter a secretary more amiable than most, one who would smile at me, treat me as a human delivering an envelope, rather than as an envelope that happened to have been escorted there by human. She'd ask questions about my day, about my job, talk weather … and amongst all the cold of London, it could feel so damn tender, so achingly warm, to be given the opportunity to be a person again. I would hand her my pocket computer on the screen of which she had to scribble an electronic signature, and as I did so, my poor, starving fingertips flooded with the miniscule touch of another, so that sometimes I'd all but find my head lifting to look up and share a recognition of this sacred intimacy of ours against the city. Of course it never came, I'd look up into the crown of her head, tilted down at the screen, then back at me as she smiled and waited for me to take back the handset. Once a secretary asked if I'd like still or sparkling when I moved to refill my water bottle. It was then I realised that I'd been broken, that no matter the self-respect I might have started with, not a jot remained. To be offered a choice of water: that was something else, had come to feel like an all but incomprehensible kindness.

You could hardly blame the secretaries for their caution with couriers, nor really for the contempt they sometimes shot our way. Four's tales of bisexual promiscuity might have been extreme, but he was far from alone in the liberties his eyes took. Some couriers were lascivious all right, the city had brought out their animals, with London like one big, look-but-don't-touch dance: the billboard sex, the shop attendants, secretaries, women dressed for show at every turn and couriers pedalling between, panting and slaving like beasts to keep themselves alive with a roof over the head. In a dead-end job you soon realise why the world's poor end up reproducing at such a rate: down there the idea of genitals fast becomes one of the few things to brighten the rest of your life, and plenty of couriers seemed to find it hard to step out of the animal and back into the human once they got from their bicycles.

All puffed-up they strode into the offices, leant elbows on desks, peered forwards: '*Lovely view, darling!*' They requested phone numbers, took pot-shots with their eyeballs, lobbed them like ping-pong balls at goldfish bowls, as if the cleavage of those open blouses were fairground stalls, a little fun amidst the hard life of the roads. Orwell touched on it, down-and-out in London he talked of the tramps robbed of their manhood because, in society's aversion to their appearance, they saw a reflection of themselves: a mirror image of their lowly rank and the revulsion it inspired. The same judgement seemed, however, only to have robbed the couriers of inhibition, and so many went about the city spurred by the hope that what had happened to Ben might one day be waiting for them.

The nearest I came to it was one late afternoon on Bateman Street, Soho. I'd waited fifteen minutes for a woman to come downstairs and sign for a parcel, was standing around in an anteroom within her apartment. Orange-faced and with sunbed skin, grey hair bleached back to blonde, eventually she appeared and fumbled a signature. White wine on breath, French manicured nails tapping handset … the space around her eyes was cracked with makeup, the skin at her neck hung down to a body dressed in the clothes of a younger girl. Tight black jeans clung to her legs, shoulders under a shawl with long tassels hanging from it, a ticker tape in black and white plunged across a neckline showing cleavage … two-dimensional, flat, like a straight, strong pencil-line drawn right down the middle of her chest.

She looked at me: '*Would you like a glass of water … maybe juice?*' I nodded water, she looked at me some more, lingering, moved to a sink and kept on looking my way, chin resting on shoulder as she filled the glass. With a tick-tock of hips she rocked back over. Stood there. She watched me, watched me closely as I drank, saw her through the water and base of the tilted glass: her face distorted like some strange, brightly coloured creature in an aquarium. She made a remark as I finished up, sighed as I offered the glass back and made to leave the reception.

'It must be frightful … being out there on a motorbike all day long.'

'It's not so bad … I'm on a bicycle.'

'*Ooooh!*' she crooned, 'if I'd known you weren't driving … I'd have offered you,' she took the glass back from my hand, made sure her fingers touched all of my own … smiled barefaced at the proposition she made, '*something* …' she lingered again, nothing left to the imagination in those pauses of hers. '*Something … more exciting.*'

27 April – W1 – Docket #17

If I've given the impression of couriers as deadheads, well that's not quite the whole story. For each dear deadhead I've told you of … for every five who couldn't hold down any other job, and for every jailbird who needed cash-paying work because he wasn't allowed a bank account, there was – it must be said – one other type of courier.

They were younger, healthier, better looking, and getting their kicks in life as road warriors. Their limbs were tattooed with cycling iconography, with sprockets and eulogies in French. Their bicycles were minimalist or vintage masterpieces, and the riders carried heavy chains, locks, slung around their shoulders or fastened, clinking, from their waists. From bag straps hung sprockets they had worn out on the roads, like metal feathers in caps or claimed Indian scalps. They concealed eyes with sunglasses, or else orange lenses wrapped around the face. They wanted rock-and-roll, they wanted down-at-heel, sporadic, had *L-O-V-E* and *D-E-A-T-H* tattooed in Indian ink across the knuckles. If that was the appearance, then the truth was that they were often plain, tried too hard, wanted all the abandon of the idiots but with trimmings of refinement, panache and intelligence that were just not compatible. They would be sure to drink enough water at the pub, did not spend all their money in one night, and on those occasions when they let themselves go, you knew you would be hearing the story for the next six months … that it was never for the moment so much as the story they needed to produce in order to stay relevant, to keep up with everything they'd like to have been. Amongst them were a handful of North Americans living the dream… every time you met, you'd hear how long it was until their visa expired or how long since it had expired, at which point they became '*an illegal*'. They couldn't get enough of that word

– *illegal* – couldn't stop talking about their visas, ever in thrall to the idea of law-breaking and the romance of the fugitive.

The bohemian couriers were all, on the side, trying to make it as artist, designer, photographer, producer, musician, cartoonist. I didn't become a courier when I first took to the circuit – that was when I started working as one – the moment I truly *became* a courier was when I began telling people I was working on a book, or on articles … trying to make it as something else. Half the couriers I met were always *something else*: they were either a sad story, an explanation, or they were the talent of theirs that the world had never wanted. Couriering was how they survived, the thing they did in the meantime, the meantime … that very lengthy, that everlasting, meantime. Working with that lot was the first time I realised how many of the world's hopes come to nothing … seven billion of us kicking about and nowhere near enough success to go round. London swallowed dreams and burped couriers, just the same as New York and San Francisco. All of them like human scrapyards … piled high with junk, spirits and near misses, all picking through the countless wrecks, the infinite knot of dead-ends that prop up history for the lucky one that bursts on through.

Often I'd consider the strangeness of the English-speaking world: ever as if success-or-failure was the only currency that made any of our lives worth living. People invested their hopes in a city, and in the process of having those hopes dashed, the city fortified its mythology with struggle, became a place where dreams were made and broken, and broken, and broken. I remember talking to a rider who'd left the London circuit and his aspirations as a filmmaker, moved instead to Berlin, where he was making a decent living building websites. Back for drinks one evening, he told me of his new life.

'Money's good, job's fine, flat's nice … *I'm really comfortable in the city.*' Confessional, he looked up, 'To be honest … I'm in a bit of rut.' And I laughed, for who knew what difference there was between a rut and contentment.

∽

There's a lot to be said for relationships inside the same profession, another person passing their life in an identical manner: someone who cannot judge you for it and who shares your appreciation for the dull minutiae that distinguishes one day from another, but which means nothing to an outsider of the job.

Three-Four was like me, kept on the margins of the other kind of courier, the creative types. She was a free spirit, but without most of that ego, and sure enough in her empowerment as a woman that she didn't feel the need to be aggressive with it. She was an artist, good at it too, talented, a brilliant painter ... sufficiently skilled to have discovered that painting things that looked like they were supposed to look soon became a pretty banal undertaking, more like DIY than art. She took up conceptual stuff instead: sculpture and installation. Everyone – from her family to the couriers who saw her work – promptly decided she was crazy, cuckoo ... said she was churning out tat, that she ought to go back to painting. We weren't at the same company for long: she moved somewhere with better pay, said one of our controllers had been hassling her whenever she went out to Docklands to collect invoices. He'd suggested too hard that they should go for a drink sometime, offering to make her wages better if she did. Three-Four headed for the door instead, climbed up the courier ladder ... that thing I said I'd never do, not out of loyalty, but a reluctance to improve the unimprovable, to make my lot more amenable and so risk staying put in the trade.

Three-Four was stunning ... was *pain-in-the-ass* beautiful. A face ahead of its time: the sort of girl who's been bullied through school for being prettier than the popular girls, and is tired of the novelty of being looked at by her early twenties. Eventually, she'd pursued the only sensible course of action for a girl in that situation ... she shaved her head, at which point you realise the social understanding of female beauty isn't very much more complicated than long hair.

Three-Four's shearing revealed an odd-looking skull, shaped like somebody's first attempt in a pottery class. The trick worked a treat, so that I was the first to hassle her in a while, long enough for the attention to have become flattering again.

We first met on a doorstep in Mayfair, had both heard the other make a delivery either end of Brook Street. We walked down the street towards one another, the two of us with bicycles wheeling next to us. There was always a curiosity about meeting another number for the first time, which perhaps intensified when it was a girl, so I knew exactly who she was ... but with Three-Four, I didn't want to seem like I'd been paying too much attention.

We come to standstill, 'Are you Three-Seven?'

'*God no!*' she blurted, an affronted grin. 'I'm Three-Four ... are you Two-Two?' I blushed, though only a little. She knew my name.

It must have been sometime in April, drizzle through the mist and Three-Four with a hood up ... drawstrings pulled so that her face was wrapped tight on all sides: no ears, just a moonlike face peering out of a hood. Her cheeks bunched against the elastic of the hood, glowed rosy with cold ... rain dripped down from the forehead, hanging from the end of her nose.

'You empty?'

I nodded.

She smiled. 'Shall we get a cup of tea?'

We walk down Brook Street: bikes between us, fixed gears, pedals turning. Shoppers begin disapproving that we are taking up the whole pavement: the two of us with cleats tapping side by side, waterproofs rustling, shapeless together, each one wrapped in expensive forms of plastic and neoprene.

'They look like good leggings,' I say to her, courier small talk. She nods enthusiastically.

'They should be, they cost enough ... they're thermal, but only waterproof on the front part, so you don't get too hot.'

We talk about the virtues of expensive gear: agree it makes the job bearable, ends up paying for itself when you don't have to spend a day wet and miserable. We stand below an old catering post, one of a dozen stalls around the city that were always surrounded by groups of cabbies. The hut is made from green-painted planks of wood, an old typewritten page of prices is slipped inside a plastic wallet, paper fading a sun-bleached yellow. Below the prices a note is scrawled, irritation in the handwriting. Pinned there for the benefit of the cabbies, ever in need of energy to keep them going on the roads:

> *After the seventh, each spoon of sugar is*
> *charged at ten pence – thank you!*

The stallholder leans out and over us, the ledge of her stall obscuring her face except a nose and kindly eyes perched on top of the counter. We order teas, are answered by the sound of steam coming out of the cabin, two cardboard cups appearing. Three-Four unzips a pouch on her belt: an *A–Z* and tobacco appear, stuffed inside with some paper and a blue banknote. She offers coins up onto the counter, smiles at me, 'You can pay next time.'

Through the coming months we'd listen closely for one another's deliveries over the radio, learn where the other was, and at the end of the day figure out where our final drops had left us. Now and then we'd casually pedal towards the part of the city where we knew the other to be, then realise – nonchalantly – that we were actually nearby ... might as well say hello.

1 May – WC1 – Docket #18

Headed for Great Russell Street: Trade Union House, roads are shut. Police and traffic cones have cut off Clerkenwell, a crowd is up ahead. Today is their day. I see banners, I hear a band, brass and drum on the afternoon air: the spirit of the people is making itself known through the capital. I see plain-dressed teachers, see sailors, rail workers and nurses, I see firemen in the shining buttons of their uniforms. Whistles, megaphones, chanting. They make their way across London, the traffic at standstill as the embroidery of the banners goes shining with the sun, loose threads pulled free on the wind. I smile to myself, roll slowly up behind. The chants change, they alternate, find voice and chorus behind the megaphone. I see some mouths open: hands cupped and voices calling out, red lips giving way to the black holes of wide open mouths, unashamed and proud. They sing out, beside other lips muted shut, others mouthing half-hearted … unsure as to the extent of their convictions. Whatever the uncertainty, slowly, slowly out it comes … a call rolling between the bricks and above the engines waiting at a purr all around. I glide alongside, they hit a vein, the call rises.

> *'The Workers!… United!… Will never be defeated!*
> *The Workers! United! Will never be defeated!'*

And in me something stirred, a spirit awoken, rising a moment only to be struck straight back down by thought. Goosebumps turned to something else, for rousing though it seemed … surely they were all living in the past? None of those voices were any different from the politicians' and all of them a hundred years behind the times. Sure, the unions were still important, but if it had not already passed, very soon would come a day when the workers could be replaced by either a robot or a faraway worker who didn't speak their language and could be made to work for fewer rights and less money. Humans were fast being made superfluous to requirements, and united or otherwise, in order to emerge victorious, however terrifying, the people would have to learn to value themselves as more than only workers. Just as the couriers would have to figure out what to do when one day their dockets dried up for good ... so the workers would need greater purpose than a safe job in a factory.

9 May – EC4 – Docket #19

My favourite thing about couriering was often the streets themselves. I was still a fantasist at heart, in love with history ... duels, pistols and highwaymen was where I kept my head for those hours when it started to rain and there was still only a concrete city all around. I came to feel an imprecise ownership over London. Long ago I had learned streets and postcodes, but come May, nearly halfway through my second courier year, I also knew all the rat runs, potholes and cambers, the hidden gardens and courtyards you could cut through.

Even more than its physical presence, it was in those street names that I saw the city as it once had been ... a time before the offices and identical chains that now fed and watered us all. There was Cheapside, *cheap* the old English word for a market, and Cheapside still the only street in the Square Mile with a significant number of shops upon it. The stretch had been singled out for development by the Corporation of London, just beginning their endeavours to create a '*world class retail experience*' ... whatever that was supposed to mean.

From Cheapside ran Poultry, Wood, Cloth, Bread and Milk Street, and Friday Street too, where a fishmonger had once sold his catch. I would cycle through, imagining a time when life had been only the regular supply of about ten different commodities at a marketplace. Near the Leather Exchange you found Tanner Street. Around St Paul's Cathedral was Pilgrim Street, Paternoster Row, Carmelite Street, Angel Lane, and streets named for friars white, black and grey. North of the cathedral, London Wall ran east, beside the crumbling remains of the wall itself ... the last major infrastructure project of the Romans before they too did the sensible thing and quit the city in the fifth century. Along the wall were all the old entrances to the city: the gates of Lud, Alder, Moor, Bishops and Ald. Running just behind the eastern edge of the wall was a street called Houndsditch, which it was said had always smelt foul because the corpses of dead dogs were thrown there from inside the city … wind blowing the rotten smell back over the wall. Bunhill Row led north from the Barbican, and the spot had been a cemetery since Saxon times, with its modern name an Anglo form of 'Bone Hill'. Beneath the ground were the remains of thousands of Christian nonconformists, lying in a graveyard of dissenters that ranged from Daniel Defoe to William Blake and a number of the Cromwell family. Moving west and the church of Mary Le Bon still stood in Marylebone, Fetter Lane wound down to the Royal Courts of Justice. Lamb's Conduit Street led just north of Lamb's Passage, and the path the animals would have taken ended at Coram's Fields, where a few sheep still lived in a petting zoo. It didn't matter if my leaps of imagination and historical detective work were amateurish and unfounded, I enjoyed myself, and with them the hours passed more quickly.

Most of all I loved the streets in honour of professions that no longer existed. There were streets for stonecutters, wheelwrights, gunsmiths, apothecaries and druids. Then there were names that brought colour and character, a storytelling of what had once been there. There were avenues for rose berries, where the roots of almighty plane trees folded the asphalt and lifted kerbstones as easily as if they had been pebbles. Beside it was a square for cold baths, there were pear trees and plum trees, emeralds, nightingales, priests on crutches and a Saracen's head. I found yards of bleeding hearts and venison haunches, lions of red and white and black, hills of garlick and artichoke beside places of mermaids, yeomanry and knights. There was Horatio, Hermes, Orpheus and Othello … all legend, mythology and fairy tale for me to pass by upon my bicycle, transported to places that seemed so much more magical than the city in which I lived, stuck fast in a world of all-too-solid flesh.

Cycling by St Paul's remained a favourite route of mine, that tiny kink in the road outside its churchyard: the quick left-right flick on the handlebars, the rolled bodyweight. On clear days, when the weather was good, I'd take detours to ride past the cathedral, staring at the bold of the white stone against the blue of the sky, thinking back to the ride around the world, the night in the New Mexico desert, talking to a homeless man about the books he'd read of London, of how he longed to one day see St Paul's. Sometimes, when the bells were ringing and I had no work, I'd stop in the courtyard, ears listening and the hairs on my skin vibrating as bells rang out and left the air to shake with some love of god. I thought of days before science explained everything for which religion had once been required, before days of electronic volume, and I thought just how miraculous those bells must've sounded back then ... how quickly they must have compelled a peasant to give the church one-tenth of his income or crop.

I scoured London for its past, married it to things I'd seen on my way around the world, the things I'd learned in books and essays. Forever I went circling the city, trying to piece it together in ways that could help me make sense of the time I'd been born into. If history had unfolded to create the society around me, I was desperate to discern the patterns by which it would start to become a better place. Don't get me wrong, I was under no illusion that there was once some sort of golden age ... the world had always been bust, but the peculiar thing, and what frustrated me most, was that people had come to think it fixed. At last we'd arrived in the best of all possible worlds, had been flattered by the future. Excitably we mistook the technology and haste of modern lives for a sort of progress and industry, a mania of false efficiency in which our sense of self was quickly lost.

On a daily basis I'd find the ghosts, the phantoms from bygone ages, those who'd dared challenge the system as they'd found it. I travelled back to days before we arrived in a world robbed of gods, a land without alternatives. Ho Chi Minh was on a blue plaque washing dishes in Haymarket, Simón Bolívar had been statued-up and surrounded on all sides by Belgravia billionaires, my dear William Blake had had his birthplace found, demolished and transformed into nothing more meaningful than a franchise curry restaurant in the chartered streets of Soho. I'd see the number 14 bus, terminating in Putney, and in it I saw Thomas Rainsborough, the Putney Debates and their radicalism. So it was that London's number 14 bus came to me as a rolling, red apparition of:

> *'The poorest man of England has a life to live, as does the greatest, and therefore, truly, if a man is to live under government then he must first, by his own consent, place himself under that government.'*

On Liverpool Street was the Sir Robert Peel public house, a market named after him up in Camden too. Peel had always been a hero of mine: he'd rebuilt the Conservatives after they schismed over the Catholic Emancipation of 1829 ... then sacrificed the lot, tore it apart when he repealed the Corn Laws, the tariffs that kept the urban poor starving for the profit of the landed aristocracy that backed his own party. They ousted him for that one, and he left office expressing only a wish to be remembered with warmth in the homes of the British poor. There he was on Liverpool Street, in only the hollow ghost of his spirit: a man who cared more for his values than his career, but vaunted in an age where the politicians had been made only administrators, guided by little more than a hunger to win elections by whatever means.

There was Milton too, waiting for me in John Milton Passage, with words written in verse as effortless as if they had been prose. Writing by the light of candles, Milton had grown steadily blind, but nevertheless gave the last of his eyesight to Cromwell's request that he should lend his pen to a defence of the fledgling English Republic, a nation governed by the rights of man rather than monarchy. They were all only ghosts, and each had had their memories and sacrifices so resoundingly betrayed. They had been made vessels of celebrity, emptied of all meaning in order that they could be admired without complication. Nelson Mandela had been gobbled up more thoroughly than all the rest combined ... they'd put him in bronze on Parliament Square, deleted the insults, the incarceration, the '*terrorist*' slurs. Long before he died, they'd stripped him good and proper, edited out his subtext: *It is acceptable to break bad laws! You may have to take arms against your oppressor! Injustice must be resisted!* They'd bleached Mandela free of all he'd fought for, not least the fact that he'd *fought* at all in the first place. By championing his nobility, it was hoped that a little of it would rub off on our own establishment, though in place of his spirit they left only a gentle, old man ... smiling warmly, an aging pin-up to remind us the world was fair and that black people could be presidents too.

Some figures I held closer than others. Riding by the benches along Embankment I would see Orwell's ghost, down and out and sleeping on cold nights and foggy mornings. It gave me heart, comforted me so much to know that Orwell would've once been there in flesh and bone ... that he would've agreed, would've told me I was right and to keep on believing the things that I believed. That comfort didn't last long. Soon the inaugural *Orwell Day!* rose up to put pay to that method of mine, for just as they'd got a statue of Cromwell – all boots, spurs and sword – kept just two hundred metres from the house of the Queen, so too had the surveillance state decided to make a hero of George Orwell. Dumbfounded, clueless, I realised sadly that my heroes were also theirs.

The whole thing made me nauseous: a frustration born of nothing more complex than the dislike of lies, the grubby idea that as adults we were meant to unlearn all those principles of honesty, sharing, fairness we'd been taught as children. It had been figured out that by paying lip service to everything, you could attach meaning to nothing at all. History had stopped happening, and if there were apparently no alternatives to our style of government – its flexible cocktail of officialdom, selective capitalism and selective democracy – then with that foregone political conclusion disappeared all sense of past or future, as if change had been rendered impossible and we were to henceforth spend an eternity running on a treadmill of the same.

One afternoon I hurried through backstreets, looking for a fashion warehouse hidden in the alleys off Carnaby Street. Frustrated, I sprang from an alley to a courtyard. And there he was, looking at me: Mugabe Amin, some stock African tyrant … the name wasn't important, neither the country. Big shades shining, a military tunic beside those famous words on the poster:

> *The only thing necessary for the triumph of*
> *evil is that good people do nothing.*

And as my feet stopped their haste, I looked up and read those lines. All around it seemed people had lost the will to question the system ruling us, the evils it overlooked and meted out on powerless people around the country and world beyond. In a £50 theatre production and stock bad-guy, it was as if *Evil* had become only a freak occurrence of half a century ago … something brought in dramatic form from where it had once existed elsewhere. A word like 'evil' was never attached to the conduct of our corporations and their compromises in the name of profit, nor to politicians, monarchs and their friendships with brutal regimes abroad. At the same time, we had become such infinitesimal, exhausted parts of the same giant meat pulveriser that none of us could envisage how our own robotic and scarcely satisfying nine-'til-fives might be part of the malice waiting further down the production lines we were part of. Evil seemed to have prevailed so far, wide and free that to me it looked like only a new normalcy … one barely noted, and in the face of which nobody did a thing.

14 May – EC3 – Docket #20

In the arches of Aldwych you'll find a man who carries his life's possessions in a chequered, plastic laundry bag. He wears trousers tucked inside a pair of wellington boots, old corduroys the same mustard shade as his nicotine beard. He recites poems from an old, beaten book with pages the same colour as the nicotine beard and the corduroys ... the book close up to his nose, so that you know his eyesight is on its way out. I hear him coughing, and the sound of that man coughing is one of the most recognisable sounds of all London to me now. Just like the smells of London have stuck with me, so too can I still hear this cough. He's got the catarrh of cold nights and tobacco pasted deep down in his lungs, so that when he starts to cough, it sounds like wallpaper being pulled off a ceiling, scraping bit by bit. The guy shakes: you see his eyes bulge, gape, shat out of their sockets so that it's like he's ready to die each time, seven earth-trembling coughs just to tickle the stuff loose. With the eighth cough he bursts, you hear it barrelling up the trachea, hitting the top of his mouth and into his throat, like an arrow to the bull of an archery board. His eyes relax, loosen with relief, he spits the ball of phlegm to the pavement, it rolls over itself in dust. He shuts his eyes, and with contentment, his chest heaves slowly back to calm.

I'm close by Strand ... it's late afternoon, radio crackles:

'*Two-Two ... Two-Two, come in. Rush coming down now.*'

I'm all right with that ... £3.75 will take me over £40 for the day, homing in on the big Five-O. I press the button on my radio, '*Roger-rog*', and the silence crackles before breaking off. I look down at my pocket computer, it bleeps, I tap with the stylus. The job comes. I'm sitting Strand. The pickup is near London Bridge. The job is going to Victoria Street. I have to go all the way east and then all the way west … one side of the city to another. The radio crackles again,

'Sorry, Two-Two … I know it's a push, you're nearest to it, you've got a bit more than fifteen minutes. Just do your best … nobody's expecting you to make it.'

The radio snaps silent. The last sentence is what seals the deal, is what means I'm going to ride like Miguel Indurain and get that envelope … put it where it's gotta go within the impossible deadline I've been given. If they'd been high and mighty about making it on time then I'd have slacked right off, almost out of principle. Being told that they don't expect much from me, that they're waiting on failure … another matter. From this point on there is only one outcome, the petty glory on offer is worth much more than £3.75 … make this and I'll be holding my head high for the first time since the world record.

Even as I'm explaining this, I'm already in the Blackfriars tunnel, riding the curve, riding black-white-black-white slices as I go in and out of the lights above … burst into daylight: full in the face so that the rods and the cones of my eyes trade places. Jump. And momentarily I can't see a thing. It's been raining, rained all afternoon long, rained solid until half an hour ago but now the sun's out so that the black asphalt is shining with the reflections of the passing sky above. I jump off my bike, we're in the loading bay … I half throw it down against the wall, the thing pings on a metal rail, kicks out feedback and shakes, rattles to a standstill as I disappear down steps. I hold banisters on both sides … *click-clack-click-clack* … cleats skid over the ridges of the metal stairwell. A door opens, a desk with a clipboard to sign, there's my quarry below it. I take the envelope, I scribble. I'm gone.

Four minutes have elapsed by the time I'm riding back: think I'm being flattered, flattered by a tailwind. I'm riding 25mph, only without a car's windscreen and metal around you, on a bicycle it feels more like eighty. I drive on, force the legs, mouth open like a basking shark, it all goes in: a crane fly hovers straight at me, disappears down the hatch, if you're lucky its wing hits a tooth and gives you opportunity to spit the body back out, *phff, phff … spit!* … gone. Early plane tree pollen, the seed on its tiny parachute and into the gullet, a pigeon, heading towards your face … duck, you duck … pigeon pulls up and out of the way. Down below it starts happening, rumours start: I can feel the moment, it's coming. Here comes that little burn … old friend … you and me we're sworn adversaries, but deep down, deep down we quite like one another.

It comes in the thighs first, seeps in, lactic acid on its way to the muscles: burning, starting in the legs, legs say stop. I look down, down south, legs turning on but pleading for a let-up. I straighten, stern, this isn't about £3.75 … this is about honour. I brace, I snarl: out it comes, immortal words, words now known all through cycling. Jens Voigt growls with me: '*Shut up, legs! Shut up and do what I tell you!*' I can feel it … it keeps coming. I can feel my face: my forehead turning pointed, jowls widen, broad corners of the jaw move outwards. My face turns triangular, I'm forcing aerodynamics into my head … mouth like a locomotive engine room, the boys shovelling in the oxygen, pulling it out of all the world in front. The legs, they go screaming for reason, pipe-up: '*Either take it easy or we'll* …' Not a chance.

We keep the hammer down, we keep the hurt on and I pull back on to the Thames and its tailwind flooding with the river. The pack of hounds are raging, they barrel after me. Eight minutes. A truck is up ahead, I'm in its dirty air. The truck punches through the atmosphere like a fist, creates a slipstream just behind it, but just behind the slipstream a burst of divergent gusts: air falling back into line from separate directions … a plumage, a chaos of airstreams that knock you this way and that. I heave on pedals, I need that slipstream, I heave on the pedals … *one-two-three-four* … I lean forwards, burst into the slip. I'm in, made it … face still triangular but at least I've got a tow. We motor, me on the rear of the truck, the truck accelerating up to speed, an eighteen-wheeler keirin race and then *flame rouge*: brake lights explode in my face, red everywhere, braking fast. I duck out, bag strap tickling the tail bar as I fly down the outside instead, roar down Embankment with legs breathing and lungs pedalling ... everyone's putting in a turn at the front ... all hands are on deck, eyes gaping and nostrils peeled wide. Twelve minutes. On the dark road I see my unfeatured silhouette as it shimmers and rocks in the wet, trails of spray thrown out by my wheels. I jump an amber-turning-red, straight on to Parliament Square, that grand trough and Big Ben on my left. I clear the Square's first flank, lean into the right-hand turn, banking right and then flipping back upright and slightly left so as to peel into Victoria Street. And I bank right and then slightly left, and I suspect then that I'm perhaps going to make the deadline that was supposed to have been impossible ... but it's more than that, more than just time. I peel into Victoria Street.

And at this time of the year, in this time of the late afternoon, the sun sits low in the sky, sits perfect at the far end of Victoria Street, with its offices high on each side of the road. And so it happens, the sun has set the wet road incandescent, and that sun has itself turned orange to mark the end of another day. It shines full down a blinding road: piling off high office windows, redoubling the intensity of that light into a solid, glowing corridor that hits me square in the face as I speed into Victoria Street, ride this road of pure gold, steaming through a silver corridor of late afternoon, all high on adrenaline and petty triumph. Senses explode inside the light. It's ecstasy ... it's as if God exists, and then a moment later ... it's as if he doesn't even have to, for everything is beautiful enough already. I'm smiling ... smiling big. I tell you, right now is a good moment to be a courier ... you don't get this kind of euphoria in many jobs so close to the arsehole of society.

16 May – SW1 – Docket #21

'*Hold tight there a moment, Two-Two … I've got work in front of me, we'll have you moving soon.*'

Ever since I first found this spot, whenever I stop by, it's always with a bewildered amusement that I ponder the thing. Park Lane: two million pounds of land purchased for black-carved statues in memorial to Animals in War. A horse is pulling a cannon, behind a dog with its paw in the air, the dog leading the way as a mule plods slowly at the rear. Of all London's memorials, this one is far and away the best. My favourite part is the inscription, proud over the statues:

> *To the animals who served and died alongside British*
> *and allied forces … they had no choice.*

It never ceased to amaze me. Even in the memory of a dead animal, still whoever it was couldn't stop themselves from bringing sides and nations into the thing: as if an elephant cared which flag it died for, or else perhaps to ward against their expensive memorial accidentally paying homage to the memory of a Nazi donkey, only following orders behind the cover of its nose bag. '*They had no choice*'. That too sounded so much better than '*We made them.*'

'*Two-Two … Two-Two?*' The radio comes through, distracts my thoughts, restores me with purpose.

'Two-Two … Two-Two.'

'Got three for you, all picking up at the same address on Eaton Square: if you don't mind dropping down for them?'

Five hundred metres for three dockets is passable business, perfectly agreeable. 'Not at all … on my way, roger-rog.'

I pull into the flow of traffic, Park Lane another inner-city motorway but backed-up with nothing moving beyond 20mph. The road tilts downwards, I'm faster than the traffic, switch between lanes, up the middle of the buses and the cars, shards of daylight switched on and off between large, dark vehicles. I round Hyde Park corner, roll further down the road towards a commotion where two drunks grapple, shout, so that I turn away from my curiosity and double back across Chester Square. Over my shoulder sits Number 73, the far end and a pretty little garden with police on the door, machine gun on chest: the taxpayer's guard given Thatcher until her last day. Thatcher, the Saudis on Curzon Street, US Embassy at Grosvenor Square, Turks at Belgrave and Tony Blair on Connaught. Whether the hypothetical enemy were Irish, Iraqi, Kurd or terrorist miscellany, the need for a gun to keep someone safe seemed a good measure of a record in politics, how many noses they'd been willing to put so fatally out of joint.

At Eaton Square I lock up my bike, fasten it to a black-painted railing around the private garden. I'll stretch my legs a little, remind them how it feels to walk. Someone close has ideas to the contrary: "Ey … 'ey yu … yu cannot poot thet there.' I turn round, he's a way off but walking towards me with purpose. Thick, black eyebrows, thick black hair and a Boer with olive skin. They've given him a navy blue blazer with gold at the cuffs and the front buttons, but still, we're the same rank. I can sense it in the way we're squaring up to one another … primitive instincts, I can tell we're about to make one another's jobs and lives as difficult as we possibly can, fight it out while a banker cleans up and the weapons manufacturers nearby are signing off a bribe to the Middle East. He slows his march, closes in, arms up by his sides.

'Yoo cannot poot thet there.'

'It'll be gone in five minutes.'

'Not the point, mate, it's the rools, someone might want to use the garden.'

I looked through the railings: one of those magnificent private gardens, always empty, gardens that the public at large was not allowed to set foot upon, and that the residents themselves had no interest in setting foot upon. I smile.

'It doesn't look very busy in there.'

'Never is ... but thet's not the point. Someone sees a bike locked oot here and I'll git it.'

He shrugs his shoulders. I nod, smile. He shrugs. He smiles. Successful disengagement.

'Wot yoo dooin 'ere?'

I tap my bag. 'Courier ... picking up a delivery.'

'Ah ... curier ... 'owz thet pay?'

I smile, 'Not the best ... not going to be living on Eaton Square anytime soon.'

He laughs, short, from the throat ... holds the sleeves of his blazer, continues undeterred. 'They pay per delivery, or yoo get a weekly wage?'

I don't like this conversation, slowing my replies, 'Per delivery.'

'So when it's quiet, you doon't earn money?'

I nod, nod once. Deep, slow and unmistakable. I look at him, he doesn't get it, asks more questions of how and where I earn my money: what's good and what's bad pay. The guy's obsessed with money, has spent too much time watching the stuff come nowhere near him. He strokes a hand across the black stubble around only his chin, his cheeks smooth and freckled. I see the crest of a family on the gold cufflink of the jacket they gave him. As I answer his questions, I see him relax, visibly relax ... his dark eyes go from keen to soft. He puts in, 'Money in Zooth Afrika is bed ... but pay here, it's quite good.'

He looks at me, almost a sympathy to his gaze, as if he's assumed a position of superiority ... he's the breadwinner in our relationship. I sense that he enjoys my company, because he earns more than me, which can't happen often in Eaton Square. For a sweet moment – and thanks to me – that Boer feels like he's winning, like he's the wealthiest man in the whole conversation. He loosens up, cheers. Having discovered I pose him no threat, that he's getting wealthy quicker than I am, he confides his plans to me, shares some wisdom: the masterplan.

'Wot yoo need …' he leans in, he whispers. 'All yoo need,' he clarifies. I wait. '*Is an idea.*' I look at him. He looks at me. The start of a smile. An air of confidence. 'If yoo ave a good idea … then thet's eet … then yoo can pay people to work for yoo … thet's 'ow yoo get rich. My father taught me thet.' He smiles, like he's blowing magic at me. 'It just takes an idea.'

I look at him, perhaps a little underwhelmed. He leans back out of his confiding … satisfied, the sorcery over, the spell worn off. I don't really know what to say. Settle.

'And what's your idea?'

He shrugs, moves the padded shoulders of his blazer up and down, shrinks a little. His father had obviously popped it before sharing specific examples of economically salient ideas. He qualifies, 'I doon't know, not yeet … yoo have to pick the right one.'

I look at the guy. I don't tell him the truth, don't tell him that it's his father who's the problem, that we wouldn't have been having the conversation about how to get rich had he been the son of the Duke of Westminster, or heir to the Eaton Square estate he was instead telling people not to lock bicycles to the railings of. '*All you need, son … is an idea.*' As far as inheritances went, it was hardly glittering. You don't get rich, you're born it: it's as hereditary as eye colour. He didn't see that social mobility was stagnant, the fellow hadn't been in the country long enough to figure out that ours was no promised land. He *believed*, no crisis of faith in sight … neoliberal communion rising out of him like I was back with the hobos of the United States. He just needed an idea, and once he had that idea he would put it upon the altar of sacrifice to receive his blessings of affluence. Just an idea, only one … and if it never came then it was his own fault, full personal responsibility, the buck stopped with him.

17 May – SW1 – Docket #22

Now and then, riding on the circuit, you're given the opportunity to feel you're doing something vaguely important. For me, the problem with those moments was the way they left me to confront what a small and replaceable cog I had become, and within the very system I'd always dreamed of changing rather than serving. When Lehman Brothers went bust, I cycled three times to their Canary Wharf offices, delivered the receivership notices from HSBC, Bank of Scotland, Santander: each envelope confirming public knowledge that the debt they had borrowed from one another had gone from good debt to bad debt. Lehman had screwed up $600,000,000,000 of collateralised mortgage obligations, and I was to be paid £000,000,000,007 for pedalling the six-mile round-trip that delivered three sets of confirmations of this very fact. That felt like a pretty good representation of how the economy worked.

Now and then I would go to the House of Commons, went skidding on my cleats through the barricaded crowds on the morning of parliament's reconvening. On the occasion of a 2010 election victory, I was obliged to deliver flowers to an incoming prime minister: blue gladioli with yellow narcissi amongst them, a tribute to the colours of a new coalition government I'd be living under. You wouldn't believe the pain it caused me, it hurt like hell, knowing I was only the delivery boy for politics I thought so little of. Cursing and spitting, I pedalled helpless towards Downing Street, the bouquet alone upon my back. En route, paralysed with impotent rage, I stopped with the flowers at a public toilet. For me to say what I did with them there wouldn't be decent, but by the time they arrived at Number 10, I felt better.

That same month, with oil spilling across the Gulf of Mexico, turning the Biloxi sands black where I'd once slept under a pink dawn, I couriered a handful of documents and demands to the offices of BP, down in St James's Square. I read the news reports: the explosion at the Deepwater Horizon well, operated by the firm of an engineer I'd once met in a Texas café. I read of the femidom they planned to insert to stop the ruptured oil pipe, of the billions of polystyrene capsules to be dumped in the Gulf, soaking up the oil to make the deadened sea look clean again.

It was sitting empty on the steps outside BP that I first met Seven-One. Seven-One was some fifteen years older than me, late thirties, but slowly I somehow came to feel a responsibility for him. Another of life's beautiful losers, Seven-One was scarcely capable of holding it together week-to-week, but less concerned by his own fate than a do-gooder like me seemed to get. I suppose that, even then, I still hadn't given up the idea that life could work out all right for everyone, that a guy like Seven-One could learn how to keep himself in check. He was a lank, towering man, always stubbled, with eyes ringed by set, drug-induced shadows … his ears well-pierced, and his mouth, mostly gums, bereft of most of its teeth on account of fights, crashes and industrial accidents. He smiled like a baby, a huge, red mouth that showed directly whatever mood was in his soul. Seven-One was a lot of things, but he wasn't complicated.

On the steps that afternoon we said our hellos, said them a second time – sincerely – once we'd realised we worked for the same company. Knees up, bags slumped beside us, skin of our legs peering in places through our jeans, we sat eye-height with the hub caps, shining, of Jaguars and Bentleys. We waited for work. Seven-One slipped an old, beaten tobacco tin from his bag, put it down to the pavement with a scraping of metal, unfastened the catch. I watched him roll his cigarette, hands in fingerless gloves, oil deep inside the web of fingerprints and behind his nails. He placed a wiry tangle of tobacco into a paper skin, pinched it down to size and rolled it out … lifting it to mouth, where his tongue slipped out like a third lip from between empty gums. Seven-One was newer on the radio than I was, left me a slight sense of courier seniority, despite his age. Along with Two-Four, he went on to become the person I was closest to at the firm. He sparked his cigarette, inhaled.

'How you findin' it?' I asked.

Seven-One exhaled smoke, answer tailing out on the end of the plume, 'Done it before, haven't I … a decade ago, mate … used to be able to make £400 quid a week back then, brilliant money in them days,' he leant in, nodding at me. '*Know what I mean?*'

'Know what I mean' was stuck like a question mark on the end of every second sentence Seven-One ever spoke. Seven-One didn't speak, Seven-One boomed. With his fist, he gave me a push to the shoulder, 'Know what? What I can't get over is how *clean* it is now.'

'You mean the city?' I ask. 'The streets?'

'*Nahhh* … the *driving, mate!* I remember a cabbie stamping on a courier's head once,' my eyes gape, Seven-One opens his even wider, as if to confirm. He nods eager confirmation, breathes down cigarette, 'Down Farringdon it was … and the air too,' Seven-One blew smoke. 'The air, it's so much cleaner!'

I mused, welcomed the historical perspective … an idea of improvement, spared Seven-One the truth that the same particles had only been made smaller, invisible, and that there were now more of them.

I go on, 'What have you been doing since then?'

'*Me!?* I've done a bit of everything me. Mainly steel fabricating … fabricating and erecting. I've done buildings all over this city, know what I mean?' I knew what he meant. 'You know that one on Rosebery Avenue? Down the bottom at the junction … that one's me … loads of others too. See those?' Seven One held his cigarette in his lips as he spoke, pulling off his mitts and turning over a pair of huge, grey hands, wrinkled like animal hide as proof of his labours. 'That's what ten years working with steel looks like. Know what I mean?!' *I knew what he meant.* And then Seven-One looked up at me, 'What d'you do? You don't sound like a courier.'

Whereas in many walks of life you feel self-conscious for sound-ing common … as a courier you're conspicuous for sounding smart. It's not even a matter of accents, more the finished sentences over the radio, the tendency to express things precisely. Everyone thought I was getting well-fed by radio control, thought they heard my voice a lot … I suspected it just stuck in their head amongst all the gruff.

'I studied politics,' I said, simple and awkward.

'You've got a degree?' quizzed Seven-One. I nod. 'Then why you wasting and risking your life as courier?' Seven-One gave my leg a shove, 'If I was young and had a degree … I'd be off getting myself prospects.'

'Degrees aren't what they used to be,' I offer, by way of apology, self-conscious at my wasting opportunities Seven-One had never had. 'But I know what you mean, there are probably easier jobs out there.'

Seven-One took an intake of breath, nodded and sucked his lips in between his gums. 'It's a hard job … what makes it easier though…'

I wait for the hint, the tip on courier politics, fitness or naviga-tion. Seven-One continues, 'If you've got the money … what really makes it easier is a bit of Charlie.' He nods in at me, eager-like: 'Y'know … *nose powder*, mate … cocaine!' Seven-One pulls the back of his hand over his nose, gives a snort and then a laugh to himself. 'Sets you marching, it does. *Know what I mean?!*' I knew what he meant, but just in case I didn't understand, Seven-One stood up and began goose-stepping to illustrate the point. 'Have you ever tried working with it … *awoah?!*' he gasps, smiling, 'only a little … mind … it's brilliant stuff, mate, makes life *so* much easier!'

That was the thing with Seven-One, he just liked to have a good time, didn't know how to look after anything else. He was short-sighted in the extreme: point-blank consequence-blind, couldn't see a course of action any more than one step down the line. Despite that, he'd actually set himself up fairly well, bought a flat in Bristol on a fat mortgage, a housing benefit tenant covering most of the repayments, and Seven-One living for free in a squat and working the roads of London to make up the shortfall. He called the house his 'pension', touched the wood of his head in saying that all he had to do was stay on the straight and narrow for another fifteen years. And things'd be swell.

For all his excess, I soon learned that Seven-One knew London brilliantly. His brain was like a pickled onion, bleached white by hedonism, totally etiolated, but with the veins of the streets all perfectly preserved inside. He knew by name the alleyways off the dead ends, knew backstreets by both new names and those names they'd worn fifteen years earlier.

After thirty minutes, and still sitting on the BP doorstep, the sound of '*Two-Two*' came crackling down the line with a job. I stood, picked my bag up, swinging it high and letting the strap fall back down over my head.

'What's your name?' asked Seven-One.

'I'm Emre ...' sticking out my hand, 'what's yours?'

'You won't believe it ...' Seven-One gave a chuckle, as though he liked being asked the question. He stuck his hand out: 'I'm Roger.' And he laughed ... that big, toothless red smile spreading over his face. 'Gotta be the worst name going for a courier ... every time someone says anything, I think they're talking to me ... *know what I mean?* Roger-Roger-Roger ... all day long!'

I laughed, couldn't help what came out next. 'That's like in *Catch-22*.' Seven-One didn't know what I meant. 'With the Major who's name's Major, and gets promoted to Major Major, so that he's Major-Major-Maj...'

I trailed off, Seven-One was looking vacantly at me, the dark rings under his eyes swallowing his eyelids as he squinted, trying to focus in on what I was getting at.

6 June – E1 – Docket #23

After the rain, with a flash and then a flood, suddenly there comes fire at the western end of Wigmore Street. Up in flames it goes, burning at the close of each clear day between April and September, framed either side with five Georgian floors. The street sets to an inferno above the tarmac, the last circle of hell lodged and raging just round the back of Marble Arch. Everything roars, ablaze, you hear screams and shouts, people running from the flames before you realise that here is only the normal noise and the regular chaos of our city.

It was the diesel that set the firmament. In 2010, London had Europe's worst air, the foulest of any from Athens to Rome. Painted red with nitrates, benzene, sulphur … not to mention the tyre particles and brake-pad dust, it all poured out of the engines and off the wheels … particles splitting the spectrum of its reds and oranges. A few hundred miles closer than at any time since dawn, the sun turns gigantic, pulling eyes to watch as it goes bellowing out the last of day. You can't help but stare … blink, then close your eyes to shield your retina … so that fifteen identical suns, each dressed in a ball gown of purple, stand proud and spinning on the back of the eyelid. The *tap-tap-tap* of a taxi carburettor winds by, turning the handle of the projector as you open your eyes again.

Oscar Wilde once mused that the paintings of Joseph Turner were the first time sunsets became a celebrated concept in society, entered popular media … reached that point at which a construct somehow becomes more splendid than its natural existence because it has been recorded, has had its essence captured on human terms. Feet up on bicycle frame, I sit, a head free to wonder, and I know I am a rich man in all currencies but the one London cares for. Sky turns red once more, and the white-painted walls of Marylebone go bathed in blood: a Macduff-is-dead sort of shade, slipping moment by moment down the city. Along the street walks a nanny, a boy in one hand, shopping in the other. He pulls her arm, a good tug, from hip-height, '*Look, Melissa ... it looks like the sky is on fire ...*' and she hurries, pulls him onwards by the arm, his legs rattling to keep up as he sings high, unbroken vocal chords ... '*London's burning ... London's burning ... fetch the engines, fetch the engines ... Fire! Fire! ... Fire! Fire!*'

The humans turn silhouette, that old weakness of mine. They all undress, remove clothes so that naked shadows walk down the street as silhouettes of black and nothing more, everyone humbled to an outline. Up close their skin is warm, the colour in eyes and hair stands out, this moment when the sun smiles and resolves to make its world fleetingly that bit more delicate. With a distant whistle, it begins sliding from the face of the earth, leaving only black chimney pots to stand like chess pieces against a purple sky.

છ૭

A wind blew through, pushed forward the rose head, flush pink petals full with the afternoon's downpour. The head tipped, the scent poured out, the collected water following after ... emptied like a jug, falling to the concrete with heavy slap. Three-Four and I sat together on a bench, a night some weeks of meetings in the making. She leant at my side, our gloved hands held together, the word 'waterproof' written on a finger of hers, 'windproof' on a finger of mine where I'd gone for the cheaper range. Between us, we'd be unstoppable in any weather. Courier romance is a peculiar, practical thing.

Our bikes were leaning on one another: handlebars, pedals, cranks all held tight together, the leaves of a hedge pulling them in and peering green between alloy wheels. We were both in our work clothes: she with a denim skirt over black leggings, me with a sleeveless body warmer over a black hooded jersey, the two of us covered in black Lycra and neoprene. Where the light fell we gave off a dull shimmer, as if landing on the blubber of two seal pups, washed ashore on a bench in the city. We cuddled, not that that word seemed right for it, somehow too tender: we held one another, warm skin pressing at skin-tight layers. Two beers stood open beneath the bench, the glass bottles giving a chime each time one was resettled on the concrete, the timbre lower as they emptied. We didn't say much to one another … we hadn't much to talk about. Never did have, in truth. At the same time, we'd become close enough to pretend the silence was owing to comfort, to think we'd found a match.

A man walked by: two Rottweilers pulling at their leads, the silver chain catching the moon, necks clutched by collar so that the dogs breathed in with a pant and hiss. Three-Four wet her throat, swallowed a mouthful of beer, licked the remains over her lips before starting to speak, '… had one really good run today.' I listened, made a noise of interest as I drank. She went on, 'Two in the City going to Westminster, with a pickup for St John's on City Road, then Robbie had two more for me in Westminster, to bring me back to the City.'

I gave a nod, an impressed smile, 'It is satisfying when it runs in a perfect circle like that … did you cross Westminster Bridge to get back to the City?'

Three-Four looked at me, a little disbelieving … her eyebrows arching, plucked back into the thinnest of lines, the only feminine grooming she indulged. She fixed a glare on me: doesn't say a word, it's all in the look. She shook her head, patronising her like that, brushed me off and went back for her beer. As couriers, we all seemed to pride ourselves on having figured out that the large loop of the Thames, which had its tip at Somerset House, meant it was quicker to cross west to east by taking the inside line across south London. Three-Four put down her beer with the low note of an almost empty bottle. She turned, smiling playfully, crooked teeth. She pushes me away by the chin, leans at me.

'You think you're so clever … don't you, Two-Two?'

I laugh, she slaps the back of her hand at my waterproof chest, which crumples as she rolls her eyes. I push her, smiling back as she smiles at me so that … *lo!* … we were smiling at one another. She went to hit me again, gritted teeth as I caught her hand. Eye contact. We looked tentatively at one another, her wrist held in my hand and the couriers living out the same love-clichés as the billionaires, the only difference that ours were on benches with dog walkers for occasional chaperones. After a moment more, we must have realised we had nothing to say to one another, kissed instead.

A part of me liked being with Three-Four on the benches. I enjoyed the closeness: the warm against the cold, simple humans in the city, set together beneath London's few stars. Those moments of halfway romance could come to feel like acts of resistance, rebellion … as though the urban could not stop something of the human remaining after all.

'Do we have another beer?' Three-Four cut in my thoughts.

I nod, point at my bag, 'One more … we can share it.'

Three-Four leans forwards as I realise something … something in my bag, incriminating. She can't find it, she *mustn't!* Double-quick I reach down.

'*Wait! A minute!*'

Damn. Too late. I shrink.

'What's this?'

She lets out a laugh my way, hoists it by the cables as if it were underwear, holds it naked in front of me: a tangle of wires and power pack … my battery charger. She pokes me with a spare hand.

'Planning to get lucky, were we, Two-Two?'

Red-handed … I turn meek, nothing for it but impish … bashful-endearing my best hope. Three-Four might as well have found condoms, liquor and lubricant. A courier's radio battery lasts a day … a day and half a morning if you're lucky. The battery has to be charged each night, or else you can't work the following day.

A courier has to sleep in the same place as the battery charger, and if the battery charger was in my bag that represented contingency for sleeping in a room that wasn't my own. I ignored Three-Four, reached past and pulled out the beer, leant its crimped cap on the metal arm of the bench, knocked it off.

ભ

We rode towards her flat, down the canal towpath: flashes of bright pink from the peak of her cycle cap as we passed under street lamps, light splitting overhead, shooting off like the points of a compass. I followed as she pulled further ahead, denim skirt up-down over the old, cobbled sections: grooves between stones wide enough to snatch a wheel, so that the best way to pass is to hold the bars firm and straight, power through, ducking your head to avoid the low, sloping belly of the bridge. Drips of water fall with a pattering echo through the bricks, the underside of every second bridge illuminated as Three-Four keeps disappearing into tunnels of green and blue that cast bright, dancing shadows on the canal. We corkscrew past locks pissing water downwards: cow parsley and columbine tumble out of the stone and a slime of green-black moss smeared between the old and the new water level … a smell of moist weed waiting on the air. The branches of trees brush out of the way for us to sweep by, twigs whipping back at me after Three-Four has ridden on through. She pulls at her brakes: turns sharp and sudden through a narrow gate breaking into streets and brickwork. She's pedalling hard, unrelenting, makes me work just to stay on her wheel, gives me a dressing-down and asserts herself in whatever this relationship is to become.

The brickwork of housing terrace turns gradually to grand, white stone office, and then the buildings give to London Bridge. I pull alongside as we roll under the City, bursting like a firework: London glowing like phosphorescence in a rotting log kicked down the trail, kicked like a flint-laced stone down a path, sparks flying as London kicked and – there it was – the white dome of St Paul's, the red tint from the Blackfriars Bridge, a million earthly stars of orange and white and yellow, sheer light and life amongst the death of darkness. Flags flutter on the wind as humans set about defying the night time: the arches of Tower Bridge, and then the estuary birds … down feathers of their undersides aglow from the city, the birds flying back from the metropolis to the waters of the Kent sea.

Bicycles on shoulders, we climbed a staircase, the carpet peeled from the floor to leave only hardened glue … wheels tipping to bounce against the banister. Three-Four reached the top. Keys scratch lock, door opens. On the floor was a mattress, a double on a bed frame of freight pallets pushed together, a popular style of courier bed. It was a small room: books around the skirting board of two walls, a basin in one corner. With a reaching foot, Three-Four hit the switch of a lamp on the floor, knocked the head of the light downwards to cast a corner of the room white … a bright triangle cut from shadow. There was a large window ajar, a fourth-floor breeze blowing in and London waiting outside the house, some way from the centre, so that a night sky had risen. Framed inside the window, beyond the wall, waited the city, its blackness flecked white, the scene cut as if a postage stamp with stars strong and deep, shining like oil paints built up out of the canvas.

Three-Four threw down her bag as she leant her bicycle against a wall … put her radio on to charge as I lay my bicycle against hers. With a fumbling, the pedal of my bike dropped between the spokes of hers, slipped through the opening of metal with a sound of tension pinging free. The frames collapsed against first one another, and then against the wall, tyres lifting briefly from the ground as they moved through the air. Coiling, the drops of the handlebars swept out, bound close, would not let go their grip … the cable of her brake went looping outwards and up, falling down to catch clumsily around the lever of mine. The light from the lamp cast a brightness against the two bikes, the scene of their entanglement shot large in shadow upon a wall, entwined in clutches of the most simple engineering. All night the bicycles were knotted so, the light of the lamp caught in a crescent across half an aluminium wheel rim, shining in the dimness of the room.

Out of night and into dawn, the room grew pale. That crescent of light upon the wheel was sucked in, absorbed by the brightness of the new day, rolling upwards with the first moans of traffic and the thump of a helicopter overhead. Propellers pounded at the sky as the last of night was beaten down, and inside the room an alarm sounded, so that with stinging eyes, and tired hands held together, Three-Four and I left for work.

Seasons

The weather grew warmer. In the still waters at the banks of the River Lea, on the first days of milder temperatures, larvae hatched to pupa and then took to their wings as flies, rising with the thermometers. I rode through them on my way home, millions of the things and still more each day the temperature lifted. The air would grow thick, the air itself started flying, perforated … all of it hovering, swarming. I would swallow mouthfuls of air: it got inside the eyelid, the ear hole, hit tonsil until you gave in and coughed. On the occasions that we met, Three-Four and I would take it in turns to wipe the dead flies from off the balls of one another's eyes … peering upwards, holding still as a finger dabbed against the whites, the pink inside of the lids. On mild evenings, riding home over the marshes, you watch the grasses shorten to meet the playing fields, where Caribbeans play games of makeshift cricket against Bangladeshis.

All over the city, plane trees crept into seed, dropping their endless dusty clouds … feathered darts that rushed through the streets on the winds. The pollen collected in great, golden drifts along the kerbside, carpeted the piles of horse dung left behind by mounted police. Pollen stuck against my eyeballs, lodged in my throat, leaving me to cough for hours on end as I rode about town, as I rode home and went on coughing into the evenings.

By the time June arrived, London was enjoying a string of consecutively warm days. The people started coming over mystic, an annual murmur of 'summer's here' went blowing through the parks, only for the weather to cool again and the population to bewilder just as fast. People set to guffawing that they didn't understand what had happened: how could it be that it had been hot, but now was not? In time it warmed again, though the people were dissatisfied with the new temperature, felt short-changed, convinced it had been warmer in the past. Still they made the most of it. Always *make the most of* it ... we English, we pour all of our optimism into making the most of crummy weather, haven't the energy for any more once that's been done.

Above the building sites, in the nests of the tower cranes overhead, you saw the crane operators fixing themselves some shade ... sheets of newspaper going up over cab windows, bare feet resting on door panels a hundred metres into sky. Below, I'd figured out at what time and where the sun would pick through the buildings to cast small pockets of sunlight amongst skyscraper footings. I would detour towards those few spots, taking a break with an apple. The office workers did likewise, all of us gravitating towards the precious light and – where it could be found – some square metres of turf laid down in the concrete.

In the parks, folk stripped down to bras and vests, shortened shorts, unfurled their toes and finally got to lower the sunglasses that had waited hopefully on top of heads all spring. Towels and mats were rolled out, people fell asleep, awoke in colours of white and pink: long rows of them, scattered like shrimp on the artificial grass of a fishmonger's stall. Flirtation made the parks a tough place to wile time: skin and serotonin all about, so that everyone came over a bit less frigid, thawed and cheered right up. People became more attractive, and at first gradually, but then eagerly, London rediscovered a hunger for having itself a good time. The problem was, before they got down to business, cut to the chase late evening ... first they had to have conversation all afternoon, leaving me to listen to hour on hour of spoken foreplay, their noses and hands getting closer with each emptied bottle of cider.

Fruits were always my favourite calendar, and soon after the parks had filled, out came the peaches. I remember my first: a fortnight after they'd appeared, all too firm, outside the grocer's stall. Soft to touch, I brushed off the furry coat upon the skin, could feel the fruit just beneath the surface. My favourite place to eat a peach was that bridge where the abandoned golf course met the train tracks, a stop-off on my way into the centre. From there I'd watch freight trains rattle at rails moving north towards Essex and eventually, I guessed, the Port of Felixstowe. The tracks whistled under the nearing weight of shipping containers, and I savoured memories of the USA, with these British versions so short and quaint against the three-mile trains I'd been smitten by in the Sonoran Desert and down the Pacific Coast. Holding my bag of fruit, upon the lowest step I'd sit, beside long grasses that had overrun the old course, concealing a sign of rusting metal that once marked the ninth hole. With a peach it was always a hesitant first bite: terrified of a crunch, of bad, unripe flesh. That first one of 2010 slipped perfect against my palate, taking me back to Serbian evenings at dusty roadsides, sitting on a stool beneath the tree from which a farmer sold his fruit.

1 July – WC1 – Docket #24

High Holborn, midday, going west. A van comes alongside, a contractor's vehicle, some basic utilities-type name on the side of it, the name of a town in Middlesex. The window is down, a forearm out of it and resting on the door panel, a warrior tattoo wrapped under outdoor labour suntan. I can feel something different about to happen: the van is going too slow for this to be impatience, to be abuse, but at the same they're driving too close to be just passing by anonymously. It rolls right up beside me, we move along together as the passenger leans out: unshaven, blonde hair up in spikes, the name on the side of the van printed again on his polo-shirted chest. He's talking, talking to me, but not clearly, half-hushed and scarcely trying to make himself heard over the city. I just hear an O sound at the end of words I don't catch. '*What's that?*' I call back, traffic moving around us as if a rock in a river … our two vehicles curious there on High Holborn, scooters and taxis parting to flood past.

'Which way's Soho?' Comes at me, clearly this time … who knows why he didn't just say so first time around?

I start pointing, 'You're headed the right way, Soho's up ahead, take the left fork …' and I fade out, he's hardly listening, saying something else, trying to shout a mumble … a sound like '*oot*' is all I catch. Dammit man: speak plain or don't speak at all. I shout down, a little impatient, '*What are you saying?*'

He looks right at me: van and bicycle side-by-side. A pointed nose, ratfink eyes, a foul face, the sort that originates from an ugly inside. Thin, pale lips, a cutting face, snarling like a bent nail. Finally he says it, says it clear.

'Which way's Soho … I need a prostitute!'

I pucker up my face, give the sort of look I was always being given myself as a courier … a wash of contempt.

'*A prostitute?*' I respond. 'Why don't you get a girlfriend instead?'

He gives a laugh, sniggers a snort, then drops simply: 'I've got one.'

I shake my head, like I'm disappointed in him … disappointed we've got even anatomy and a gender role in common. I shake my head, 'Well get one you like having sex with then.'

He leans a little, gets excited, the driver chuckling beside him, a pair of boys. 'It's not enough though … I need a prostitute as well!' The van picks up speed, starts to accelerate, pipes up beneath the bonnet as it begins pulling away. The man's head is leaning out the window by the end of it, disappearing into the traffic with the final, desperate words: '*One girl's not enough!*'

Sex was all through the city. Soho wasn't the only place in London with sex shops … only the most brazen about it. You can pick up a foot-long dildo off Sloane Square, there are vibrators in Knightsbridge. You never see anyone go in, never see anyone come out, but the window displays are lavish … woodwork immaculately painted, ever under a fresh coat of gloss and the bricks around it cleaned down nicely. Even without all that, rent alone in those spots would have been confirmation that the stores were making a pretty penny. Those places catered to the man who wanted a dominatrix dressed in leather corsets or Nazi uniforms … to the woman who wanted her underwear crotch-less, sex without the nudity … not unfaithful if the pants stay on. They sell whips, chains, cuffs … they were all at it … books on how to tie a safe noose, save everyone the embarrassment when it all goes wrong and an aristocrat is found hanging, blue, asphyxiated with cock in hand. When you can afford any possession on the face of the earth it must take an awful lot to get satisfied, get pleasured, have your eyeballs roll upwards and start looking for your brain.

Putting aside the sex shops … still the phone boxes told the same story. Always in central London too, never out in the sticks … the poor areas where people are constantly having aspersions cast against their character. Oh no, it's the comfy ones who go picking up trafficked women while the wife stays home. Renewed every day, those phone boxes were constantly revolving artefacts, exhibits from a society that thought nothing more evil than paedophilia and nothing sexier than a schoolgirl. Asian, ebony, Slav, Chinese: as long as she had pigtails and resembled somebody else's daughter on her way to class. That was what the market wanted. And yet it went well beyond the conventional: there is no capitalism purer than that one found stuck inside a phone box. By some quirk, it turned out there was a market for sex with pre-operation transsexuals – a penis and breasts – so that eventually, even the old pervert in a Soho backstreet, dressed all year with hands stuffed in a heavy wax jacket, would start to seem like a pretty regular guy.

The only sex that existed independent of any obvious need for a market place was found in central London's gay community, where the guys had no need for prostitution. So long as you'd figured out how to stick your fringe on end, and had a dog small enough to carry, ugly or otherwise, there'd be someone prepared to service your needs, at least out of kindness. The community even had a name for that, called it *a charity*. That one was a self-regulating market, staffed by a free-for-all of men determined never to spend another night alone, convinced life was about making love, or some other word for it, and nothing more. For not so very long we were joined on the circuit by One-Seven. Austerity had cut the funding for a clinic where he'd conducted HIV tests, and he found himself in a stint as a courier on his way back to work. He told stories of denial … of all the straight-gay men he'd see, wives blissfully ignorant as the husband went through the entire gay community, never a condom in sight, and not a word to the wife because it didn't count as unfaithful if it wasn't with another woman. One-Seven was fairly glib about it: 'To be honest it works fairly well ... until one day a guy finds out he has AIDS.'

Florists were best of all. If you want to find out who's in bed with who in London, open a florist, or at least start delivering flowers for them. The affairs, gentlemen's clubs ... the bouquets sent from Mayfair's most exclusive addresses: luxury hotels and hedge fund offices ... it wasn't only the taxpayer those guys were screwing. You take their hand-tied bunches to the ivy-covered building off Curzon Street, the one that any courier worth his salt has learned within a year is actually a brothel. You read the label on the flowers:

> *Dear Miss Twiggy ... I hope you're feeling better, honey*
> *... I'll come and bring some medicine soon.*

The florists had an ear for a good story, it came with the territory of doing window boxes and flower arrangements in the houses of the rich and powerful: talking breezily while re-potting a geranium. I knew florists who could tell you of the escorts who had stalked the halls of Dolphin Square every day for a decade. There were florists who knew of the illegitimate royals, bastard children who'd be housed in luxury until death ... kept on public-paid stipend in return for ensuring their traps stayed shut about the infidelity that produced them. Florists were all either gay men or large, indomitable women: people who knew how to keep you talking, took no shit and inspired a trust that most of the time was pretty undeserved. Your secrets would soon pass to somebody else. In my case, to the courier who'd stop in for a cup of tea and a chat to go with the delivery. I'd watch as the florist poured bleach into the bucket of water full of gerberas, the bleach to kill bacteria that would otherwise rot the stem from inside, and make the flower wilt before its time. With a wink and a smile I had that trick explained to me, and in each of them was such a rich tapestry of knowledge, assembled exclusively in the pursuit of how to keep people happy. MacPherson, Ecclestone, Khan: over time, the florists had come to know all the prime addresses of London, and slowly, from one doorstep to the next, so too did I.

With that lot, gossip spread like wildfire. They told tales of the peripheral member of the royal family who had once solicited a page boy … requested the poor kid sit on his face. Word had flashed through their network inside six hours, but with the story already bought and paid for by the papers, the injunctions were out in ten. I won't name the royal, the Palace would sue each of our asses to kingdom come: me for writing it and you just for reading the thing. You don't need to know the details, just know that it happened. If those guys in the monarchy weren't so swaddled in secrecy … well … we probably wouldn't think their tradition gig quite so harmless.

The biggest deal I remember dropped with a bouquet for a house in Pimlico. It went with an odd message too:

Thanks for your help – the paediatric unit.

There was no patient name, no '*the staff at*'. The florist thought it strange right away, though knew not to ask questions … processed the order and sent it anyway. Later we figured out it had been the warning message at a safehouse, the flowers a sign for: *Beat it! Busted! Scram!* We delivered the bouquet too late: tabloids like lice and the police already crawling all over the scene. An MI5 agent had been found stark naked, dead and handcuffed inside a sports bag, with the media embellishing the whole affair nicely, dutifully displaying footage of the deceased dressed as a woman, as if it were somehow in the public interest.

Another drama took us one morning to Tower Hamlets: a bouquet to a hospital after a young girl had thought to research her MP's voting record and got mortally angry with the results. She saw how he always fell into line with the government: wars in the Middle East, 48-hour detention without charge, you name it and he'd support it … the only precondition that it should demonstrate a

disregard for human rights, and the wellbeing of Muslims in particular. In a startlingly direct act of democracy, she went out and bought
herself some carving knives, visited his surgery and made to run
him through. He overpowered her, escaped with only flesh wounds,
and one of us delivered *get well soon* flowers to the police guard at
the Whitechapel Hospital. On televisions and headlines around
the nation, the media went calmly and predictably berserk. They
screamed about the waste of it all, this girl some sort of polyglot:
scholarships, King's College (*ha … King's!*) and the world at her feet.
Nobody could understand why she would give up on the unpaid
internship, student debt and her landlord's buy-to-let mortgage …
all of it waiting the other side of university, and now gone forever on
account of some crazed conviction that the world was wrong.

Bandstand.2

It was late, an evening at the end of one of those hot days when everyone sighed, '*That's more like it*', and '*This is how summer's supposed to be*'. I was in Arnold Circus, sitting knees-up on a bench in the bandstand … the orange of sunset glowing on the red brick of the flats. 6:30 p.m. is taking its time, won't hurry up and just let me home with my week's attendance bonus intact. An outline appeared on the top step opposite. Somehow familiar: a long coat moving towards me, fastened around the middle, taking confident strides. He stopped in front, purposeful-like, as if he'd planned to meet me there. His hand went forward a little, by way of parley … buttons fastened on the cuffs, the man overdressed for the weather. The cuffs of the coat are frayed, the material faded. On his face a moustache, still cut neat and trim, just as before … the same flat cap, casting a dark crown across his eyes and the top of his nose.

'Excuse me, sir,' that refined accent, not posh, refined. 'I've lost my phone and my wallet … and need to call my wife.'

Just like the last time, his voice made no apologies … still proud. I smiled, started going into my bag, wanted to see how it'd play out.

'Sure. I suppose you can borrow my phone.'

Well, actually, it's quite a long call … if you could just give me some money for a phone box.'

I stopped in my bag, played along. 'I remember you'd lost your phone and your wallet when we met here once before … you needed money to call your wife then too.' I gave a laugh, good-natured, 'That's quite a coincidence.'

He scarcely broke rhythm, didn't bat an eyelid or flutter a word, just went right on looking at me, the whites of his eyes coming through the shadow of the flat cap as he leaned in with the same earnestness, spoke to me, direct as you like.

'Yes,' he said, as if I were holding him up, 'that is a coincidence.'

I laugh, go for my wallet all the same. I'm not going to rock the boat ... this guy's worth paying, worth keeping for the sake of his story. I drop some small silver into his palm, the stitching of the leather glove coming loose. He doffs his cap, drops coins into pocket, and with a slight singing of metal, they disappear.

6 July – W1 – Docket #25

You find your poverty waiting at the bottom of someone else's wealth. What you end up with in your wallet is yours, you don't worry so much about that. However little, even a bright blue five or a single gold nugget you feel thankful for, makes you feel rich. You don't find poverty in what you have, it's in what you don't have … what everyone else around you does, how quickly yours is gone. The presence of poverty is all about absence, and of all London's marvels, of all its fine attributes, make no mistake, in the entire city poverty is the greatest. More glorious than St Paul's, more ubiquitous than the Thames. The poverty there was stunning, magnificent, spectacularly achieved and with meticulous attention to detail. I will never see a poverty so complete as that which I have witnessed in London … the Kazakh villages couldn't hold a candle to the place. Even those Steppe kids, sprogs up to their elbows in horse dung, making bricks for the garden wall … those guys were living it up compared to what they'd have found in London, the brash opulence they'd have been obliged to live beside without even a space to run around in and call their own. Poverty is a funny thing… only really comes into effect once you've been bundled into a broader system and have numbers placed on you to determine the monthly cost of staying alive. If the Steppe had been outside that system, then London was its heart.

In front of department stores, horses and traps would wait to take customers for rides in parkland. Gentlemen stood in cravats and top hats at hotel entrances, holding open the doors of Italian sports cars so that their owners need not trouble with doing so. The drivers would step from the vehicles, peeling themselves out of seats and the miniscule hull of the car like magical sardines from an expensive tin. They strode towards the entrance, dusts of banknotes falling off their heels … the concierge and the doormen knelt in front and buffing pavement with fringes. Beside that would be a man in a two-thousand-pound suit, a sartorial dream: perfectly cut, nice rigid collar on the shirt, full Windsor knot in the tie … they dress him up like that, give him a toothbrush, then order him down on his knees to scrub car tyres outside Claridge's. Through revolving doors I'd go, ushered in with delivery in hand: carpets turning full, velveteen … like walking a trampoline, a cloud, bouncing over mattresses as I crossed to the concierge, standing beside a magnificent pyramid of fruit that waited to be thrown out, untouched, at each week's end.

Away from hotels, I knew shops that paid humans to work as mannequins and from which I once delivered a seven-hundred-quid négligée of lace … seven hundred pounds to half-conceal a pair of nipples and vagina. There were shops that sold yachts, that sold claret, sold port, that sold cigars, the thick smoke chugging on the wind back up St James's Street. There were shops selling cufflinks that cost my month's wages, shops selling villas and islands in the sun, shops chartering jets and vintage cars. There were the restaurants with tables decked in flutes and three separate sets of cutlery … embroidered cushions upon the seats and some of the most well-fed and positively delighted-looking folk upon the cushions. I would watch them from another world beyond the windows, a silent laughter that could not reach me through the glass as they rocked back and forth in a voyage of glee. You know the colour of the money in those places? The banknotes were certainly never blue, but neither were they ever pale orange or soft purple. The money there was always red: bright, vermillion red … same colour as the autumn leaves I'd once ridden beneath in Washington State. Fifties, peeled from a wrap as if nothing at all: each single note a day of my wages. The attendant takes the fifties in her hand, puts them straight in the drawer, no second glance at the denomination, no counterfeit-testing pens necessary. You could smell veracity on the diners.

We delivered banking books for institutions asking a cool

half-million minimum deposit ... banks that threw monthly receptions with canapés and aperitifs. Polished triggers and gold hammers
shone from rifles in the hallway, muskets and bayonets, souvenirs
from the week in the eighteenth century when they had to mobilise
the staff to keep the riff-raff out. Beside the firepower is the notice
board: the scheduling of monthly receptions in which guest speakers
give talks on ethics and sustainability ... on moral consumerism. The
customers sit there at the front, seated on red, leather-upholstered
chairs with gold fastenings ... in the evenings you see them filing in,
and they sit and listen, with half-million minimum deposits in their
accounts and social conscience in their ears. It's enough to make you
burst, my gaskets took a hammering. Half a million cash deposit ...
Ethics?! In this world you either have a spare half-million to open a
bank account, or you have ethics, the two don't mix.

I watched them pay for all they lacked ... learned fast that trickle-
down economics was based on the idea of people paid minimum
wage to display some charm and manners to folk so indecently
wealthy they were excused both. They paid for other people to have
taste for them: bought bouquets of flowers with mint and rosemary
and sage stuck fragrant amongst the foliage. It was exquisite taste
... but someone else's exquisite. They paid for common sense ...
paid attendants to remember to remove the receipt from the box of
chocolates they paid someone else to pick from a shelf. They bought
their opinions in magazines with high and mighty titles assembled in
the lobbies: *Economist, Banker, Spectator* ... each with Swiss watches
separating articles that were only opinions made palatable, coher-
ent and easily repeated by those without ideas of their own. Where
passion would otherwise have been, they bought other people's
talent, other people's flair: Cuban dancers, Indian sitar players, Viet-
namese painters. Paid for the refinement of some champagne farmer
outside Epernay, paid two bottles at £1,475 a go, paid me £2.50 to
deliver both ... three full months' wages corked and ready to pop.

At the same time, I held all those memories from the world: the

Kazakhs were drinking camel milk out in the Steppe, the Lemoines picking pecan nuts by the tens of kilos in Louisiana. Deep down I knew that in all those fluffy, immutable ways that don't help pay rent, I was richer than they were. And yet still it was sensational, stupendous, because after seeing all that, I was left to count my deliveries and get to the bottom of whether I had earned the fifty daily pounds I'd come to treat as some watershed of satisfaction. I would count dockets, deduct the amount of money I had eaten to keep going, and there, right there waiting, after all you have seen, that ... *that* is poverty. The most spectacular poverty imaginable, for in those moments it could not be more acute ... the awareness of all you do not have.

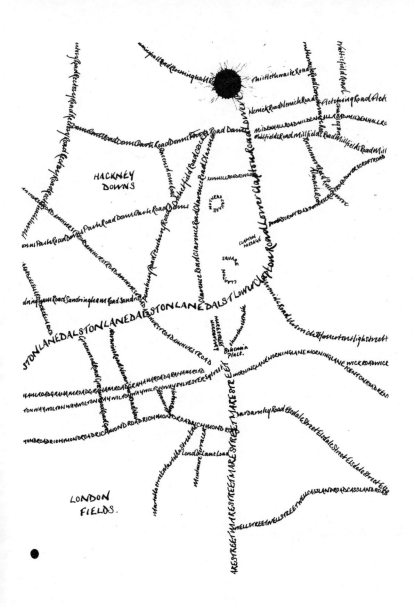

Part III

KEEPING ON

16 July – IP17 – Dunwich

The Saturday night nearest the July full moon came round again, a night always good for the soul. Once more, I showed up at London Fields Park … a late light: the shade the French refer to as between dog and wolf. All around is Lycra, wheels and half-empty pint glasses clinking between laughter. Twenty years ago, the founders of the ride had needed a legend, a myth … needed something to help get it off the ground. They said couriers had started it: friends drinking after work on a Friday night, daring one another to ride until they hit the water, until they reached the sea. The couriers had cycled all through the night, and then, with the sun rising, they had come to the water at Dunwich … 120 miles away on the Suffolk coast, where ten centuries earlier there stood a booming hub of the wool industry and, come 2010, only a pub and small hotel.

The story wasn't true. Like I say, they'd needed a myth: some form of romance to help build the thing. The people responsible for the Dunwich Dynamo were not and never had been couriers … I was proud to count a few of them as friends. One of them, the owner of the Lamb's Conduit bike shop, the finest in London, had bought me a copy of Voltaire's *Candide* when I returned – so miserably – to London after my record. Between them all, you knew they'd lived a lot of life … a group of guys with hair starting to thin on top, and with no claim to rock and roll beyond knowing what was good for the human spirit. They never sought credit for their idea of the Dynamo, still don't, desire no recognition beyond the wish that people turn up and enjoy themselves. Now and then, as cycling became ever-hotter marketing property, they'd joke about cashing in and selling the ride to an events management company, making their retirements a little easier. Yet you could tell they didn't mean it

... that it wasn't the way they thought about life. Often grim, grizzly and outwardly cynical, theirs were some of the warmest hearts you'd ever know, who would look out for people where a dozen twenty-first-century friends, bombarding you with exclamation marks (!) and professions of *awesome*, would sink so quickly without trace. Twenty years ago they had created that courier myth, and although it endured then and will no doubt endure into the future, there's no need for it, not any longer.

By the time the nineteenth episode of the Dynamo was underway it had already established a legend all of its own. It needed no embellishment. Thousands of us went pedalling out together. Collectively, you feel the weight of London lightening. As dusk lands, and then gathers, riders begin leaving the park to pick their way out of the city along the Lea Bridge Road. You don't go too soon, for leading is more trouble than simply following those turnings in the night ... keeping to the wheels of those who have made the journey before. Out the north-eastern sticks of the city we ride, out of the trees of Epping Forest ... all two thousand of us with evening newly down and all the night ahead. Chatter strikes up: people talk pannier bags, you hear stories of the couple just home from cycling in Argentina, reassuring the girl setting out next week for Mongolia. At this point it's just a ride, still only a ride, only a question of miles and tarmac as we all go pedalling through the coming grey, stop-start traffic and receding concrete.

It's the night that does it. The road comes alive: a dragon takes up the trail and if there is any one thing that any person riding Dunwich will always remember it's that trail of lights ... that flashing red that winds away in front of you, blinking and flickering and glowing as darkness comes down. They light lanterns. The friends who started the Dynamo two decades ago still go out in front each year, leave London hours before the rest of us. Tiny jam jars with candles inside of them glow yellow, glow white within the night ...

each placed to either just the left- or right-hand side of a junction, a roundabout exit, so as to mark the turning you should take. The flame gutters as the wind pushes over the rim of glass, blowing a sound into silence. That same wind pushes us on with an invisible hand, coming up from the south and blowing that pale, pedalling yawn of cyclists along the road.

We ride, we all ride, all of us together … you're never alone on that road, a whole legion of strangers with whom you have all the right things in common. I hear snippets of talking as the bats flutter frantically above the road, serrated wings cutting at moonlight as the caught-breath conversation goes pitter-pattering with the in-out drizzle. I listen and, my word, but the bicycle … it sure brings out the best in people. '*The thing to do is toast the mustard seeds in a dry pan for a few minutes before you get started*' comes from the left, as two girls ride gradually by. Over my right shoulder, '*It's really interesting the way the road slopes like that, just gently sort of.*' Cyclists, or humans riding bicycles, whatever you call them … they sure pay attention to the little things, the tiny bits of nonsense that make a life worth living.

Gradually it takes me. The road takes me under the crumbling, crestfallen towers of old churches, roofless stone gables reflecting the moonlight as the tarmac leads you down through hills and into the village of Sible Hedingham. Stuck to each lamp post are signs, printed on bright white paper where '*Shusshhh! We're sleeping!*' shines under the same moon. Each year the village hall stays open all through the night, the villagers serving up soup and flapjacks. Flapjacks … damn … but after Dunwich you don't want to see another flapjack for a long time. The hall is packed: waterproof from wall to wall, some of it crawling inside a sleeping bag … the scene like some sort of refugee camp on the edge of Essex. Around the hall, people sit hunched over Styrofoam cups of soup. I get in line: wait my turn, wait my turn, get to the front. The flavours are red or yellow, and they call it minestrone or vegetable but the reality is that it just tastes bad ... you pick your favourite colour and enjoy the warmth on its way down the throat.

After the rest stop things change: the food pulls the blood from your brain into your gut. The sleep comes to take you away, off the road and into some space above the fields. The stars float by above, tearing the sky apart as they trail like tiny comets back down the road. Other riders pass you: packs of them, road crews, chain gangs. Their skin is wrapped up tight, aerodynamic helmets, heads inside casks faster than a human skull covered in hair. They ride in enfilade, jaws rolling above handlebars, musette over shoulder. You hear them coming, the deep rims that dust themselves free of night like brooms upon a stone step. I hear the hum, purr of the tyres, and, looking down before me, there move my feet, my-feet, my feet. I watch my wheel ahead, some rudder on the sea ... the wheel above and the road rolling under as night looms ever onwards in front. Up ahead I see the skin of white legs, showing on top of long, black football socks pulled up to thighs. Up and down the legs go on, black topped with white, so that in time I see only two pints of stout pedalling along the road.

It takes all kinds. Dunwich draws us all in, every type of rider. Each year there's a man with a large Labrador and an even larger basket. The Labrador curls in the basket and the man drives him through the night, the dog turning round on itself every now and then, sometimes sitting up to yap at passing bats. You see a girl, a pair of denim shorts and riding a pink Pashley with a wicker basket. Her boyfriend puts his hand to her back and pushes her into the incline hanging over us. If you meet a girl or guy on the Dynamo, or if you find someone who will ride it with you, keep hold of them ... they're special.

The sleep is what does it. As ever, you don't tire in the legs so much as in the head. Six hours in and I start swimming. The lids get heavier and the vision melts. Some of us break from the road, crawl onto a soft lawn of Suffolk and sleep under a tree. I stay awake for the silhouettes, always and again those silhouettes. White moonlight cuts black shapes from the high stalks of dandelions, cow parsley and bramble thicket. I could look at those silhouettes all night long, drink from the things after my water bottle runs dry … and as the dawn begins breaking and the sky cheers from black to blue, you pass out of the final woods: a guard of honour formed by trees, cracking branches together like quarterstaffs above your head. The country-side opens, opens wide, lets out a yawn and then … and then … there it is. Glowing at the end of the road is a giant, warbling ball of red crimson, warbling … turning to a baby's mouth that screams at being woken for the new day. The sun chases down the road, flashes by the trail of flickering red so that the chill of darkness passes and there comes the warmth of day to take its place.

Hours of half-light roll slow as the lanes of Suffolk begin to twist. A central reservation of dusty gravel appears, kicked up by the tyres ahead so that your eyes sting once with fatigue and twice with the mist of debris on the air, dandelion parachutes taking up the breeze. The day rises, grows bright, and there you see sun shining through the flowers that line the walls of those roads … high banks of mud cut directly from the hills and lined perfectly with poppies and poppies and poppies. The sun comes through those red petals as the flickering lights of the cyclists are switched off and instead we follow that trail of poppies to the sea. The heather of the heath is last of all, a soft purple, the same colour as those burst veins in the legs of the middle-aged cyclist, snaking into Alpine switchbacks about the calf and down into the ankle.

As one, we move over the heathland, wind dropping for the coming day, a warm smile resting somewhere just behind many lips. Dunwich arrives a whole lot faster if you set out simply to ride through the night. Forget the 120 miles, you just keep riding … in the company of friends, or in the company of only yourself, that's all you have to do. The finish line of a beach comes: shingle pulled from the seabed and thrown back down forever, crashing over on itself as the sun glints off rims and reflectors and spokes all thrown down on the beach, a sea of bicycles washed ashore from some better place. The tired limbs of cyclists stretch out to rest upon the stones, beneath the boughs of old boats, where other riders crouch with kettles and tiny stoves, pouring boiling water over bags of tea. Clothes stripped, we step down to the waters … stones pressing soles, pressing toes, pressing soles. You jump in – you have to. You have to jump otherwise you'll never go past the waist. Cold is a state of mind … it's not cold, it's euphoria. Under those waves, somewhere just between the shingle and your head beneath the waters … once more, right there, all life is waiting for you.

22 July – EC1 – Docket #26

It was in the advertising that the change felt most apparent, and after six months cycling deserts, coasts and countryside, the determination of a city to constantly nudge me towards new purchases, through images of some ideal self, had become conspicuous. '*Tired of feeling tired?*' ... '*Smart has plans but Stupid has stories*' ... '*Adventure is the new Mini*'. Riding by, my infernal brain clocked each and every word, compulsive as you like, as if those lines were supposed to have been worth reading. Time after time I longed for my own illiteracy, to unlearn the ability to read, would've gladly given up Stendhal in return for never again having my consciousness breached by a real estate developer's slogan of '*Your future in our hands*'.

The brutality of it drove me crazy, clueless as to who had granted all of those brands and hawkers of advertising space the freedom to invade the sovereignty inside my head, split the peace where thoughts of my own could otherwise have taken shape. The blank canvas of a mind after 18,000 miles away showed society in a new clarity, and it struck me that the duty of advertising was to instil in people a small sadness at their own life and who they were, a discontented doubt to be filled by the service or product on sale. If the advert didn't create that sadness then it had failed in its purpose. That we would convert all corners of our city to such a sad psychology made no sense to me, and when I once said as much to another courier, his glum response was only: '*What else would we look at?*' Poetry, art, equations, maps, designs ... all a society might have stood for, or advanced by, had been taken down and replaced by only a set of sophisticated *For Sale* signs.

New cafés all seemed to have about them something eerily similar, a confirmation of this new and perfect order. Notes of an acoustic, melancholic love dripped from endless music in soundtracked lives. If not that then the air chimed an electric, saccharine optimism. The happiness industry was already working full-tilt by then, cranking out ideas of homogenised joy so that people grew terrified of anything else. Boredom, a little disquiet, waiting … it had all grown unacceptable, not to mention the possibility of feeling sad once in a while. Only happiness remained, as if any other state of mind were some admission of personal failure. That too was key: it was all about the individual, like everything else. Each one of us bore responsibility for our own happiness, there was no obligation placed upon the makers of society, those with power, to create a fairer place where it might have been a bit easier to find happiness to begin with.

Of course, it was no more possible to be consistently upbeat than ever it had been, and in a sleep-deprived city, nourished by caffeine and crash diets, a nervous anxiety filled the seconds, flickering its charge through the hanging light bulbs. I remember a girl, dressed in soft features and an embroidered shawl, the letters H-O-P-E tattooed on knuckles wrapped around the handle of a coffee cup, so that I wondered what it was she was even hoping for. The second hand held her phone, thumb gliding – as if a twitch – through endless images, a face that always moved from longing to vacant in proportion to how long her thumb hovered.

Throughout those cafés went a small legion of flexible, *freelance* workers, so positively titled yet without half the rights, security or pay that would have passed for normal to those only two generations older. Graffiti in the toilet of one café I visited drove home the point, was left up in what must have been agreement, even after most others had been painted over: '*You can't change the world, but you can change someone's world.*' With everybody adrift amongst symbols and straplines, it was as if – gradually – drip-fed unexamined messages of what life was supposed to be, we had lost the ability to envisage or dream of any alternative way of being, only to purchase and mimic the lifestyle imprints assembled in front of us.

24 July – SW1 – Docket #27

Above all others, one day really drove home the effect London had started to have on me. With a single bouquet of flowers in my bag, I made my way out to Knightsbridge, via Pimlico and Belgravia. Something about delivering flowers always left me feeling sad, guilty, as if I were some sort of gangmaster … looking down at the pretty little heads of my delicate captives, all set to die with some stranger who had received so many flowers in a lifetime that they seldom seemed to appreciate the things anyway. Flowers meant people who would call the florist in three days and complain that some flowers had wilted, who would phone up after just one to complain that some had not yet bloomed … as if nature ought be as controlled a commodity as all the others we consumed. Another irritation was the reaction flowers earned from the security guards, receptionists, chauffeurs and builders waiting around outside. Every time it came, unfailingly, clockwork and just the same: *'For me? You shouldn't have!'* and they set to chuckling at their own humour. Please, for the sake of whoever's doing my job now, don't say that to the guy bringing in the flowers. He's heard it twice already that day, and every other day, too … eventually, I promise, someone will snap.

I rode through Vincent Square: red brick, black railings with locked gates, lush green grass in the centre of it and then more locked gates, locked gates, locked gates. At the heart of Vincent Square is a private garden that doubles as a playing field for the local private school. Cricket wickets, football nets, hockey nets, tennis courts: you name it, they had it, while the children of the schools I cycled by on the way home got only grazes and concrete. On the field, the boys ran around in knee-length shorts, burgundy polo shirts, a burgundy-yellow cap in the school's colours, and a yellow neckerchief folded in a triangle and tied in a neat knot. I cycled by, looking at those little humans, locked in some social quarantine destined to reproduce its own order.

I arrive in Knightsbridge: a large apartment building, a driveway sweeping around the front. The waters of a fountain slip either side of long, wide steps, each step the size of your front room and three of the things leading up to large doors. Doormen and concierge stand all over the place, holding the door for a family walking out: coloured saris and a white suit with a matching moustache. Indians. Indian billionaires were good, Indians were real good ... they'd taken their caste system and discovered it not so very different to our own class system, only a couple of letters different, perfect assimilation and the key to being British: be rich. Real damn rich. Once you've got a stable of horses with which to play some polo, once you've inherited your grandfather's Rolex ... then you can go about fitting in. On my way up the steps, the Indians pass me by: I smell perfumes, see gold handbags fumbled. I watch them pass, less than a metre distance ... corner of my eye and I'm sure there's a sneer on the lips of the family head, breadwinner extraordinaire. The fellow looks pretty narked that even with a five-million-pound house he still has to clap eyes on pieces of shit like me. But enough of my opinions, give him the benefit of the doubt, perhaps it's just my shoulders talking.

The reception looms over me and my bouquet, mainly peonies: plump head of petals opening along a single split. *Hell!* I feel bad, leaving these peonies to die with such people for company. The receptionist has dark hair curling tight back in on his head, aquiline nose, North African Arab for certain. He carries himself with a real air of dignity, self-contained ... keeps his dignity to himself, puts it out sparingly. He picks up a phone, calls the number on the card with my peonies. No answer. He looks at me, doubtful. 'Go up, I think they're home.' I look at him, dubious, I'm always hurrying, don't want to waste my time going up to a shut door. 'And if they're not home, I'll just leave them on the doorstep?'

The receptionist's eyes flash no, flash an *are-you-crazy* sort of a look.

'You bring them back here, my boy … or someone else will take them!'

'From the doorstep?' I exclaim. Face contorts, not sure.

'Yes, from the doorstep!' He leans in, sort of smiling, a knowing whisper: 'You think you can trust these people because they're rich. Let me tell you,' he confides softly, 'they'd steal from their mothers … things are always being stolen, especially on doorsteps … these are the worst kind of people!'

Warm inside, I head for the lift. It was always reassuring to find someone else in on the joke … the myth, mirage. I ping up through the floors: a courier with peonies looking back from the door of the lift. There's a girl next to me, perhaps scarcely older than myself. She peers at her reflection, then closes in on it, pulls a grimace-smile. She checks her teeth: examines for signs that sometimes she eats food, pulls a herb out of the nook between two teeth … doesn't care what dental upkeep I see, I don't exist anyway. She gets out first, leaves me alone with my reflection and the peonies. We ride the remaining floors, up to the top … a half-million increment in the apartment price with each ping. This one's rich, this one's loaded: we're antepenultimate floor, we're penultimate, we keep on and *Bam!* Someone got lucky, someone got penthouse. Boy … someone must have worked real hard to get all the way up here.

I ring the doorbell. Wait. Nothing doing. I ring the doorbell. Wait. Nothing doing. A scuffling sound comes to me, comes from behind the door … concierge was right, someone is home. Scuffling grows louder. They're on their way. Right behind the door. They should be answering the door right now, but no, instead the scuffling retreats. I ring the doorbell. Wait. Nothing doing. You learn that about the super-rich … they really don't like answering the door. They don't like answering the door because they're not used to doing things that don't earn them money … because all their

life is planned and my ring at the doorbell is not on the itinerary…
because they don't respond well to being summoned, even by their
own doorbell. I ring a final time. Footsteps near, coming back, latch
switches. Door opens. There she is. She doesn't like me. She looks
surprised, put-out, aging but not old. I reveal the peonies – *ta da!*
– as if to explain myself. I read out her name, she extends a bone of
arm with skin hanging off it. I hand her the peonies: farewell my
friends, so very pretty, I'm sorry it has to be this way.

With a wave I part from the flowers, but I'm not done, not yet. I've
got my halfway-regular social experiment to conduct, my very own
voyeurism meets rights-of-man act. I'm not bursting, but I might
have been, and when a fellow human delivers something to you, and
says he needs a piss, social obligation has to take over. 'Excuse me
… but you wouldn't mind if I used your toilet quickly, would you?'
I turn polite as you like, a regular ambassador for proletarian good
manners, a *mother-raised-you-well* mode of address but still … she's
miffed, amazed … her eyeballs swell but, credit to her, she subsides
and steps aside. She waves a bone of arm, croaks: 'Second door, the
left.'

Into the toilet I stride, carpets plump as ever, a cosy affair: marble
walls, dried flowers hanging, matching towels. The maid has folded
origami into the next sheet of toilet paper that will smear over a
backside or dab dry a genital. Looking down at me from a six-foot
canvas, looking down from under orange hair, holding her knee …
is none other than Mrs Egon Schiele. Schiele who had scandalised
the cities by his enthusiasm for young girls, Schiele who depicted
cocks and labia and stares in all fearless glory. Schiele had talent,
Schiele had balls. So up he went, six foot high, to kindle some sense
of passion and scandal, framed politely amongst all the good form.
On the table beside the sink was the parfumerie: twenty fragrances
from the most renowned houses of the world, others from names so
priceless they've never even found their way into the ears of com-
moners like us. Each bottle was all but full, each of them different,

so that his and her need never go out smelling of the same artificial pong two days in the same month-and-a-half period. I left the toilet, turned on heel and made my way out, the woman standing back in her front room, a short demand of '*close the door after you*' uttered without so much as a turn of the head.

Oh, but none of that was the breaking point: up to that moment the day was nothing more than par for the course. It was on the way out of the building that it happened, on the way out that I realised just how I'd been poisoned by it all, contracted a strand of resentment that had left me with an almost sociopathic hatred of wealth and the wealthy. I marched out of the building, through the glass front: fountains spewing down the pebbled steps, beside chauffeur-driven cars parked up in the driveway. From almost nowhere a child came running towards me. He didn't notice me, just as the woman checking her teeth in the lift hadn't noticed me, just as nobody else in the whole city noticed me at all any longer. I'd long ago turned invisible, so that the young lad just went right on running, as if I hadn't even been there … as if I were a net curtain, an apparition.

He was dressed in school uniform: socks pulled to knock-knees, legs bounding towards me, rattling around and around. Seconds before impact, I could see we would collide, especially as I wasn't about to break stride. He would hit waist-height, and as that little child came running full pelt into me I continued moving forwards, watching. Until. *Bump.* I couldn't care less. I made no effort to catch that ball of infant as it bounced off me to land on its rump on the forecourt. Wide eyes looked up in confusion: he saw me then, found out I existed after all, flesh and bone all right. And I simply walked, unperturbed, back to my bicycle. It's then, when even the children are no longer innocent, that you know something's wrong with you … when a young life resembles only one more little person waiting to grow up the same cunt as his parents.

20 August – E1 – Docket #28

There was a brown stain in the white ceiling above. Water damage spread long and wide, like some tea-stained map of Russia. Six months prior, a tramp had moved into the upstairs flat, not far from Cable Street. He'd made himself at home a while, eventually realised the flat's copper piping would fetch a pretty penny from the gypsies out in Walthamstow. He pulled out the pipes, every last one. The water poured through.

I lay on my back in the bathtub. One of Three-Four's legs either side of me as I look up at the stain. Three-Four was fiddling with my face, a finger in a scar, tracing old stitches. She has fingertips like thimbles, callused hard from life at the handlebars.

A few plants had been placed in each corner, a grubby towel mat left on the floor. The walls had long lost their paint, turned to a patchwork of pale yellows and dark greens, some kind of internal camouflage. Wide, grey floorboards spanned the room, each full of splinters, though generally you'd spend so long in the bath that the soles of your feet became good and soft, so that pruned, wrinkled skin grew plump, and it was quite simple to pull a shard of wood back out as soon as you felt it passing in. Three-Four had dripped lavender oil in the bath, the room smelt Provence, filled with steam from the almost scalding water. The mirror-condensed, footprints, all shining wet, did a lap of the room where Three-Four had jumped out to fetch soap. With a coarse, wiry mitten, she moved suds around my shoulder and started washing at my arm. She pulled the thing from the armpit down, bicep squeezing out of the way, slipping between the press of thumb and fingers as she forced her hand up and down towards my elbow.

Three-Four and I would take turns washing one another. For an

170

hour each evening, we became one another's *soigneur*, grew devoted to the other's cleanliness. You got as good as you gave, being thorough was an investment in the scrubbing down you'd be given afterwards. I watched steam winding off my leg, rising from the water, the reflection of taps in the still surface. Two candles were glowing, glowing once against the corner of the room, twice against the water, splitting a touch of pink from floating discs of lavender oil. We shuffled, made to move, knees and elbows lifting and raising: *click-click-click.* In a bathtub or bed, courier intimacy always sounded like a game of backgammon ... four knees cracking and clicking as they're moved, joints that memorise a million pedal strokes and release them one click at a time. We repositioned, swapped places while trying not to slip on the bottom of the tub ... Three-Four's legs so dotted by bruises you'd think she were a cricketer, little puffs of navy and black all over her thighs with Three-Four always clueless as to what caused them.

With a small slip, she splashes down in front of me, faces my way, candlelight shining in the silver ring through one side of her nose. She sticks a leg out of the water, puts her other ankle on my shoulder and lets out a grin, indicates that it is my turn to scrub. I pick up a calf. Three-Four's calves were something else: masterpieces, filleted, ribbed ... like someone had stuck a palm leaf up under the skin. I'd have liked to have shown Three-Four's calves to the Lycra-wearing roadies who'd make boyish remarks about girls riding bikes. Where cyclists are concerned, calves don't lie ... the only way to develop a calf like that was to ride a bicycle endlessly, and to ride the thing well. I pick up Three-Four's artillery, one of her engines, I squeeze at it, the muscle trying to get out, slipping from under my grip, winding up the skin as Three-Four gives a happy little moan. She lets her head fall back, looks up:

'Do you think he got much money for the pipes?'

'Probably not bad,' I enliven, some of my favourite information on its way out, always after opportunities to make political economy relevant. 'Copper prices are high, have been for a decade because China needs so much for wiring and industrialisation.' Three-Four is underwhelmed by my titbits, I try more. 'There's more than two-pence worth of copper in a two-pence coin.'

Three-Four closed her eyes again, let out her most contented face. She spoke calm, distant, 'I don't understand why you care so much about this sort of thing, Two-Two ... economies and all that.'

I went on scrubbing, top to bottom of her leg, my arms rowing, doing lengths up and down, short stubble tickling my forearm.

'I don't understand why you don't.' I replied. 'Doesn't it bother you that your whole life is taken out of your control, that you're powerless?'

In general, the more worked up I got, the harder I scrubbed. The harder I scrubbed, the less concerned Three-Four was about powerlessness.

She laughed, kept her eyes closed, 'But why don't you just enjoy having a bath, Two-Two?'

'I am enjoying having a bath!' I laugh back. 'I'd just like to have a bath in a slightly fairer world.' I pressed the point, 'I don't under-stand how you can be so satisfied just delivering post for people who don't give a shit about the consequences of their work.'

'I don't care who I deliver to,' began Three-Four. 'It's the riding ... *I just love it.*' She paused, paused before becoming animated, a little flustered, spoke excitedly and without troubling to open her eyes, '*I love it, I just fucking love it ... I just love it all.*'

I look at her, lying there with her eyes closed, with calm on her face. I wondered what it felt like up there between her ears: if she thought any further than those simple sentences, if they offered all the description she required of life. I wondered if there was a tangled mass of unexpressed emotion in there, all the more frus-trated because she couldn't articulate it, or if she was simply content with no more. We both go quiet, I watch her, steam winding off the water, snaking in the candlelight. Her head is back, her neck up, peak of her throat lifting like an atoll out of the bath, the purple of nipples half breaking the water. She looks so peaceful, her short, wet hair sticking down on her ears and forehead. Her lips move, ever so slightly, as if to talk, and then they close again, as if deciding whether to say something.

'I think you think the world's unfair because you're unhappy … and if you were happy, it wouldn't bother you so much.'

Three-Four opened her eyes. Sure in her verdict, she looked at me.

27 July – EC2 – Docket #29

At the top of the whole lot was the City, the Square Mile: the world's largest offshore tax haven, moored like a pirate ship on the banks of the Thames. The guys in Sloane Square, Mayfair, Belgravia … at least with them you could see the actual human beings, with that lot you could see who the winners were and who was living it up at our expense. The City was different: with the City it was faceless … stark and sheer, the pirate ship with black mice pouring into it across the bridges each morning. By night, the ship was left at anchor, deck eerily deserted, creaking and rocking as the gales came flooding up the Thames or along the A14 from Stratford. Packs of wind would come howling down river and highway until they arrived and met with right angles of glass and steel. The winds thrashed against the rocks, dashed themselves to bits and a hundred separate gusts ran barking into the City, chasing their tails around the footings of each building. Litter, newspapers and the dead leaves of the Square Mile's few trees were all picked up by the lifting and falling of gusts. At junctions, the packs would draw, barking, to a halt … a wet nose would proffer forth, sniffing out which road to take, testing the air for a smell of whatever life was still present.

Underneath those right angles, even after the suits had left each day, still you could feel the presence of their ideology in the cold and lifeless streets. EC2 was the global home of voodoo economics, casino capitalism. No matter how many scandals broke, still you felt down there – with new buildings ever rising – that the ideology was holding strong, and the very things that had caused crisis were apparently to bring about recovery … who better than a banker, after all, to resolve a banking crisis? The clue was in the name … and so the public heard how we had to pay large bonuses to reward talent, even where all it seemed to have done was incentivise risk and fraud. We could not regulate the risk, so we heard, or else the market … sorry, The Market … would sense interference and be impeded in otherwise solving our every problem. As the years wore on, they told us we had to lose jobs and accept a lower standard of living to avoid a deeper crisis in which we would have to lose jobs and accept a lower standard of living. Remedies were also consequences, and though it seemed simply fearmongering, tricks and power games … the people had been made to believe in it, would not bite the hand that fed them, no matter how meagre the meals might become.

On the margins of the postcode, you found the watering holes that lubricated the industry. Three strip clubs had opened within half a kilometre of Bishopsgate since I'd arrived in London, another every time the ribbon was cut on a new skyscraper. Early in the evenings you'd see them all getting started, every one of the men with a wrap of notes so big they needed a clip to fasten the things together. It entertained me to think anyone could ever reach a point at which they had so much money they needed a clip in which to keep it tidy. Once they'd bought a clip to keep the stuff in they'd start waving the thing around: a book of clipped notes was worn like a ring upon their fingers, with predatory men doing everything in their power to buy alcohol for any woman inside a twenty-metre radius.

All across the island, the bankers had divided people. Most of the country was convinced we were paying them to take us to the cleaners, while a few remained of the opposite opinion: believed they put food on our plates, were the only thing keeping the country going. Whatever differences of opinion, after twenty minutes in the City on a Friday night, one thing became certain: none of them had very much class. Ever on their way to soused, from Thursday lunchtime they would all be building up to it. Even as builders and road workers were begrudged every tea break, you could find ten thousand banksters and bankeresses sinking pints and spritzers before high noon Thursday, only just halfway through their working week. All of them had found the same way to dress, they had all seen *Wall Street*, been inspired by Michael Douglas showing them how to finish the day: collars slackened off, ties untied and hanging down exposed chests as bankers went rocking a hard labour chic.

The whole thing was sex, was hormone, and I don't mind telling you exactly how the financial crisis came about, although even that title was wrong, for '*crisis*' makes things sound somehow surprising. '*Crisis*' had been a stroke of marketing genius and, by all rights, the thing should really have been called *financial inevitable*, at the very least *financial chaos*. The word *crisis* leant banking an air of expertise to which it was not entitled. If everyone in the country had spent a few days wandering the City, instead of watching the edited versions of TV news, then the mystique would have soon worn thin. They'd all have laughed out loud … pointed fingers and called it for what it was, told it straight. The so-called financial crisis could be traced reliably back to the fact that the City of London was an enormous dating agency, an orgy and a lonely hearts column that just happened to have an international Ponzi scheme attached. I saw it playing out on the streets of EC2: attractive young women ecstatic to be taken seriously as professionals at last, talking engrossedly to older men who were ecstatic to have found a woman to at last pay them some attention. Then there were the lookers – alpha-males and alpha-females who you felt needed the City's sense of power to match their egos. Others, more human, stood awkwardly by in ill-fitting clothes, a certain despondency in them, as if trying hard to dress up to their own part in the show.

☙

One Friday evening, no energy for the Foundry crowd, I headed to a pub at the northern edge of the City, ready for a drink to end another week. It was a small place, down a side street, a couple of tables in red-white tablecloths outside and a waitress practising politics. She slid down two plates of food at the table, spoke of her home in Andalusia. She talks youth unemployment, goes about finishing a conversation from before my arrival: something or other about working all week long for only her rent and bills. The crescendo follows, the same as always: '*But at least I have a job.*' A brace of bankers sit, their eyes at her breast-height, legs spread wide and purposeful, as if accommodating *pétanque* boule testicles. A hand rests on each knee as they listen eagerly, suck at their teeth with sympathy ... coming over all social justice, noises of '*it really isn't right*' and '*it's okay for some*'.

Two things I learned from my years on the streets, my brushes with the wealthy: 1. Most of them like to think themselves poor, or at least ordinary – they want to empathise with your difficult life. Nobody likes to admit that they're coddled, cosseted, have it easy ... nobody wants to be the bad guy, wants to be *that* person. The easier your life, the faster you learn to talk as if it's hard, while those that are really being made to sweat tend not to want to draw attention to the fact. 2. Mostly the rich will be nice to your face. Bankers included, they're an amiable lot, perhaps a bit obnoxious in passing, but generally fine in conversation, maybe even warmer than your average individual, eager to compensate for the bad impression of their job. It was only with the people they couldn't see, couldn't touch, that they were able to be so robotic. Once all of the flesh-and-blood lives, all of the hardships, had been aggregated down into a single spot price, when all the living people's mortgages were bundled into only a collateralised debt obligation ... it was then that they didn't give a shit, buckled down into *only following orders* and set about happily shafting the invisible multitude.

I finish fumbling my key in its lock ... leave them to it as the Spanish girl starts explaining the plight of Spain, talking locksmiths refusing to change locks on foreclosed houses. Her adoring audience sits wrapt in attention: ready to revolt, swear allegiance to the *Indignados*, food going cold but the waitress offering a splendid scenery, a spirit of the kind not found up a bankscraper. They vanish behind me as I cross the threshold, into the pub, a few lonely heads turning round while the rest carry on starting their weekend.

With a drink, I sat alone at a small table, pulled up a short stool, set to scribbling in my notepad. Slowly the pub filled ... the chatter-spotted silence went to chatter and then to din, the bar disappearing in a swarm of suits. A handful changed from out of their uniforms, turned civilian and switched back to plain clothes. The tables filled up. Outside the pub the crowds were smoking, one to the next chugging away, drinking cigarettes right down to the butt ... smoking the ends of fingernails as the electric heaters came on and humans attempted to heat the night, make the whole world warm where once the July weather might have done as much on our behalf. I watched the crowd of bankers out front, jostling and reverberating, numbers multiplying, all bathed in red from the heat lamp ... faces glowing hot and orange like some new species of biohazard contained inside a laboratory.

A stool scraped beside me, a hand reached down, an arm with its sleeve rolled up. Soft face looks at me, *'D'you mind if I sit down?'* I gesture he be my guest, he takes the stool, sits with his beer and a book: Graham Greene. The guy wrote a book a year, safe territory, but I'm reservedly surprised.

A short while later, I pause at the end of a page, lift my head to look around before going on. He rises, pops up out of *The Quiet American*.

'What are you writing?'

Writing in pen and ink, in the twenty-first century, is a pastime that looks so deeply personal it becomes eccentric, so that people always take an interest in you. It is as if you're performing a great act of exhibitionism, a public spectacle of the private that leaves few better ways of encouraging strangers to talk to you.

'Nothing much,' I answer, bat back politely: 'What you reading?'

He holds the book with his thumb, flaps it by the spine, 'Just Graham Greene,' a hint of apology. 'I sort of like him.'

We smile at one another. Banker or no, this guy's not so bad. He has spots on his forehead, down the side of his cheeks too, skin as smooth as an apple. Fair hair shines in the light, floppy, swept to a side parting and ready to float away – the guy's birth-side of twenty-five for sure. Above his top lip looks to be the thin growth of a day or so without shaving, stubble a few millimetres long, but unnoticeable at a range greater than two metres. It always unnerved me that the economy had been entrusted to those not yet old enough to grow a beard … still, you can't hold only a person's age against them. His shirt is tucked tight into a pair of jeans, brass buckle on brown leather belt. Tasteful-looking, all in all. A thin, navy sweater hangs over his shoulders, arms falling at his chest, like a piggyback given to a lifeless child. He carries on the conversation, I watch him, watch his eyes: real shine, the spark of good childhood, opportunities, blue skies.

'It's good to have a read and drink sometimes after work, rather than going out with the rest of the office.'

'You work around here?' I ask.

He nods, looks apologetically back at his book. Some of the bankers had justifications: would tell you they worked with corporate responsibility, or were fighting the bad guys, were working with the money-laundering taskforce. Others were barefaced, told you they wanted to get on the housing ladder, while still more didn't even care to justify. I wonder which he'll be.

'I work in derivatives … and risk.'

Technically, I suppose that makes him a good guy. Looked at another way, if he does the job badly, then he's the one responsible for the bad guys running amok. He shunts his head sideward, as if to dodge a judgement. He goes on, 'I monitor things like the ratio between capital and liability.' He runs a hand across smooth cheek and chin. A little bracelet of red thread, a Buddhist number tied at his wrist.

I straighten up for a pacifist's confrontation, bring out financial trivia, 'Isn't the world derivatives market five times bigger than the actual world economy?' I snark. 'You guys must have a lot of work to do.'

He nods, laughs with a breezy guilt. We talk banks: Goldman helping the Greek government to diguise their debts, exchange-traded funds and JP Morgan owning half the world's supply of copper, sitting in a warehouse somewhere while the value rises. We discuss Goldman making profits on a hundred consecutive days of trading, like winning on a hundred games of blackjack: tossing a coin and calling it right a hundred times over.

'Goldman … they've really got problems … there's no ethics left in that place.'

I almost scoff, then it dawns on me that it only made sense: the bankers had their own bad guys. Just as the secretaries had the couriers to feel a sense of superiority next to, Goldman Sachs had provided the rest of the industry with something worse, an institution next to which they could feel clement.

After a while he smiles, kinda uneasy, 'Are you a trader?'

Now it's my turn to laugh. I'm not dressed in my finest courier rags, but still, not much more than jeans and long sleeves, 'Do I look like I work in a bank?'

He gets nervous, offers again, 'Then you're a programmer?'

I shake my head, terrified that some slender knowledge of finance, expressed with confidence, can lead a banker to believe I know exactly what I'm talking about. That was the problem: they respected nothing more than confidence, and assurance, because deep down, most of them hadn't so very much of their own. They hadn't had the collective confidence to question the culture of their industry, just as individually they once hadn't had the confidence to envisage any future for themselves other than that one offered in the graduate scheme. The banking crisis was, as much as anything, a crisis of self-esteem. That avalanche of poor judgement had been driven forward by minions who may well have disliked their jobs, many of whom were not even so very well paid for doing them, but who felt validated by the address on the letters they opened, the logo beside their name on the business card. They were people straight out of the mould … individuals made by and for the machine. At the same time, it said something of the confidence of the rest of us that, even after such failure, we still looked to them for answers.

'I'm a bicycle courier,' I clarify. 'A messenger.'

He smiles a little, more excited about my job than I am. 'That always looks like a fun job … you guys come into our office now and then,' he pauses, excitement in his voice. 'They smell of the outside. In winter, it's almost like you can smell the cold on them, you feel it coming off the clothes.'

That flummoxed me. The guy had been reading those books after all … had a writer waiting inside and trying to get out.

'Everything in an office, it's so set and orderly … everything has its place. When you guys come in, it disturbs it all,' he laughs. 'It's like a challenge to the structure of the place. I quite like it … it breaks the monotony.'

I smile back, my heart warmed to think that one of the suits I've been walking past might have felt that way about my turning up, 'Sounds like you're more interested in us than most of your lot.'

He shrugs a long, pained shrug, a scrunching of the face to go with it, 'Lots of the people I work with aren't very interesting … but it's too easy, for guys like you, on the outside, to just call us all "bankers" and then be done with it.' He seems to rise a bit, like he's speaking for himself, from the heart, 'We're not all the same, and lots of us would like to make the industry better.'

I look down at the table … guilty of being caught wrong in one more judgement, but curious as to how a spirit like that survived in the cold of a bank, how he excused lending his life to their name and to their work. We've both finished our drinks. I look up.

'Would you like another?'

He shakes his head, slips Graham Greene into his bag as I realise I've just had my company knocked back by a banker, hit a new low.

'I'm heading home … back to Clapham,' he points outside. 'Looks like rain.'

I nod as he gathers himself, stands, looks down with an out-stretched hand. 'Nice to meet you.'

We shake hands, 'And you too.'

He stepped out of the pub, the hard sole of a shoe on floor-boards. The crowd of red-lit, heated smokers parted to let him out the doorway, and I watched as he strode purposefully through them and across the road. He stopped in front of a railing opposite, he unlocked a chain, swung on to a saddle, and cycled away.

2 August – WC1 – Docket #30

It got hot. That British summer was especially timid, suffered chronic stage fright, but sometimes, every once in a while, it knew how to let you have it. On those days, you realised that for the previous part of the year nobody had really minded the bad weather at all … the overcast and grey simply provided the most obvious subject for complaint. Weather was an easy gripe, the stuff changed on its own and without anyone having to do a thing. It was the mortgages, cost of living and falling wages that got everyone so irritable, clouds were only a scapegoat for neoliberalism. As soon as the sun came out, people merely complained differently: too humid, wrong clothes, heat oppressive. It was too hot on the buses, too odorous on the tubes. The cyclists, smug as ever, soon seemed like the only ones enjoying life at all.

Scorching and ablaze, August arrived: the whole city is evaporating, even the buildings sweat. Skyscrapers burned like glass bonfires, reflecting concentrated sunlight onto concrete and asphalt. It melted. The car parks smouldered, the actual parks went haywire, berserk: people ventured out, shit-scared they'd start smelling of themselves. They'd come prepared, aluminium tins in every handbag or rucksack, hissing with vaporised meadows, sea salts, calendula, apricot. Above, the sky sat like a hot sponge, soaking into the streets and dripping heat. Beneath a few of the quieter roads, those running uphill, you hear the underground rivers, streams and sounds that took me back up to the Alps, carrying on them a far-off memory of the cool. The jets of Heathrow, of City Airport, engines on roads, air conditioning pumping cool air in as hot air spewed out the back and onto pavements. The rubbish piles start warming up: a thousand different stenches, drifting out the alleyways as dustbin lorries go stinking round, all sour and curdling. Like a band of incontinent rats, the taxis struggle: thinning oil pisses black from the underside, trailing them down each and every street. Punch drunk with heat, nobody knew what to do.

The pubs were always the first to capitalise on the uncertainty. They put out chalkboards, screamed *PIMMS,* and in no time at all everyone had fallen into line. I knew a courier who had a good earner on days like that … capitalism at its finest… he'd go round drunk punters, collecting their used jugs of Pimms, helpful-like, and returning them to the bar to claim the deposit on the jug for himself: £10 a pop and worth four deliveries. I tell you, all the best nous, all the really good ideas are kept locked away amongst the poor, where generations of necessity has honed wits to sharper points.

❧

The radio crackles. I'm Holborn, central and rolling slow, unenthusiastic for two jobs pulling me two ways: Victoria and Camden. Ridiculously bad work from the controller, a child could've done it better, a split like this says either he hates me or is just plain dumb.

'Two-Two, One-One's got one going south. Meet him Great Russell Street, swap it for your Camden job … he's going north'

That's more like it. One-One was the only one of us who partially retained a name beside his number. He was *One-One-Louis,* from Sicily … a London courier for twenty years and still scarcely a word of English in his head. '*Onmaway, onmaway*', he always yelled quickly into the radio, then plodded slow across the city, his broad shoulders rocking this way and that. One-One inhabited a different wavelength to the rest of us … alcoholic I suppose, either that or just softening in the head. He worked part-time, or rather, started at noon because he couldn't get out of bed before eleven, made up hours by working into the evening, towards night, long after the rest of us had gone home. He had elephantine features: boils and swellings, red and blotched skin around youthful, blue eyes, a head of prematurely grey hair. One-One-Louis was gentle, real gentle, loved grappa: it made his eyes sparkle just to speak of it. He would talk of the shop on Old Compton Street that he visited once a month, a present to himself. Kissing his fingers, he swore it was the best grappa outside Italy.

I ride towards where Louis is supposed to be waiting, I ride through Bloomsbury, the heat easing as I start to move. Air hits sweat and cools, my man-made breeze sets to work as I pass the coach park with French and Belgian buses lined up. Portly drivers in sunglasses sit reading *L'Equipe*, a foot hanging from the window. *Voyages, Vacances Lefevre, Reisen*. You pass the coaches and then hit the kids. My word ... but they're only children. Such innocent things, sent by schools and parents to a foreign land ... packed up on death marches around Bloomsbury and South Kensington. On days like that they really suffered, the poor little mites, press-ganged into culture by adults back in France. Cuneiform tablets from the reign of Nebuchadnezzar, restored frescos and all the kids want is an ice cream.

They beat the pavements: long lines of them, like the British Empire marching Malaysians into the interior to mine tin. They trudge, deadweight, move one at a time, fastened with invisible shackles. A child falls, topples to the pavement, this after the eighth hour of science and natural history. The teacher steps to the back, jerks him up by the arm. Poor little Pascal. With flush cheeks he falls back into the line, stepping up to the British Museum ... if he survives, the V&A will be waiting to finish him off. Eventually the gangmaster calls halt: sweater around shoulders, he lines them up in front of a wall, girls and boys starting to realise what the opposite sex is all about. Giggles ripple up and down the line, they pinch and punch at one another as a teacher tries to convince them to stop flirting and listen about the Bronze Age.

Nearing the British Museum, I smell the hot dog vendor, where sweating onions light up the air a hundred metres in whichever direction the wind's headed. Most days the smell's delicious, but today it's too hot for food, there's no appetite … you can't eat. Across the road is a tartan shop, full of Scottish knitwear for Koreans and Japanese to take home to Asia, and standing there against a boarded-up shop, coming into view, I see the outline of One-One Louis.

Louis had heard about my round-the-world, learned about it over the radio while I'd been away. A lifelong cycling enthusiast, he'd taken my achievement straight to heart. After my return, whenever I saw him, he'd give a little exhale of recognition and surprise. It was as if everything that happened in One-One's head caught him off guard, as though he was only ever expecting as little as possible, and so even the slightest event took a mental effort. He smiles when he sees me, just like he always does, clueless as to anything other than the fact he recognises my face. Louis gives a breath, '*Ah … Two-Two … Ciao … Two-Two, ciao … campione del mundo … ciao!*'

It's so hot. So … stunning … hot. The air sits still: exhausted and stagnant on the cauldron of the street. Louis sees me, still computing. '*Ah, Two-Two … ciao, Two-Two!*' he speaks in his normal Sicilian, speaks at a hush, like the walls have ears and everything's a secret. I look at him, confused. I check the weather. I'm not mistaken, it is definitely hot. I look at One-One. He's wearing football socks pulled up to his knees. Long shorts cover the rest of his legs. He's wearing a fleece. A body warmer. Everything zipped up tight. A scarf round his neck. Fluorescent jacket over the top … that's fastened up too. A hat. One-One is wearing a hat. I've got sweat coming off my ankles and One-One Louis thinks it's still January, nobody's told him about the weather.

'One-One! *Man!* Aren't you hot?!'

Louis is gone out, like I've shit in his hat, 'Hot? Me? *No* … I a-like the heat … *Heat! Heat! Heat!*'

One-One's face is even more swollen than usual, crimson too, looks like he should be burning up … the swellings are casting shadows across the lowlands of his face. A face like a termite mound or an anthill but still, he's unperturbed. Louis looks to be in good spirits. I ask how he's keeping.

'Not so good, Two-Two … a-not so good.'

One-One leans-in, conspiratorial, he gets closer. I can feel the heat off One-One-Louis. He feels like a volcano, like scorched earth policy in a desert oilfield: he's raging, voice at a whisper, barely audible as he turns the gauge of a Bunsen burner and roars it in my face. Just looking at the guy is making me sweat: it's trickling down my calves, dehydration coming, like I'm chewing balls of cotton wool. Any moment now and I'm going to faint, going to wilt if One-One doesn't stand back a half-step.

'Two-Two, Two-Two, tell me … a-what d'you eat-a?'

'*What do I eat?!*'

'Yes … a-what do you eat, in-a the evenings?'

I hadn't expected that. I scratch my head, 'It varies, Louis, you know, something that fills you up, carbohydrate … a big meal.'

'Ah, *big* … a big meal!'

'Yes.' This was peculiar, even for Louis. 'Yeah, like pasta or something.'

Louis lights up, like he's recognised an old friend in a crowd, something that makes sense at last. '*Pasta!?*' he whispers, a memory returning, '*You think pasta?*'

'*Yes!*' I repeat, give his shoulder a slap. 'With olive oil and Parmesan.'

I look up, take stock: am I giving pasta advice to an Italian fifty-something?

'*Ahh,*' One-One becomes pensive, distant, looking straight through me, staring back to Sicily. 'I get-a 'ungry … in the night I get-a 'ungry. And in the morning too!'

'You eat breakfast?'

I turn dietician, wipe my brow and cradle my chin as Louis snaps from his trance, '*Breakfast?*' That was a new one.

'Yes … in the mornings.'

'You think it's a good idea, huh?'

'Yes, Louis.' I'm coming into my own, the only responsible courier in all London. 'If you're hungry in the mornings.'

'*Hmmm.*' One-One holds his chin, philosophical, as if we're talking solipsism, geopolitics, macro-economy and great deeds. 'Breakfast, huh? … *Breakfast* …' and he jerks his head up, right at me, he's remembered. 'But Two-Two … I have-a a problem eating in the mornings.'

'*Hmm* …' That would cause problems with the breakfast. 'Could be an issue.'

'Yes … *Yes!* I think you might be a-right, Two-Two … you might be right.'

Between the heat and the madness, this is already the limit of what I can handle for now. I swing my bag off of me, a band of dripping cloth under where the strap sits and wraps my body in padded polyester. I withdraw One-One's envelope, he does likewise, lifts his satchel to his front, tears open the Velcro. He gives me my south run, I give him his north and watch his face drift away and turn back to vacant. Louis disappears back into his head, eyes floating off and away. He stands there, muttering things about *pasta* and *breakfast*. He repeats our conversation, under his breath, as if so as not to forget what he was supposed to do. I slap his shoulder again.

'Look after yourself, Louis … look after yourself.'

'Yess … *yess!*' he lets out, like he's excited at the suggestion, more brave, new thinking from Two-Two. 'Good-a idea, Two-Two, look after-a yourself … yes … *yes*, look after yourself.'

I watched as he pedalled away, no different to the time before or the time after. For years he went on calling after me, I'd hear a sudden shout of '*campione del mundo!*' and turn to see him smiling, a raised fist. I still see him now, though he rides by silently … my story faded, gone from his memory.

10 August – EC4 – Docket #31

'Two-Two. Two-Two?'

'Two-Two.'

'Three for you at Camerons ... going to that other BlackRock office, no rush.'

'Roger-Rog.'

BlackRock pickups and deliveries were good work to be given, not for anything to do with BlackRock, but on account of the coffee waiting just south of London Bridge, and only a hop across from the destination. It was opposite the railway arches, an increasingly poorly kept secret. On warm days, outside you'd find a couple of suits, sitting down on a hessian sack of coffee beans, getting a touch bohemian and coming over all peasant before returning to the office for an afternoon. The City had crossed the river, the Qataris set to finish their Shard, looking as mean and miserable as intended. The thing stuck inside the clouds over Southwark Cathedral, a finger straight up the backside of London, brusque reminder that petro-sheikhs were the only ones with money left kicking around.

I slip out of the Aldersgate traffic and under the hatch: roll into the low, dark underbelly of Cameron McKenna. Yellow lines are painted across one another in a grid on the floor, bins of shredded paper, a table with a light above it at the back of the loading bay. The whole area is bisected by a single line, thick and red. A short, stocky man stands over the red line in a fluorescent jacket, brown skin and narrow eyes ... he'll be Nepali, Gurkha, one of the many working as security contractors around the city. The man braces as I ride over his red line, heading for the table where my dockets are waiting for me.

'*STOP! Get here!*' He calls after me.

I look round, pulling to a halt.

'*That's not health and safety! That'snothealthandsafety!*' He snaps it at me, marches my way.

Rolling eyes, I think to myself, '*That's* not even a remotely accurate sentence', but I unclip a pedal all the same. Stop. The loading bay is dead flat, empty, with nothing but a health and safety rule to prevent me crossing that red line. In the past, I'd got ill-tempered with guys like that and their rules. For every heart of gold who takes bending their job description in the service of helping others as the most worthwhile power life affords, all over London there'd be at least a dozen eager only for the opportunity to raise their voice. I'd always ignored them outright, snarled that they were holding me up with asinine technicalities. After cycling the world, however, I'd calmed right down, realised all any human needs is to believe their life's work is worth something, that it means something and holds purpose. After the world, I'd stopped blaming the security contractor: it wasn't his fault, I blamed society for having given him only that red line and the protection of it with which to validate himself. I swing from my bike, skip on with the sound of my cleats like the hooves of a goat, scratching and tapping across concrete towards the table. I get my dockets, sign for them on a clipboard, the Nepali brushing down his jacket with the air of a job well done. He goes walking back to his post and holds his hands, one across the other, clasped in front of him.

A minute later I'm back on the road, my wheels pick up momentum, gain rhythm, bicycle silent on a stretch of empty road that soon meets the press of traffic. I roll over on to Cheapside, a crowd of people at the shops, a smaller crowd around an old man who's fallen from his feet to the pavement. I hear a woman, screaming something into a hand held next to her head. I see blood on the flagstones, blood on the old man's temple, all down one cheek: eyes dazed, a bicycle paramedic kneeling down and tending to him. White cotton

is dabbed, white cotton wool turns red and the old man begins to—
… *a bus!* Pulls out on me. A wall of moving metal appears in my
eyes. I swerve a little, gliding away from the old man, now gone
forever and I've my own life to look after in this carnivore of a city.

୧୬

That office sat right on the river, a minor private equity fortress just
north of London Bridge, rising up from shadow and looming over
the Thames. The building was set back from those around it, made
more ominous still by the fact that BlackRock seemed to be making
money even as everyone else in the world was losing it … not that
any company calling themselves BlackRock was about to lose sleep
over popularity. Private equity was one more grey area in the financial world everyone had given up trying to understand. BlackRock
bought ailing companies when their stocks were down, had earned a
nickname as part of *vulture capital*. They made profit flogging whatever remained of value, then sacking the workforce and fetching
what price they could in getting rid of the rest. When horse meat
eventually started turning up in lasagnes that were supposed to have
been beef, it was no surprise to see private equity like BlackRock had
passed their wands over most of the offending companies.

Before I cross the river to the coffee that makes this a decent job
to land, I first must go down to the dungeon, step down to the post
room and drop off my dockets. Post rooms, like loading bays, were
always especially disappointing. For those who said we were a post-
class country, who bought into the New Labour, nineties optimism
that said we'd all been gentrified together … I promise you the class
system is going strong, and that you can find it in the loading bays
and post rooms of the city and no doubt beyond. Those are the
moments when you discover class … when you're told there is a
place for people like you, and that it is out of sight.

On my first visits to London's most prestigious addresses, I'd strode through the revolving doors, all full with the importance of legitimate business upon the premises. There were fountains and tropical plants, bronze sculptures, secretaries bedecked in suits and shined trimmings. I would walk through those revolving doors, and before they had even finished revolving, before I could even finish appraising just how nice a job had been done with the decor, a man in a suit and earpiece was on me. His arms spread wide, ready to catch me like a giant human glove, so that next thing I knew I was being ushered back the way I'd come, hearing only impatient words of a loading bay or post room. Back out the door I'd be dispatched, round the side and down the steps: '*left and left again*', '*right and right again*'. As a courier, you fast lose track of the number of times you've heard those two directions ... sent on elaborate detours and administration procedures rather than a recipient's desk just beyond reception.

These days I know my place, that and I've no patience left to fight it anyway. I take the steps, down three flights. I know what's waiting. He'll be in there, he'll be in there until he kicks it, down in his lair of envelopes and franking, pushing back against evolution ... a man kept alive by property rights, industrial agriculture and the partial successes of the Enlightenment. Today, just as yesterday, I find this post room at the rear of the building ... through an alleyway and at the foot of the last flight of stairs. He's still there, sitting just the same, as the heavy door slides slowly but effortlessly. Open.

You look at him, as he sits in a room without natural light. In those places were no plants, no fountains. This is the engine room, the boiler house, the cooler. Here, once again and as always, is my rightful place upon the premises. In the BlackRock post room you find a man sitting in a chair behind a window. He takes your delivery and gives you his name, has thin hair pulled over his scalp, and his eyes have taken the hue of life underground, turned wormhole. His cheeks droop, so swollen that his mouth seems to have shrunk inside his face. His chin slopes into his neck, slopes into his chest and breasts, slopes into a stomach, slopes into a huge pouch of fat that smothers his groin and lies squashed between two thighs in the largest trousers that still prove too tight. He has crumbs on his chin and egg yolk on his tie, an escarpment of human, has lost the will to partake in this interaction of my delivery for his name. His tongue is suffocating, he can scarcely talk, and he would slip from his chair were it not that the weight of his buttocks hold him in place. I hand him the delivery, slide my pocket computer and stylus through the hatch in the window. I already know his name from the dozens of previous visits, and on the screen he places one more of those scribbles that marks his life and his identity in this world. I don't hang around, I hurry back upstairs, breathe relief. These places suck out your spirit … they drag you down to their level, destroy your illusions, they age you fast.

Empty of BlackRock I cross London Bridge, where the traders at Borough Market bake buttery pastries and sourdough breads, and for five pounds, a fishmonger performs magic with shrimps and a grill. The strongest smell as you turned into the market was always the coffee beans, roasting right under you on the corner of Park Street. A few moments after the smell hits the top of the nose, the sound comes into the ears: the unmistakable ringing of a coffee shop. There were the puffs of people blowing at hot milk, tiny noises of delight at the pretty patterns in the froth. As years passed, and tourist brochures added the destination to their pages, the flickering of camera shutters joined the hum. Broadsheet newspapers were shaken out and ruffled, shared between friends who then sipped between expressions of eloquent dissatisfaction with the state of society that, an hour later, people had generally decided hadn't treated them so very badly after all.

The best noise in that place came from the basement. There the laxative properties of caffeine and milk had gone to work all through the lengthy queue for a single toilet, waiting in a room beyond a small vestibule at the foot of a flight of stairs. I'd get in line, watching my fellow toiletees, feet crossed as … *Boom!* … *Kablammo!* … whole barrels of defecation were jettisoned, thrown overboard into the water. Explosions of shit and gas rang like mortar fire from behind the locked door, noises by some margin less sophisticated than all the chatter above. The artillery was followed by a hissing, punctuated by a self-conscious, pressurised vapour as the smell of jet-propelled shit would come seeping with alpine freshness from out under the door. Cold against the skin, the pong carried on that pressurised mist, a high-pitched smell with an undertone of pure shit. With a scraping, the bolt slides back … a sheepish face appears, resolutely lowered, like there's an anchor on the end of his nose. He watches the floor as he walks free, past the long line of waiting eyes, the people, who know exactly what it is he's just done.

Soon I'd started taking an interest in London's toilet etiquette in general, found an ethnography just waiting to be written. There was all the obvious stuff: the temporary toilets up in a Hackney Park in summertime, a makeshift cock-hole sawn into the chipboard between one cubicle and the next, nothing but a phone number that spoke a thousand depraved words beside it. Better secrets were in the offices of the software developers … the programmers with their bathroom cabinet ajar and rows of medications for removing haemorrhoids off of their backsides. They might well have been lords of the new economy, commanding wages and respect beyond any of the rest of us, but underneath that prestige, despite their status as sorcerers for a tech age, the coders all had piles. It was hardly surprising: each of them would spend days on end just sitting on a chair, stuck in their code holes, trapped in lines of programme that tied them in such knots they clear failed to notice as the capillaries in their anus went breaking, bursting under their own bodyweight. At the other end of the social spectrum were the public toilets where the deadbeats passed out or hid, each and every cubicle with the lock kicked in, the doorframe broken through where an angry drug dealer or fed-up park attendant had dragged their sorry or semi-conscious body out of there. From a half-shut cubicle you will sometimes hear a lighter, repeatedly sparking with the sound of a fix scored. Moments later a pale-skinned, lank-haired dead-man, his crack head pounding like a woodpecker, stumbles out and back into the world, talking determinedly to himself, throwing out his arms and still holding the last of a tinfoil joint.

Luxury hotels were my favourite. The toilets in those places were something else: a man in a waistcoat and a towel on his arm, calling people '*Sir*' as they passed him by. Along the urinal trough, one of those that runs all the way to the floor and along the length of a wall, they had positioned a visor at a 45-degree angle. Your shoes would fit neatly beneath, to save their being splashed by any piss that sprayed back out of the porcelain. The throne itself … oh my … but that was a stroke of genius, a philosophically thought-through toilet, for the chute went straight down, then sloped backwards rather than forwards so that the rich had not to see the banal smear of their own shit trickling down the bowl on its way to a sewer. There must come a point at which a fellow's status makes it hard to accept that his innards contain a digestive tract as stinking as any other. I'd sit, pondering the world from that million-pound cubicle, mine the lowest-earning backside ever to grace the thing. I thought back to squat toilets in Kazakhstan: that one with an old fridge door doubling as a cubicle door, my eyes peering out above the egg tray … those toilets where the highest luxuries imaginable were wooden supports to sit at angles beneath your heels, taking the pressure off your quads as you squatted in perfect contentment.

That sort of place was still in my mind the first time I trialled the facilities at the Connaught. Standing at the urinal you finish your business, shake it off, try your best to ignore the attendant who waits patiently beside you. He stands right over your shoulder like some formal pervert, ready should you need any help. You turn to face him, so close and attentive you almost expect him to fasten your zipper and smooth down the creases in your trousers, the man with untold subservience brimming in him. He gestures you towards the faucet, turns on the hot – those hotels know a thing or two about a good boiler, there's no waiting, it comes straight out: steaming, piping. He puts his own fingers in there, scalds himself … adjusts the temperature with the cold, apologises for the wait. He takes the soap dispenser and waits with his hand above it: you cup, he squirts, squirts into your hands. You lather as he waits over the faucet to stop the water without you lifting a finger. Once rinsed, he fetches a towel to wipe down the splash upon the marble surface above the basin. With a second towel he pads dry your hands, right in the webbing and so that you don't have to. He does everything for you, for me, delivery boy, just in case I'm an informally dressed millionaire.

With that lot out of the way he stands back, to attention … almost a salute, nobly taking up his position in wage servitude. Nothing has really changed in two centuries, the one difference the hourly number: a sixty-minute unit to correspond to the same rank people had always been left to. A priceless bit of numeracy, respectability, some pretence that only numbers differentiated that man from those he was born to serve.

12 August – Lift Shaft

We all get in. Silent, close together … I wonder if they wanted to be here? Umbrellas and handbags and briefcases line up beside me: hands and arms shuffle to avoid accidental contact. Grey coats and black trousers stand to attention beside tobacco and mint and then a perfume with too much frankincense. I wonder if this is how they expected it to turn out. I wonder what they feel inside, if yellow is the favourite colour of anyone else in here … if their parents stayed together or divorced, and whether or not they ever got over it? I wonder if these two square metres are all we'll ever have in common, if I've ever stood beside any of them before. I stare at the back of a head in front as it goes on staring at the back of a head in front. I wonder what medication each of them is on, how many of their loved ones have died and if, as children, they learned to play a musical instrument they've since forgotten. I wonder if they've donated blood or signed up to donate their organs in the event of their death, if they'll give their eyeballs to medical research. I wonder if one of the two women here is pregnant without knowing it, if the men's middle-aged prostates are growing irregularly. I wonder if they're in love, if they ever have been, if they're happy or if they're sad. The lift glides upwards, so that I feel my insides rising or my outside falling … the steel doors separate, and silently, we all get out.

13 August – W1 – Docket #32

My bag's light. I'm empty, south side of Berkeley Square, outside the hedge fund headquarters from which Northern Rock were advised all the way to a taxpayer-funded bailout.

Radio crackles: '*Hold tight, Two-Two, we'll try and get you moving soon.*'

My skin crawls. Berkeley Square is possibly my least favourite location to be left empty in the whole city. Fresh from those 18,000 miles of world, the unreality of London still keen, I remembered the days when I fantasised about taking a chainsaw to the plane trees that stand proud over the square: toppling them through the window of the Bentley dealership, branches turning glass to smithereens and then flattening a few hundred thousand pounds of brash automobile. In my head, I dreamt of leaving only a perimeter of stumps and some sawdust.

This vision of mine had been furnished by Four-Six, who had spent some months living back with his family on a Hackney estate. He'd told us how the council had planned to fell trees on the estate, so as to cash in on the land with a new development. His mother had fallen out with her best friend because she said she needed the trees while the other parent, that bit more strapped for cash, knew her family needed the money. They offered the residents' committee £25,000 compensation per tree: a hundred thousand for four trunks meant about five grand per household. Twenty families eventually turned down the money and so blocked the development, said they'd stick with the trees, though not until after heartache and disputes and the end of friendships. With that lot left to fight it out among themselves, three miles west a carefree wind tickled the leaves above Berkeley Square. Radio crackles – not for me.

The unfairness got to me. Every morning and night, I would cycle in or out of the centre, into the emerging *banlieu* of London where new billboards had started going up on the road east. The tone of the hoardings was dominated by a cocktail of Olympics froth and vague social responsibility: '*Your London! What part will you play?*' adorned photos of people from all working-class races, smiling in overalls and hard hats, the same style of image that surrounded construction sites I'd cycled by in Communist China. More and more posters appeared as the Olympics drew nearer, billboard after billboard, but only ever in the poorest parts of town. They put them up, directly asking what people planned to contribute to our great city: how they could express civic gratitude, feel included in the magnificent whole that was London? You didn't see any of that guff in Berkeley Square. Where the streets were cleanest, safest, greenest, and brimming with the rewards of other people's labour ... down there the idea of social contribution and society at large had sunk without trace. Social contribution was for other people, because who really needed a society once they were already rich? Radio crackles – not for me.

Berkeley Square did show the one contribution the super-rich were still willing to make, gladly even, positively falling over themselves for a piece of. Benches. Benches was it ... garden furniture ... whole waiting lists of millionaires eager to get in on the generosity, have a piece of the action. Eventually the council had to put up restrictions on the things ... '*Only for those with a direct connection to the Square*' ... such was the popularity of a bench as a means to give back after a lifetime profiting from others and dodging (optimising!) taxes. Dozens stretched from end to end, benches lined up unrelenting either side ... super-rich determined to give something back, but never so generous as to miss out the dividing arm rests that might have inadvertently given a homeless person the space to nod off. Theirs was legacy with caveats: in those benches you could be sure they were going to *do their bit!* ... but never more than a *bit* ... and only ever *theirs*, lest they accidentally wound up taking care of more than their fair share of decency. Radio crackles – not for me. Each bench inscription put my nose further out of joint, waxing of how the departed had loved London ... always London ... and I wondered what the residents of Berkeley Square knew of the city I saw, wondered if they had ever found themselves in Tower Hamlets or in Leyton. They loved *London*? Come off it ... they loved *Mayfair*, loved *Knightsbridge*, were well acquainted with the route back to Heathrow and the first-class flight to the equivalent streets of another city. How could they ever have loved? Those who were not even possessed of heart enough to see the injustice in all they took for themselves.

Radio crackles – this time it comes crackling for me alone. 'Two-Two ... it's gone quiet. No work on. Come back to the centre, we'll find you something.'

16 August – SE1 – Docket #33

Car drivers were the only ones whose mood actively deteriorated as the weather improved. Windows down and breathing one another's fumes, sunlight toasted them through the windshield, like ants under a magnifying glass and the poor things shrivelling before your eyes. In the heart of the city it was terminal: nothing could make them happy, they blamed everyone else for causing the traffic they themselves were part of. From inside cars they waited, resenting everyone else for each misfortune, and even as they spent their life shut within the very thing that made them poorer, lonelier, angrier.

It was one such hot day that I came across Three-Six, just south of Blackfriars Bridge. Three-Six was an interesting case, another good guy who couldn't keep a handle on things, let down by life and no match for as much. Three-Six had been fired from half the courier firms in London, either for offending clients, working intoxicated, or a combination of the two. In the bottle cage where most of us kept water, Three-Six carried an empty beer can – not that drink was his problem. In the empty can a row of holes were pierced, and on good days, when he'd earned enough, Three-Six smoked crack to help pass the working hours. He was never discreet. The first time I saw him he was doing it, clear as day, on the steps of Great Marlborough Street. Had Three-Six been less brazen about the actual smoking, still it was clear as day, for his teeth … his teeth read like a Class-A drug test. They were yellow, they were brown, they were black, they were a shade of blue-green, bluebottle hue on the crowns. Three-Six had teeth the colour of death … the things hanging on for dear life, ready to drop, rotten to the root and there for all to see because Three-Six, somehow, seemed to earn or borrow just enough to ensure he was always smiling. He knew not to overdo it.

That day Three-Six was straight up sober and waiting to pull away from the junction as I saw him. I scarcely knew the guy, no more than to know that I liked him. More than anything, Three-Six had mental health demons … he wasn't aggressive and gave a wide berth to anything that resembled trouble. Unlike some respectably dressed people all through London, left alone Three-Six would never have harmed a soul. Standing by, I go waiting on work in the pedestrian reservation at the centre of the junction. Three-Six stops for the lights. *Red.* Our *'Alright, mates'* go back and forth, we clasp hands, Three-Six heading down to Elephant. *Amber.* I start stepping back from the road with the words … *'But you're looking after yourself?'* Some arsehole is right behind Three-Six: typical schmuck, fresh out of puberty, has spent his entire wages on a finance-deal sports car and is now revving engine, firing horn and rolling forwards even before the light has turned. *Green.* Three-Six, he clips into his pedal, *'Yeah … I'm OK … thanks, Two-Two'.* Sports car window is down: manicured beard, jewellery, crystal stud in ear and an ugly, scowling face turning red as the lights go green. Three-Six and I wave a quick goodbye as Three-Six rolls out of the blocks, into a rhythm, but the car's been driven right to his back wheel … the driver isn't prepared to wait for him to pull away, would rather drive clear over him instead. He's blaring on the horn, calling Three-Six each of the few insults he can think of, shouting out the window in a way that would be impatient even if there were some drama here.

It's inevitable. What's going to happen is already a dead cert, all bets are off: *engine revs*, car jerks at its tyres and axles: *acceleration-brake-acceleration-brake*. Ten centimetres, five centimetres, two centimetres. *Tig. Gotchya!* A thousand kilos of steel with a combustion engine plays tig with Three-Six's 900 gram back wheel, snaps it out from under him. From where I'm standing it's all slow motion … I'd clairvoyanted it a few seconds earlier, with spokes and wheels flashing, flying up and down as if the tarmac were a bouncy castle. Three-Six crashes down on the road in front of the sports car, stops the traffic, upstart whelp included … red-faced and stationary in his vehicle.

That guy was nothing new. I'd been nudged at lights in similar circumstances: some loser who'd bought a car allowing him to feel like a winner … an all-powerful general, hussar, epaulettes all over the shoulders and with only the push of a pedal to feel a hundred-strong cavalry at his command. Three-Six is on his feet, is throwing his bag off his back, is rightly furious. There's nothing like seeing your life flash before your eyes to piss you off, especially with the culprit sitting comfy in an armchair over your shoulder. Quickly, I'm on it. Even in circumstances like that I'm not one for conflict: credit to my parents, they instilled that one in me, arch-pacifists with everyone but each other. Three-Six throws himself at the bonnet, I pull him back, he storms round to the driver's door. I barge in front, can smell his drug-sweat … the guy smells like a goat. For a bystander, the whole thing must have had an air of the comic to it: Three-Six and me, both in our hard-bottomed shoes, skidding on metal cleats as Three-Six keeps pushing at me and I keep putting myself between him and the driver. The driver: he's not so tough now, is shrinking right back down behind the wheel, melting into armchair and bleating, '*He should've got out of my way! He should've got out of my way!*' The real trouble is that it is Three-Six who now looks like the psychopath, even as the killer goes on looking remarkably normal. Three-Six and Two-Two go roaring back and forth: '*Calm down, mate! He's not worth it*' … '*I'm gonna fucking kill him*' … '*He's a nobody*' … '*Forget it!*' We shout at one another as I go on pushing Three-Six away from the intended object of his GBH conviction, Three-Six determined to get at him.

Over Three-Six's shoulder, over on Stamford Street, and just as I'm wondering how long this can last … I see a beautiful sight, I see an angel. It's grey and red, blue lights … thank the lord but I can see a police van. Between clutching hard at Three-Six, I start waving my arms, the first time I've ever seen a copper in a London moment where he might be useful. He's there in the driver's seat, he's looking at me ... there in navy blue overalls, sitting comfortable, sitting comfortable. I wave, frantic. He still seems to be sitting comfortable. And if the bastard doesn't stay put! If he doesn't leave me to it. The arsehole, the coward!

I must have held Three-Six back a full five minutes, five minutes that felt like an hour before ... at last ... the police force arrive in force. Five-strong: two squad cars coming down just as Three-Six's rage has burnt out ... the two of us still skidding back and forth, but slower, subsiding. Three-Six is leaning against me, collapsing in half an embrace, like ruined boxers, as a copper steps in and a hand reaches for his shoulder. The officer summons the standard response from police confronted with a cyclist who has just witnessed the possibility of his life abruptly ended, is understandably less than happy about it ... '*Do you want to get yourself arrested?*' he asks Three-Six ... That comes straight outta his mouth. Three-Six yells, 'He knocked me down, *he drove right into me!*'

I look round at the copper, aghast at the idiocy. He has bleached hair, tattooed arm and thin lips, out of which it is about to get even better. Here they come ... the sublime words, right on time.

'Why weren't you wearing a helmet?'

It drives me off the cliff face ... steam from the ears. As if a helmet were some sort of lucky charm, a forcefield that kept your entire body safe from all danger ... retrospectively improved your chances in even those incidents that – no thanks to the driver – hadn't involved a head injury anyway. If drivers were told to drive safely, rather than cyclists told to armour themselves against dangerous driving, well Three-Six and a good many of us would never have had to find out how tarmac tasted anyway. I guffaw, step in, square up and very near get myself arrested. Blue in the face, I shout so loud I'm scared my face might break – a megaphone, 'Wearing a helmet doesn't stop people driving cars into you!'

Two years later and Three-Six was smiling. Eventually they'd given him the same sum I got for my own bounce on tarmac ... the go-to, default £2,000 ... a trauma payout to cover the flashbacks. The insurance companies were the only way to punish dangerous drivers ... you had to hit them in the no-claims, the police didn't give a hoot, especially not where couriers were concerned.

2 September – E8 – Docket #34

It was over. Three-Four and I had our romance come to a head at a party one night, the whole thing fizzling out in one. We hadn't enough in common, had nothing beyond postcodes as far as shared interests were concerned, the limits of her world scarcely left the congestion-charging zone. The party was at one of the regular courier houses, an address that had stayed in the community for years: cheap rents and a room passed reliably to another rider when an old one left. There was a must of degreaser and oil on the air, scent of courier starting to seep into the mortar: you could smell the rubber of tyres, the fish scale talc they put inside tubes to stop moisture gathering. The hallway was full of bicycles, an area down the side of the house, beneath a plastic sheet of roofing, was also full of bicycles, with a second tier stacked on top of the first. Outside the house a lamp post had been bicycled, one bike locked on top of the next, until a bicycle tree had taken root. The lamp post went swallowed whole in wheels and frames, a sculpture of twenty bikes spreading up across the pavement and into the road.

I stood in the kitchen next to a pile of polo mallets, helmets with face cages, knee protectors and shin guards: the equipment for the bicycle polo that had by then become the latest feature in London's bicycle subculture. Three-Four knew everyone in that house, counted them as friends. I knew most of them to no more than two degrees of separation, counted them acquaintances. It was a party for the bohemians and punks of the circuit, the real dropouts didn't do house parties, parties required too much organisation. Those guys were tapped into the squats and illegal raves, others drank alone, others drank together in East End boozers where none of the fashionable riders would ever have set foot.

The last party I'd been to at that house had all but slipped into lore. A few of the riders had taken ketamine, one in particular coming over deranged-heroic when in the kitchen he'd found a mouse not quite killed in a trap. The rider had perched, squatting on a stool, holding the seat of the stool in one hand and a hammer in another. After a half-dozen blows he managed to stop the mouse darting out from under the hammer, guts and fur pasted everywhere. Come the party that evening, the author of the tale had a hammer and a mouse tattooed on his upper arm.

The kitchen smelt of damp, a whiff of sour milk coming from a bin with pizza boxes sticking out of it. The place was never well-kept, though most of them gave the impression they liked it that way. Whatever my reservations, you could feel the love of a community inside those walls: the postcards from riders in San Francisco and New York, flyers from alleycat races in Tokyo and Warsaw.

Looking around I recognised faces, saw guys from the West End photography agencies, the reprographics outfits who employed their own staff. Those were couriers paid well, and working on the margins of the creative industries, so that the whole thing had sometimes gone slightly to their heads. Even talking one-on-one, you could still feel a little like a gooseberry with that band: a third wheel, as if you were hanging out with them and their image. Often there came moments when you would sense the distance of their gaze and attention, when you realised you were only the prop, the social mirror in which they watched the reflection of a personality they were cultivating.

The corridor was packed, rammed, everything wall-to-wall courier chatter: postcodes, close shaves, grievances with controllers, a soundtrack of the reasons I tried not to socialise with couriers. The smaller a person's life and ambitions, the more complicated they make every little thing: people talk over the same drama six months at a time, without ever realising they're doing it. After a year is up they start giving speeches no less ardent about how sometimes you just have to let things lie: a dramatic denouement of the old drama. So long as there was drama, they were fine.

Looking back, with hindsight and a little distance, I guess I've learned to love them all a little more. To the last, the messengers were special people. They had spirit: it was impossible to do that job for even a single day without it, to choose it over office jobs, hanging clothes on racks, scanning barcodes. At the time, I guess I focused on their flaws rather than the meaning they'd managed to find … how special and harmless that was. I sometimes wonder what they'll make of it if this story ever gets read: an honest tale, a betrayal by some ratfink, or just a book on other people's shelves that few will ever even hear of? Three-Four had the right idea, I suppose. She took them as they came … liked the subculture and derived a belonging from it that was part of who she was and made any tedium worthwhile. Even if she would grumble about them when we were alone together, while amongst it, she accepted the courier way as her own.

Up the stairs, uprights in the wooden banister were missing or splintered while rubber-tyre marks smudged black on the walls. At the head of the stairs a door was ajar, revealing the end of a long, sprawled-out leg. The rider lay motionless, a tightly-bound fillet of calf hanging off the bed, foot still inside the heavy plastic and ratchets of a cycling shoe. Waiting in line at the toilet was another rider, hood over head, one hand stuffed in the pocket of a jacket zipped up tight. His thumb picked hangnails from the finger of his other hand, oil marked thin spirals on his fingerprints, and flesh tubes opened holes in his ear lobes. One hoop goes through his lip, two hang, as if a bull, through the septum of his nostrils. I get in line outside the bathroom, I say hello.

The guy is laconic. 'I don't recognise you.'

I shrug, not sure why he was supposed or needed to. He goes on, claiming authority, like he wants to know how I got in. 'Who do you ride for?' I tell him. Return the question. He smirks, only a little, but enough. He replies.

'I'm a mechanic … not a rider.'

That made me smile, was one of the hierarchies among couriers. '*Mechanic*' had a nice ring of wisdom to it, skilled labour … the bearers cherished the word, proud to have made it off the road. Society had become so deskilled that suddenly, especially with the wave of fashion the bicycle was riding, younger mechanics had started thinking themselves witch doctors and shamans. *Knowledge is Power* was the strapline, writ large above posters offering maintenance courses, wrenches clenched in fists as though the guys identified as Black Panthers or Sandinistas. The door opens with the lifting of a latch made from a spanner, the mechanic leaving our awkward silence.

In the corridor below the stairs, I watched a sprawl of peaked caps, helmets, some shaved heads, one tattooed skull … all laughing and talking noisily. The couriers often left their bags on, relished the martial quality, the heavy straps and hanging buckles. Some kept their radios on their chest, spoke via radio to those in different pubs around the city, communicating meet-ups for later in the evening. Gradually, I found my way back to Three-Four, gave a playful shove to her shoulder. She looked round as I apologised, 'I'm leaving.'

'What? We just got here.' She's hurt. 'It's only eleven o'clock.'

The two riders she's been talking to have broken off their conversation, pause in silence as they catch the friction with a knowing glimmer. The scoundrels … you can sense the two of them clocking a female courier about to come back on the dating scene. I shrug, put my hand on her forearm, apologise again.

Three-Four liked me enough to follow into the street, pulled me round as I unlocked my bicycle from a railing.

She smiles as she asks again, 'Why are you leaving?'

For a girl with a half-shaved head, her front teeth crooked from the bottle once smashed into her face … Three-Four sure looked gentle sometimes. I look back, somewhere in me a little bit of sadness, a thought that I wouldn't have minded fitting with their scene, enjoying life inside a tribe.

'It's not my sort of thing … you know that.'

'But it's *mine*.' She held one hand in the other, leant in, earnest about it all. 'Don't you think you could put up with it a while … because I'm happy here.'

There's nothing else to say or do, all I can do is stammer. It's always been this way … always me failing to make adequate investment in our relationship, she deserves better. Three-Four hops up to the low wall with the railing across its top. She hangs on, lets her arms stretch as she falls back, swaying side-to-side. The night was foggy, street quiet, Three-Four's dangling shadow in the yellow-tinged mist of a street lamp. A taxi comes down the street, the noise of its fan rattling past and away. Playfully, she says it, 'Have you ever thought that … *maybe* … you could have fun?' She rearranged herself, arms back behind, smiling as she leant in at me. 'That you might even enjoy it … if you just wanted to?'

I go on unlocking my bicycle as she steps down from the wall, comes up, holds me by the waist. By the sides of my jacket she pulls us together, faces close, hers serious but soft. She says it, real simple.

'I like you.'

I give a short laugh … don't know how to take any of it in the way I suspect she wants. I fall away, allow her to hold me as my head rolls back, eyes closed, remorseful. I'm not going to insult her with an apology, like some customer-service facility. I know I'm not for her just as much as she's not for me, I've simply been the first to call it. I warn her off: it's lunacy, doomed to failure. 'It won't work, we're different … hurt feelings, it'll be messy … really … *it's a bad idea!*'

'I don't care!' she snaps, eases into me, sidles, grabs me by the forearm, stuffs my hands into hers then straightens up, indignant.

'Please let me go,' I ask.

She shakes. She shakes her head, her waterproof body and her arms with me held in them … 'Nuh-uh'… is all I'm getting. She turns defiant, like I'm a cabbie or a truck trying to force her off the road.

'I don't care about getting hurt … I'll lose everything but I'll never let go of your hand.'

Damn. But if it isn't the simplest souls that say the most beautiful things. I've still no idea how anyone got so uninhibited as to drop a line like that. Me and my words … half-musical sentiment on tap forever and there was Three-Four, letting slip iambic pentameter like it was a sneeze. She shakes her head as she says each word, in rhythm even. She bursts to a smile, chin pointed up, head held high in a total rejection of my wishes … she almost sings the words. I'd never seen anything so precious as Three-Four socking me with that one. My eyes soften. She's not lying either, it wasn't an exaggeration: she's got my hand in hers and isn't letting up. I shake my head, not with the same hope she had, but slowly. I unpeel her knuckles, clinging corpse-tight. She shakes her head, less certainty this time, as if a child who doesn't want the old family dog to be taken to the vet, like shaking the head and being hurt enough could make it all OK. She mouthed it, didn't really put any air into the words, her throat wobbled. 'Please don't go, Two-Two … please stay.'

⁂

Soon after, we visited one another, swapped back borrowed tools, spare radio batteries left at the other's house … she missing a pair of waterproof overshoes she thought I'd taken for myself, withholding a favourite cycling hat of mine in retribution … the 'spoils of war', as she liked to call it. We only saw one another at work after that … already at different companies anyway, no need to hear the estranged voice over the radio, to meet up and exchange dockets. When we noticed one another approaching, we simply cycled by. We didn't stop. Passing on the streets: two couriers on their bicycles, two more strangers who set about pretending they never met. I suppose it hurt for a while, the better memories float to the top, the slow ache at the way another human is there and then is gone … ends up holding a part of your history.

7 September – W1 – Docket #35

Out west the clouds regrouped, storms drifted up, rumbling, gathering at a distance that looked like Heathrow. The storm clouds stack up, anvils along the horizon's length as the hammer drops, hammers a pin to manacle and shackled thunder follows lightning and hammer drops again. Sparks fly hot, chains rattle as lightning strikes and hammer drops, thunder marching, toe-to-heel as hammer drops and all the manacles shake. The clouds, the clouds they haul a heavy shadow out of the horizon and across that land towards where the city waits.

It hits my cheeks: the air has grown cold, there is ice somewhere high in those clouds. Mid-afternoon turns dark, the clouds moving steadily our way, a whole horizon heading straight for us. All afternoon they'd shuffled darker: grey to deep blue, booming lightly, so that in the cool air you felt storm coming. Gradually the shades sank deeper. As four o'clock neared, the last of the white cloud died, and a blackness settled over the tops of those buildings on the western skyline.

Couriers pay a lot of attention to the weather ... like urban farmers, street sailors, like anyone who spends their lives outside. The statistics said that in London it was only raining for 6 per cent of any one year, not that that cheered you once you were wet. That afternoon was one of those weather systems that continues to look distant even as it slowly starts turning above you. A plane came in overhead, the calm roar of jet engines at a steady pitch: jet stream sinking a solitary line of silver into the black, like the chain of a plug vanishing into a sink of dark water. The plane disappeared, swallowed slowly into cloud as the winds picked up, churned at its jet stream, pulling at the chain so that it thickened, kinked, jerked

away, and then. Finally. Pulled up. The plug lifted. First with a crack
of thunder, and then a slow, ill-tempered gurgle. The first drops of
water began seeping out, fell, pattering down on to London.

Beside me on a dark Soho street is an old Victorian matchmaker's
building. I look up at the family name, painted on the wall with a
paint that over time has faded into brick. I look around at London,
thinking of a time when marketing strategy was simply to paint the
family name on the premises wall in big letters. A moment later, the
crack comes again, the black sky to the west turns to black sky plain
and simple, and effortlessly, matter-of-fact, a deluge strikes down.

Radio crackles. 'Two-Two … *Two-Two!* Tell me where you are.'

I groan. Really? This is unbelievably bad luck, this is vile: it starts
to rain and first thing they do is send me out for a soaking.

'Two-Two here,' I'm reluctant, circumspect, 'sitting west.'

'Get yourself to Berkeley Square … bottom Davies Street. Six'll
meet you there, he'll give you two jobs.'

'Roger-Rog.'

I sigh, moan resigned curses. There is nothing for it, there is no
alternative. The only thing taking my mind off the misfortune is the
oddity of the job. Positively strange. Six doesn't give me work, and
nobody would ever have thought to take work from Six to give to
me. Sky flashed lightning – everything bursts in a moment of white
– takes a photo of the frozen scene decked in rain, windscreen wipers
stroking cars.

I stand in the bandstand at Soho Square, have been waiting empty
here, happily so … one of those occasions when it is worth more to
stay dry than earn £2.50 for getting wet and ruining what is left of
a day. I pick up my bag, drop the strap over my head, shuffle the
thing onto my shoulders and pull my jacket around until it sits back
in place on my chest. Hood up. I move on to Shaftesbury Avenue,
pull my scarf over my mouth, still cold, pull it over my nose so
that I feel breaths trapped briefly warm against my skin, until the

moisture – lightning, *flash went off, long and hard. Frozen* – until the moisture soaks the scarf and the wind blows colder through the damp. London is back in black and white … sky blends tarmac with only the shade of concrete between the two, red buses somehow darkened, every car a black cab, jet-black … city's cold.

At Cambridge Circus there is that man, hair tied in plaits of fraying rope, bags almost a shade of purple under each eye. He's dressed the same as ever, a T-shirt with '*Jesus loves me*' written large on its front. Jesus doesn't love him. I watch as he waltzes sad towards disinterested professionals on their way to offices, a copy of the *Big Issue* unsold in each hand. I roll down Chinatown: hood up, low on my forehead, just over my eyes so that the droplets sit on my field of vision like games of marbles, like glass blowing. Suspended from my eyebrow are ten bottles, *hanging on the wall, ten green bottles, hanging on the wall, and if one green bottle should accidenta—* Water trickles on to my nose. I shake my head, the bottles go flying, shatter all around. I ride on south, ride by a branch of Bank of China, just like the one I once rode by in Lanzhou.

Even with the rain to dampen it down, still Chinatown smells, smells of frying sugar. You see the smell strung up in windows … birds, three on a string, deep-fried and headless: bright crimson against the grey. You hit Theatreland: the shows, the lights, the queues of teenagers who wait through long hours of the day to glimpse their heroes for ten seconds of the night. They wait in line to catch them on their way to Stage Door, just before that time when white lights come up and breathe life into everything, those evening hours when the miracles happen and people start to believe again. The hoardings stood proud over the theatre door: 'Performance of the twenty-first century', or else 'Play of the decade'. The theatres and critics were glad of 2010, they were happy with the new opportunity for gravitas, a 'new decade' now that the 'new century' had gotten old-hat. Down at the end of history everyone was in a hurry to get to the future… new milestones in time to make anything that bit more significant.

Piccadilly Circus is up ahead, our daylight turned so grim that the neon reflects off the mirror of the wet road …. Sanyo-TDK-Coca-Cola … white-blue-green zips in the spray from my wheels. I paddle through it, the alternating colours follow me through the circus, one fluorescent tube at a time, tailing after my black silhouette aboard its wheels. A burst drain is bubbling out of cracked asphalt … a small pond forming in the road, carrying pebbles down the hill to Haymarket.

Six was a strange case. Six was richest of all of us, or rather, Six should have been richest of all of us. Six was fed, well fed by radio control: they gave him the most jobs and he whined more, and sooner, than anyone else if his wages were not as he hoped. He wasn't greedy, quite the contrary: Six was broke. Every weekend the entirety of what he earned would disappear up his nostril. Six was well and truly hooked. When we came across one another and he talked of heavy nights, I would ask with concern if he was looking after himself, and you could always hear the failed catechisms of his stints in rehab: '*Don't abuse it or it'll abuse you*' he would nod by way of answer. It abused him. One night at the Foundry, I'd seen Six pleading coke from Four. Four had himself a tiny chamber, a little glass vial with twin valves … one valve you covered with a finger as you put the other to your nose and snorted. Six near-begged for a turn on the thing, a sad sight in a grown man, but dignity didn't bother him in moments like that. Four knew he had no money, was exasperated, and you could tell he'd been through the exchange before: '*OK, Six,* but you're only having a little bit … remember, mate, *these ain't sweeties!*'

Every Friday, Six had to cycle out to Docklands … pick up a cheque for the wages that couldn't be paid into the bank account he didn't have. Six couldn't have a bank account because the terms of his parole meant he wasn't allowed a passport, and without a passport or any other form of identification to his name, he wasn't allowed to open an account. As such, every week Six lost the first percentages of his wage to a payday loan and cheque-cashing outfit, the whole bind another of the innovative ways figured out to make sure that once you're poor, you stay that way. From all that time on the down-and-out … at the very least Six was no wimp. Sure he knew how to complain some when work wasn't forthcoming, how to beg for his cocaine too, but Six had done time inside for robbery, had spent long enough on the streets to have been hardened. He didn't stir easily.

When I found Six that afternoon, he was squatted down, stooped on a step in the shadow of the WPP offices. Head between knees, Six has turned ghost-faced, looks ready to vomit. He lifts his head when he hears my cleat unclip its pedal, white hair falling out from under his sock hat, red in his eyes. Our '*Alright, mates*' go back and forth, mine with an intonation, a question mark stuck there waiting on the end. One way or another, Six isn't all right. His voice is cracked, skin marked with a grazed patch of what looks like dried blood under his bottom lip. Six is in a real funk: shaking, trembling … a real funk, mouse on warfarin, unequivocally tremblin'. An asthmatic whistle is starting up, hyperventilating a touch, Six is in need of a brown paper bag to catch and calm his breaths.

'Take some deep breaths, mate.'

'I gotta go… that's it for today, can't do it.'

'What's up?'

Six looked up at me, 'I hit a pregnant woman, din't I?'

'*What?*'

Six puts his head back between his knees, nods. Ostrich. Sand.

'I came flying the wrong way down Davies Street.' Davies Street was one-way. 'You know what we're like.'

Six justifies, excuses himself. He looks back at me as if to say sorry, 'I don't pay any attention to that sort of thing, I went flashing over the zebra crossing right as she stepped out.' He fixes accusation on me, hardens his tone, indignant. 'It could've happened to any of us, Two-Two, it could've happened to any of us!'

Six was glazing at that point. Jailbird or not, the bottom was falling out of his voice, it splintered on the high notes, sounded like a ceramic plate splitting on a flame. I consider what to do ... his gullet warbles, the blue swallows on his neck, tattooed from his time inside, start to beat their wings.

'She fell on her bump. Two-Two ... *she landed on her bump!*'

Six is mortified ... sure the guy's a bit of a deadhead, but a deadhead with a conscience.

I come in, reassuring, first things that come to mind ... 'But, she was all right?'

'Fucking hell, Two-Two! I don't know! She landed on her bump!'

'But she's gone now ... so she must be okay?' I'd never been so optimistic.

'Yeah, she got right up. She was shaken ... in shock ... couldn't say anything.'

Six fixed me with another stare, all loaded with reassurances, desperate for someone in the world to believe he was a good person, that he hadn't meant to do it, that he wasn't the kinda guy to go round knocking over pregnant women. 'I tried to ask if she was okay, but she couldn't say anything, just stood there with her hands on her bump ... got all tearful ... then she scarpered.'

Six is melting right in front of me, he's bolting, the poor bastard is falling apart. A lightning strike illuminates the black road, a thunder roll crosses the sky. I put a hand on his shoulder. He looks round, an uncertain smile.

I turn obstetrician, comforting-like, palm resting beside swallows and suddenly an expert in pregnancy.

'I'm sure she'll be fine, mate ... don't worry about it.' I pause, look around for something more to say. 'What was it you had on? Camerons? Morgan? Something like that?'

Six nodded, 'Yeah, it was Camerons.' He shrunk into his shoulders, contorted for forgiveness. 'You know how they get about Camerons jobs.'

Camerons meant Cameron McKenna: *CMS. Cameron. McKenna*. Camerons were one of the biggest law firms in the world and about as much concern for courier livelihoods as you'd expect in such an outfit. They set us performance deadlines, KPIs on even the deliveries that didn't need a deadline. Fifteen minutes within the same postcode, twenty-five minutes between two. Even if the document wasn't needed for another twenty-four hours, we still had to get it to its destination within half. It was all a question of power … didn't correspond to any need, they just did it because they could. If we didn't meet the target then the Camerons contract stipulated they didn't have to pay us … riders had been fired for 120 seconds and the sake of that contract. Whatever you might think of Six and the rest of the couriers on the road, it's important you know that about our paymasters. It's all too easy to start blaming the messengers for ignoring the rules of the road, stuck as they were in their ongoing struggle to stay poor but alive.

I nod, give Six a fine dose of sad compassion. 'Yeah, I know, mate … I know how they get.'

Six gives a sigh, goes into his bag, hands me two deliveries.

'I'm done for the day, Two-Two. Sometimes you've just gotta stop.'

I nod some more, take the envelopes. For today, Six and his pregnant woman's misfortunes are to be my gain. Not for long, mind you. Rest assured it will all come back round again, the cosmos works quick for couriers. I point to the underside of my own mouth as Six gets to his feet, looks at me.

'And what about those grazes … you OK?' I point at Six's face, 'Are they from the accident?'

Six gives a short burst, a quick release of manic, panicking laughter. He lunatic giggles. He coughs. There in the dark afternoon he stands, his floppy blonde hair and gaunt face, looking up at me from under a wet hat.

'*These!?*' He points, 'These are cold sores, mate … *stress*! I've got the bailiffs after me, haven't I?'

20 September – EC2 – Docket #36

It was him, all right. At fifty metres I was pondering it, at twenty I suspected it strongly. Hair pure black, same dark skin, about the right height under the tall dome of his helmet, badges shining. At ten metres there was no doubting it. He was walking off the end of Lothbury, on to Bank. Right in front of me was the copper who'd presided over that 35-pound fine for my five metres on the pavement, however many months before. The traffic lights are red: he's walking the pavement, strolling. It's past mid-afternoon, that time of day when people start taking their jobs less seriously ... when everybody realises that evenings mean more to them than the content of their job description. We come to the lights together.

The London authorities had taken to painting green boxes for bicycles, ahead of the white line where cars were supposed to stop at traffic lights. The idea was to give cyclists a head start, allow them to pull away safely, pedal merrily into the distance with everyone sharing the road nicely. The reality was that nobody gave a damn: it was just another patch of paint daubed on the free-for-all that was London's roads. Cars pulled into the box, or else where cars waited at the white line, the thing filled up with motorbikes instead. I didn't care ... for a while my feeling had been that the best way to stay safe on a bike in London was to disregard all law and just watch the traffic.

My copper walks the pavement, I get my final confirmation as I pull alongside, as his jaw comes into view: cheek, end of his nose, and there he is in profile. I roll a little way past. Look at him, look at him full in the face. We're just under the traffic lights, stuck on red above the green box for the cyclists, a bicycle painted on the asphalt, disappearing beneath the chassis of a car. I didn't like to do it ...

didn't care about the law and didn't like getting the police involved with anything, but I knew he wouldn't do anything to the driver, and it was that copper … it was him, all right. Anger took me, anger made me do it.

I call him. '*Officer!*' And he looks. I point at the car, the car that's rolled right over the *Stop* line and into the pointless green bicycle box. I shout, I glower.

'That car's over the stop line. That means the driver jumped the lights.'

Inside the car and the shadow of a driver turns our way, senses commotion. Officer looks at me, recognition somewhere deep in him. More than that, he's flummoxed by my anger, mystified, can sense there is more to this than traffic lights. He won't have long to wait, I'll reveal my motivations pretty soon, already all set to explain myself.

'He's jumped a red light … and that's breaking the law, so give him a ticket.'

Coppers don't understand being told what to do. Faced with a member of the public more passionate about the letter of the law than he is, my old foe gums right up. He looks at me, stammers. I answer for him. I'm spitting at him, I hate, I fume with my inner maniac of the city. I've been drip-fed a year of *life's not fair* and now I'm ready to snap.

'Do you remember me?' I demand it of him. 'Do you remember when we met on Gresham Street? I rode my bicycle on the pavement for five metres and you gave me a ticket, *you said you had to … you said it was the law.*'

He finds his tongue, 'I … I don't remember … I have a lot of…'

'That's all right, officer,' and I gesture to the car, bring us back to the present, the driver inside wishing the lights would change. 'But he's just jumped a red light … and that's against the law, too.'

The copper starts stammering around … birds have made a nest in his throat, nothing comes out. There are only letters and beginnings in there, passing over purple lips, full cheeks, lost eyes. I don't want him to talk anyway, I'm not done yet.

'You fined me 35 quid that day … that was over half of my day's wages … so, go on, officer … give this guy a ticket.'

This hadn't been covered in training. Emotionally complicated, stitch-up and rank inconsistency with letter of the law hadn't come up. He was floundering, flipping through his Rolodex of uncomfortable scenarios and how to diffuse them. Nothing doing, he gets something out.

'I don't remember.'

'That's OK, officer,' I cock my thumb. '*But still* … you giving this guy a ticket?'

Lights change. With a small screech the driver is on his accelerator, pulls out and away, gone … just as I wanted it. Me and the copper stand there, looking at each other. It doesn't matter that the car's gone, we both know it's not about that anyway. I've got him, all the power is mine. Righteous indignation is bursting out of me. It's clear I'm telling the truth: plain unfairness and double standards are ranged against him, levelled on him like the barrel of a rifle. I'm the public and he is my servant as I go hitting him with his own book of law. I want to pulp him, bludgeon his conscience, keep him awake at least a night.

'You took over half of my day's wages … you said you had to. You said it was the law. You've forgotten, but I've not, because you took half my day's wages.'

I'm finding the emotion now, throwing my hands at him, screwing up my face. My head shakes, genuinely, and I can't bear to look at him. I'm hurt by the injustice of it all, I hold him squarely responsible for the lot of it, every social wrong: LIBOR, the death of Jimmy Mubenga, Ian Tomlinson, Hester's payout. Every gross misconduct and glaring hypocrisy is his fault. He's the face of Power and he alone is what is wrong with the world, with *my* world. Sad, honest anger is piling up on the pavement, is going to swallow him up, drown him as awkwardness goes rising over his buffed shoes. He starts scuffing at the discomfiture, tries shuffling it away with his feet in their rubber-soled utility shoes, hopes to knock it into the gutter, away from him and into touch. I'm in control, I'm his boss, he's my servant at last. I tower up like the Lord Chief Justice, I'm the Grand Inquisitor himself. Right now I'm righteousness incarnate, a system-doesn't-work cascade and I'm going to let him have it as ... minutely ... I see him give his lip a quick, sad nibble of guilt.

And that's it ... suddenly we're through. It hits me in the heart, not quite guilt, but some strain of the empathy he had never showed me. I pull back. I slacken. I realise what's happening, I've timed it to perfection, we're reaching the ends of less is more. I've got him, I've not yet tipped into my lunacy. Stop now ... stop *now*, Emre! Keep yourself in, pull up ... *whoa-there boy* ... cool your jets. I shut up, draw my mouth ... thin and tight in mournful disappointment. I overegg the hurt ... like he's let me down and I can't fathom how he could have done such a thing. The whole thing looks like I'm a parent and he's the kid, teacher-pupil, he's on the receiving end. I turn from him, I shake my head sadly as he stands motionless. I clip my shoe into my pedal. I cycle away, leave him standing.

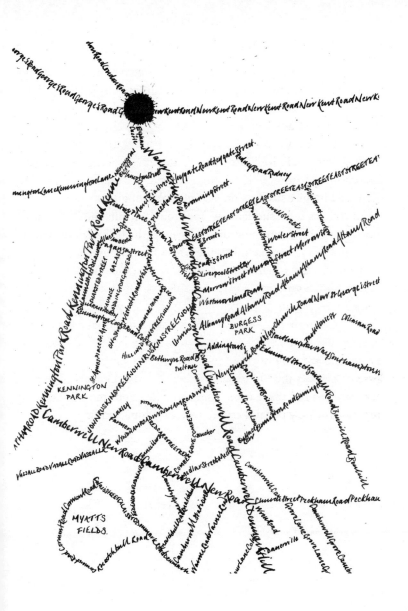

Part IV

COMING UP

24 September – SE5 – #Docket 37

Come the ends of autumn, something inside me said it was time to leave, that it was time to get out. The roads were taking me, went like tendrils and vines choking at my spirit, so that things more sinister than just nitrogen dioxide and particle dust were spreading out of my lungs. The moments of courier joy grew fewer and farther apart, interim periods harder to stomach, the vague romance of a job long gone. Evenings were a process of returning home, exhausted, to wash and then attempt a good night's sleep ... weekends mostly an aimless browse for better jobs, figuring out ways of passing forty-eight London hours holding my breath and not spending any money.

It was in that state of mind that a lifeline was thrown my way. All year I'd been scribbling, writing stories of the round-the-world since getting home to London. Eventually I'd pulled something together, created a manuscript, submitted the first thirty pages of the thing to a score of London's literary agents. I hadn't expected much to come of it, those rejection letters had been written in my head long before I received them in paper. Then, one afternoon, waiting on my phone as I emerged from an underground loading bay, there was an answerphone message. With a sense of bewilderment, I listened to the calm, steady voice of a man by the name of Hendriks, recorded from down the line and coming back my way: '...*excellent ... very interested ... impressed ... please send the rest.*'

That was startling. By then I'd all but convinced myself that only bad things happened to me, so that whatever had just started happening, it must've been bad – even if I'd once expected that the situation would have been good. Prepare for the worst and hope for the best was the outlook I'd adopted on life, but once the best was a possibility, I would set to thinking how it was only another case of the worst. The approach from this Hendriks fellow was not good news so much as – surely – a misunderstanding, and in the spirit of Groucho Marx, I didn't want to be in any club that would have me anyway. I researched, cased the guy … convinced that if he was interested in my work then he couldn't have been much cop as an agent. He checked out. Reputable. Knew his trade and still seemed to think I was good. I sent the manuscript.

We corresponded back and forth … Hendriks liking the remainder no less than the start … '*Best I've read in a long time*' was what he said to me. He took it on, sent it out to publishers, all the big names in literature. The whole thing lifted my feet way off the ground, I started writing royalties cheques for myself, got carried away right up until the knock-backs came rolling in, all the publishers very impressed by my writing … *only* … not what they were looking for. Eventually, Hendriks suggested I visit him and his wife for lunch and so, early one afternoon, I found myself on his doorstep: old stone, smoothed at the centre where others had stood before me. All around I saw a line of ghosts … part-visible authors who'd stood wearing down the flagstone in readiness for me to arrive. I rang the top buzzer … without a word there came the electronic noise of the latch opening, like the sound of a giant mosquito firing from the box.

The staircase rises, looms … turns out ivory towers don't skimp on steps. It's narrow, leans creaking from both sides, a spider plant throwing itself from a windowsill at the top. The end never nears, I step up some sort of treadmill, every bit as long as the climb I'd taken to get there from out of that childhood backwater in the Midlands in the first place. So dim and eerie, I keep on up the steps, keep on like I'm never going to make it, like what was on the other side wasn't meant for people like me anyway. It would all be a mistake, a misunderstanding. Finally the summit comes: door open, and through it the smell of a kitchen and well-loved home. I peer in, and there they are … Hendriks and his wife: grey hair, two wide smiles and nothing but warmth.

Dinner passed without a word of books. We talk politics, talk world, talk bicycles in London. I look askance at Hendriks, the profile of his face: Roman, nose like a door knocker, waves of white hair. He always spoke pointedly, enough age in him that he'd got no time for wasting words. Now and then he'd realise he'd said something that amused him, touched on absurdity, on something quaint, so that suddenly his face would turn to a smile as he let out an almost-laughter. I sit, trying to figure things out, trying to fathom what he's thinking, wondering if this whole business is about to come good, if fate will smile on me.

It's a long, grand table we're sitting at: his wife's paintings hanging from the walls, antiques in every nook. '*Buying antiques is like hunting without the blood*' was how he put it. Hendriks loved antiques: I don't begrudge him that, don't begrudge him any of it. He was a good guy, warm-hearted, almost grandfatherly ... his age had a pretty good effect on me. A man at the calmer end of life, growing up an Estonian refugee in a displaced persons camp, surrounded by post Second World War Soviet Union. Hendriks had already had to put up with the twentieth century by the time I came along ... Come 2010 he was increasingly tired with the business takeover of a bookselling trade he'd once loved. The result was a man who valued patience, time of day, courtesy and respect ... the sort of decency he felt people no longer wanted to make time for. I decided early on that whatever happened with the manuscript, I trusted him.

We get down to business: I tell him how I'm fixed, how things are sitting ... 'Not so hot on the jobs front, still working as a courier.' I sigh, my head hangs forward, I'm months passed resignation as far as jobs go, but who cares? We're not here to talk careers, we're here to talk book ... my manuscript, the one they all love but aren't sure how to market, the one about my other life, my dose of glory ... everyone's entitled to a little ... my cycling around the world. Hendriks has long fingers, moves a wave of white hair from his forehead and then folds his hands in front of him. Long fingers, long fingers go woven like wicker into a tiny basket on the table. He reassures me, still thinks it's fantastic … Hendriks always did love that manuscript of mine. To tell the truth, I think he got attached to it. I'd developed a hunch that come the time my story found its way to him, Hendriks was happy just to know there was spirit left in the world, that there were still a few upstarts kicking against the pricks.

'Emre …' a long pause, the longer the pause the worse the news. 'It needs some editing.'

I can handle editing, I shrug. 'Which bit?'

'Most of it.'

I'm vacant.

'It's too long.'

'We can cut it down, no problem. How much?'

'A third.'

'Remove one in three words?' I'm quizzical, quizzical, but he knows best. 'Sure thing … which bits should I cut?'

'None of it. It's all good, you just need to make it shorter.'

I laugh, he's joking. 'You want me to remove one in three words … and keep it the same?'

'Not completely the same.'

He looks at me askance, sideward eyes. I look back … a sinking feeling he's not joking.

'The ending … I feel … perhaps … that the ending could be tidier … the reader wants completion.'

The bloody reader, always the reader. Why can't the reader learn to read what they're bloody well given?

I summarise. 'So you want me to remove a third of the words, add a happy ending, and keep it the same?'

Hendriks gives a slow nod, a slight smile, appreciates the understanding we're working up to. 'One last thing.'

I open up my face, ask with a raised eyebrow, invite this final point.

'Chapter three,' Hendriks looks at me firmly, 'you have to rewrite it, your *ad hominem* attack on the previous record holder.'

'What's the problem with it?'

'You sound,' Hendriks laughs a little, 'well … Emre … I don't know how to say it, but …' he steadies his gaze my way, looks at me with a hint of apology. 'You sound insane.'

That was it … down went the camel's back. Never tell a madman he sounds insane … it'll only make him worse. You have keep *stumm* and hope someday he figures it out for himself. I took a deep breath, held it in the lungs, spoke without breathing out.

'Hendriks … with all due respect, the guy pissed me off.' I breathe out, 'He pissed me off enough to make me cycle 18,049 miles in 165 days. You think that's the mark of a sane person?'

Hendriks jars. '*165?*' He's quizzical. 'I thought it was 169 days?'

I sigh, exasperated by the technicality, 'Officially, yes … but I didn't deduct all of my travel time, so it was more like 165,' I wave a hand, agitated, 'perhaps it was even 162,' I swat my palm against the table, 'not that I care anymore.'

Hendriks gives a slow, pensive nod. He turns his head from me, looks out of the window.

4 October – E10 – Docket #38

Slowly but surely, Hendriks gave me some confidence, had me figuring that I couldn't remain a courier forever. Hendriks flattered me with ideas that I had talents beyond life on the road. His faith in me proved catching, almost made me believe in myself, and soon I thought maybe I was, just about, cracked up to be more than a messenger after all. *'You're too bright to keep working as a courier'*, that was his advice. The problem was, nobody calling shots in recruitment felt the least bit the same.

In no time at all, I started to discover that believing in my own better prospects had proven a dangerous experiment. Never believe in any future that relies on others to make it a reality! Within weeks the rejection letters from publishers had been joined by rejection letters from think tanks, from charities, from campaigning groups, magazines and journals too. As long as they had a department for rejection letters, every institution in London wanted a piece of me … eager to get in touch and teach me some lessons once and for all. After a few months, if I hadn't come to feel eminent, gobsmacking gratitude to those organisations using the word *'declined'* when knocking me back. 'Declined' was starting to feel like a damn compliment … like positive feedback. Chin up, and no matter the blows to the old self-esteem, I needed to be pragmatic about things … winter would soon be back, and the courier circuit was not about to be a bundle of laughs either, not quite a hoot. Round about then, however, something shifted … I finally started figuring out what the problem was, what I was doing wrong. In all of my applications there was a fundamental, one-word defect, present across every last one of them. *Poverty*.

Poverty was the issue. Poverty stinks. It secretes into your body and drips out with the snot on the end of your nose in a house you can't realistically afford to heat. Poverty drips all over your application forms, they sniff it in every word … the desperation, the fear, the *need*. For every creative, constructive thought a job might have sparked in my head, I would have four financial worries pulling me back down. Poverty fills each space where one word ends and the next begins, necessity punctuates sentences and, try as you might, *pay-the-rent* somehow squeezes on to the end of every paragraph that was supposed to justify your semi-spiritual connection to the advertised position. They think you're disgusting, miserly … a parsimonious penny-pincher with scorpions in the pockets. Worldly, artistic causes bring out the smell still worse: you reek, the stench won't budge, the more morality a job professes to involve and the less anyone wants a bean-counting scrooge like you. They want to believe you'd work for nothing … would do it all for the love of the world. Hannah Arendt should come blossoming from the armpits… salary is incidental, a perk of the job! Those guys were not after just any old somebody, somebody motivated by *money* (*spits!*) … What they want are people who want to *make a difference*, be the change they want to see in the world. Even the most *change-the-world* organisations … They didn't really want to rock the boat, they didn't want to risk so much as a change in their own office culture by hiring some upstart psychopath genuinely convinced to his bones the system really didn't work. All that was required in those offices was a vernacular of struggle, social kudos combined with a salary at the end of each month … those guys were sitting even prettier than the bankers.

Down-out broke, snubbed to the point of despair, pretty sharpish I'd come to stop knowing my left from right. You see yourself, brass-tacked, the entire universe spinning slowly around you, a bank balance haunting every thought… that fat Zero you know is always waiting patiently. What was it Ginsberg said … let me think, I had it up here once … ah yes, that's it: 'I saw the best minds of a generation destroyed by madness, starving hyster—' *Ring-ring … Ring-ring …* excuse me … the telephone … 'Yes, *who is it!?*'

'This is a call about your payment protection insurance…'

I put down the phone… *Howl!* Where was I? The phone keeps beeping, I thumb the button, it keeps beeping. *Howl!* The line goes dead. Let me go on … get these chipped shoulders off my chipped chest, once and for all. No matter how tough you start out, when life throws rocks at you … you lose a chunk here or there. When life is such a minefield to begin with, when you've no idea what a social success even really looks like and all evidence points away from things working out all right, what kind of mug doesn't learn double quick how to be risk-averse? That was the other thing about the shoulders. Phrasing it like that, talking about *our* shoulders, meant we were the ones to blame … had failed to be sufficiently buoyant about things, hadn't dealt cheerily enough with the coalface of material divide and subtle snobbery constructed overhead. The true bourgeois don't like you because you're covered with the grubby scars of financial worriment, the burning energy that you had to ignite under your sorry ass to drag yourself up to the spot in which they were born. Meanwhile, at the same time, you can't be one of the underclass, because you're too smart for your own good. You don't belong anywhere, and nothing gets any better because nobody lets you talk for the downtrodden you live amongst. Intellect apparently separates you from them … people start thinking Penguin Classics on your shelf are hard currency with landlords … and because most of the truly downtrodden don't have inclination or intellect to artic-ulate even half what's wrong, the whole carnival continues from here to eternity.

The worst part, the true fixer and Catch-22 is that once you talk about just how close to cracking you've become, then – in that same moment – by pleading mental distress, you lose all credibility. The only way to maintain a bit of standing for yourself is holding your tongue and not breathing a word to begin with, by putting up, by keeping mum.

3 November – SE1 – Docket #39

Sales began, and twinkling lights replaced Halloween lanterns as bags were filled with cut-price goods and garments. London went out in force, did its economic duty for first a thing called Black Friday and then Christmas. As I cycled beside yellow-brick buildings at the old docks of Shad Thames, I heard Nine-Three crackling through the radio, from where he waited in the Oxford Street crowds.

'I'm going to be late to the pickup, it's like hell here … the whole place is full of chavs! I can't hardly move for them!'

Laughter came from the controller, 'Can't be helped, mate, no worries.'

And I listened, clueless, as another voice chirped through on the radio, 'Chavs everywhere today, guys, must be the sales starting.'

I thought to myself, pedalling, three miles from where they spoke. But surely, didn't they realise – gruff, uneducated, tastelessly dressed and poor as the couriers were – that *they* too, were somebody else's chav?

The term had been creeping slowly into common use for the best part of a decade. A troubadour for the political Left had written a treatise on it: '*The demonisation of the working class*' his publisher had trumpeted. His heart might have been in the right place, but from inside the colleges of Oxford where he'd studied, what he'd clear failed to notice was that everybody now had their own chav… *chav* was an accessible elitism … prejudice for all! Sure the poor were demonised, the population divided, but what none of the do-gooders realised was that people were happy with the rifts … the whole arrangement excellent for self-esteem, so that the right to look down at someone poorer had come to be pretty much the best liberty on offer in modern democracy. There would always be someone with less education and money, a girlfriend with larger earrings, a shinier handbag and tracksuit.

One after another, I listened as a half-dozen voices radioed to laugh and relay their own derisive anecdotes about poor people, every one of them, to the last, himself conforming to the accepted criteria of what would have been another's textbook chav. Despondently, I shook my head … for sure, the couriers weren't always the brightest. The guys in the middle, the civil society … call it what you will … they had to get used to the fact that some of the biggest losers in the economy were less concerned about unfairness than they were.

5 November – EC1 – Docket #40

I should have listened to him. Right away, Hendriks had told me there was no money left in books, that all but the most indecently successful authors would need supplementary incomes. Despite his cautions, after a tonne more job rejections … I'd become ever more resolute, determined there was nothing else I could do besides writing anyway. The blueprint was to plug away until I penned a masterpiece the whole world would want … my career plan no more nuanced than an intent to write something that would smash through everyone's somnambulism, leave mediocrity strewn everywhere and secure me enough of an income to get a bit of roof over my head.

Hendriks' decision to take on my book, the praise it earned from other agents … like I said, I'd gone and gotten carried away with myself, started composing the inscription, all set to spend my advance and then wait on the rest of the trilogy. It didn't happen like that … it took a while for me to settle for what I'd got, contentment is a hard thing to learn but sometimes you just bump into it when least expected. Turns out that, where publishing was concerned, they hadn't been exaggerating. Books really were dead. Sure everyone still loved them, they simply couldn't be bothered to read the things. When one publisher finally took a gamble and picked me up for a song, an advance the same a programmer I knew earned in a day, by then Random House were already busily crowdsourcing their next novel. That was the future: why would anyone settle for one author when you could have a million working for free? If the death of the novel was a formality, soon the writers themselves would be seeing the same fate. My plan to wait on the lucky break and then make my way to bigtime was proving lacklustre to say the least … and yet, from nowhere … one night it happened, it really did … bigtime came a-knocking, sent the one email that justifies the next thousand times you check an inbox to make sure it's still empty.

'*Road Warrior*' ... that was big in the subject heading, along with the letters T and V. God had come for me at last! They were making a documentary, were making a documentary and ... the producers wanted to meet, to meet me! I should've smelt a rat at that point, but I was still young at heart, hadn't lived through enough to not have my interest piqued by that kind of talk. Along with the rest of my generation, raised on Disney and platitudes, I'd set about shooting for the moon and planning at the very least to land amongst the stars. Out there were millions more just like me, each one of us just floating through outer space, up with the satellites and titanium debris. I was no better, a bit more cultured perhaps, wanted to be a public intellectual maybe, a journalist ... my ruse was only a more dignified version of the hip-hop or football stardom the masses were said to be planning for. Either way, the principle was the same, all the halfway houses had been bought up: buy-to-let landlords and assorted baby boomers had a tight hold on everything between rags and riches, so that an entire generation ended up hoping against all rational likelihood that they'd strike gold. You could hardly blame us ... it was the only way left to get anywhere.

Pretty soon I got back in touch, didn't have to think too hard about the proposition they'd put my way. I left my messages on the answerphone, sat back and waited for the phone to ring. We arranged to meet one evening after work ... media came to see if I had a story in me, if I could believe my own hype and carry it off. We met at a courtyard in Clerkenwell, the tone all convivial, upbeat. Vinny wearing a wax jacket, short hair, scalp flaking over his shoulders. Thick-rimmed spectacles hang from the V-neck of the sweater as he speaks with crab apples in his cheeks. Vinny cuts right to the chase, isn't messing around. He gathers up the material of his trousers from above his knees, the electric heater in the courtyard shines on his sparkling water. He lands the first blow.

'So, Emre, obviously you care about politics ... would you call yourself a cycling revolutionary?'

That's how he begins, and already I know I'm done for. It was like being back in southern California all over again, the world suddenly so simple, packaged and heroic. A fog settles ... how to respond intelligently to a question so ridiculous? Sure he was only doing his job, just like the rest of us, but you could tell Vinny thought in pitches, dozen-word pitches to be presented to a broadcaster as potential.

I think about his question, start muttering, 'I think I have some revolutionary views ... and I ride a bicycle.'

He grimaces. I might as well have just said '*no*' and shut up, that way I could have at least remained mysterious. Right there, inside thirty seconds it was already over, media waved goodbye to me, another twenty seconds and I saw him retreat behind his retina. I just didn't get it. He screwed up his face at my mouthful of common sense. That kind of analysis really didn't slip down through the cochlea so nice. They didn't want that sort of nitpicking ... needed the two together, *cycling* and *revolutionary,* combined ... or else there wasn't a pitch. Without the bicycle in there, without a visual icon and a picture to go with the words, without all that, the programme would be doomed. I think harder, but still to this day, the only direct correlation I see between a bicycle and a revolution is that it would make a decent getaway vehicle. I stammer, decide to cut my losses, at least be magnanimous. I pause. I stammer. I wave goodbye.

'Look ... maybe you should go and find the other couriers, the guys with the image. Poland Street corner, Soho ... J.P. Morgan air vents, Aldermanbury. They're your road warriors ... if that's what you're looking for.' He shuffles his papers together. I go on, 'Only, *only* ... they're good guys, but you might find they just look the part, and aren't so into the politics as I am.'

I smile. Inside, I gasp a sigh of relief. Unbeknownst to me, but at long last I've just been liberated from my expectations. Something has just flown my shoulders, like it's not going to work out, like none of this success business is going to work out but still it's OK. All at once … I'm just so tired, I'm exhausted. The weight of years explodes, leaves me be and suddenly I just want it all to stop. I'm tired of being worthless to everyone, tired of the rejections and not fitting other people's billing. I'm just me … I'll settle for that. I wrap up, rubber stamp the deal, conclude triumphantly that I'm categorically not the guy for them. But at last, at last that's fine … because I never wanted to be anyway. I just want to be the guy for me. I smile, I can hear my lungs opening, all of a sudden I'm nothing but confidence.

'I don't know for definite, but they're the look you're after, that's what you need to get this *cycling revolution* thing across … I'm probably not your man.'

Vinny smiles, a good-dentist smile, 'Thanks for being so honest.'

He sighs, not done yet, carries on the examination and checks me thoroughly for signs of media life. He crosses my legs and taps a hammer on my knee. It doesn't budge. Vinny scratches a hand through his remaining hair, thinning, scalp blizzard falling to shoulders. Unfortunately for Vinny, I'm the only courier who broke a record for circumnavigating the world.

'Everyone at the agency loves the story … it's a real shame you didn't take a video recorder with you, grabbed some footage perhaps.'

I shrug, I'm getting the hang of emancipation, 'I suppose I felt, I don't know … I wanted people to invest something of themselves in it. If they couldn't be bothered to read a book … I guess I didn't want them to have the story anyway.'

Vinny animates, 'You're so right. I think that's a really good point, it'd be great to maybe try bringing that out in something like a film.'

'Well … really, I'm more of a writer, I think. The book is finished, I'm just waiting on publishers now.' I catch myself, don't let on how long I've already been waiting.

'OK.' Vinny moves along through his notes, 'and your record of 169 days …'

'*165* days.'

'I thought it was 169?'

'Officially, yes, but really it was 165 … I didn't deduct all of my transit time in the end. Maybe it was 162,' I wave a hand. 'But I don't care about that anymore.'

Vinny returns to the chase, 'OK … but the record still stands?'

'For a while, yes … it still stands.'

He sucks in his cheeks, sucks his teeth. I see it, he mulls over my '*for a while*'. They're the words he's stopped on … Vinny's realised he really is wasting his time, cottoned-on that there'll be a new me before long. I see a pen tapping a clipboard in his mind. I wonder if he'll ask me for the name of the new guy: out on the road already, three-quarters through and a couple of days up on my time. My boat has sailed. I'm too late for this one but, finally, inside I'm laughing. I look into Vinny's forehead, can see him setting up a meeting with the incoming record holder … they'll come to this very courtyard in a few months' time. Meanwhile Vinny's beating a trail, he's climbing into a dinghy and rowing fast back to the schooner. He weighs it up, lifts anchor, the chain is rattling around the capstan, an engine trundling over.

Vinny finishes up. 'And what do you think is different about your attempt?'

I gather thoughts, 'I don't know … not really … but I think there's a formula … to all this record-breaking and adventure … and it's insincere, and soon everyone will have heard it so many times that some of those guys … but not all of them … are going to have to think up something more to stand for, something with a bit of brain, because their shtick will suddenly get really tired.'

'How do you mean?'

'It's just …' my voice gets impatient, 'it's always the same: some guy supposedly going to hell-and-back so that someone in an office can live a vicarious adventure while they follow on the internet. Or when they watch a talk about adventure and blue-sky thinking, and how to use the lessons to get the best out of your team at work. Ulti-mately … it's just transparent, and it's dull … because really most of those adventurers are just eternal kids with the whole world as their playground … and they don't care about much more than their own thrills. They're out to conquer geography because they grew into a life so privileged the only obstacle they could think of having to overcome was a mountain with a base camp.'

Vinny pushes back, 'You've no respect for the undertakings … none at all?'

I hunker down, like I've hurt his feelings, dented a dream. 'It's not that … but mountains don't mind being climbed, and roads were built to be travelled … and it'd be so much more adventurous if they tried actually changing something in the world, rather than rowing an ocean for an investment bank.'

Vinny braces, 'Does everyone have to aspire to change the world … to change politics?'

'I'm not saying they have to …' I mull it over, slowly, 'but when you go out into the world, and you receive all that generosity … I think it's ungrateful to just endorse corporations in return. And people think I'm so political, but endorsing a bank … that's politics too, it just doesn't look like it because that kind of politics is every-where to begin with … it just looks normal.'

Vinny unbinds his fingers, unfolds legs, plants his feet and grabs the knees with a final burst of enthusiasm. He opens up the chasm of his mouth, a gaping tunnel from which there spreads a silent, little vortex. I see him licking his tongue over his teeth, forcing that wet, pink muscle deep down into the footings of his molars, tinted with mercury. Finally it comes, swallowing the courtyard and whatever future of mine had been in it an hour earlier. Such tender words … like that huge, heart-stopping dose of potassium in a lethal injection.

'We'll get back to you.'

And as he speaks, I see tumbleweed come rolling from his mouth. A stagecoach comes into view, four horses, the last ride skips town … blinkers on tight, shuttered either side of long heads. Square teeth and hanging, grey gums are chafing at the bit, bubbling white slobber as four dark beasts, hooves coming right my way, thunder with the rattling of the carriage behind. They go bearing down on me, go stampeding-stampeding-*stampeding* right over my head. The axels are springing and rattling, squeaking and creaking, jumping up and down above as I hear a whip crack. It's gone … the last stop to this town, it's over. Tumbleweed touches down and then flies away until dust is all there is left.

They'd cut back the brambles by the River Lea, the thicket with those pink blossoms that came out and floated down at the end of each spring. I'd picked blackberries there, wild ones, good and sharp in flavour, kept safe from the selective farming that takes bitter and makes sweet. I'd watched other locals, out with ice cream tubs stained purple and violet as the blackberries piled up and people discussed pies and crumbles and freezing until the winter. Those blackberry thickets were one of the few places I had seen London's strangers coming together and talking to one another. Suddenly they were all gone. They'd chopped them down. I didn't know who *they* were, we never do, but one thing was for certain. The brambles were gone. They'd flattened it. Scorched earth, trees toppled. The hole in the corner, where in the evenings a rabbit would sometimes scoot away from my front wheel, rump dragging gravel as it skidded down into a warren … that had been filled in too, Thumper out on his floppy ear and all of it gone. Gone.

You knew just what had happened: some councillor driving by with a budget to spend and that was that. Untidy, unbecoming … *Olympics*, don't you know, and who ever heard of a tidy thicket of brambles? Brambles were not what the sponsors were paying for, not what twenty thousand daily promised visitors (*yeah right!*) to the marshes were expecting.

The blackberries were gone, pink stains on the pavement where fat fruit had flown upwards on a spinning blade … falling to squash upon earth and bleed into the concrete. People would never pick blackberries again … blackberries were not to be produced in east London, it wasn't economical. Comparative advantage dictated blackberries produced by the million tonne, farmed in Oregon and then flown all over the world. The people of London could go to work instead: deep-frying chicken, topping pizza, stacking shelves or driving delivery vans. They could earn a minimum wage a politician would set but never leave bed for, and with that wage they could go to a supermarket … from which they could choose blackberries from Oregon. Not fewer than twenty-seven in a sealed plastic punnet. Never again would people suffer the inconvenience of washing pink stains from their fingertips, never prick their thumb upon a thorn or lean too far forwards to get the wool of a sweater snared on the thicket. The blackberries were gone, didn't fit with the ideal of the modern city, for you cannot have a blackberry without a bramble.

Seasons

The weather cooled again, brought with it the pears. Moss-green and flecked with brown, bruising at the surface as the form begins to fall. The first time I ever rode to Paris, on the final night before reaching the city, I slept in a military cemetery … the ground full of British corpses who had been made to die for their country, Indian corpses who had been made to die for someone else's. They keep those cemeteries well, very well, so as to help disguise the initial injustice. The mown lawn, the marble headstones, soldiers both named and anonymous … some of the dead senior – and others younger – than me. I woke in the morning, just after dawn: a cloudy white sky that had descended all the way to earth, heavy dew perched on the blades of grass, a milky light to the air, the world all silent in that early hour. I had slept beneath the old oak that watched over the cemetery, and barefoot, I ventured from my bed, out upon the grass. I can feel it now, beneath my soles, between my toes as I walked upon the dew-topped grass. All cold and fresh, it slipped between toes still warm from the sleeping bag. Those droplets slipped their blades of grass, and soaked my feet with dew. The memory of that dew upon my feet, is how pears taste to me, as autumn falls.

A Bangladeshi man sold fruit, up at Bakers Arms marketplace. A few of us used to take turns to do a run to the market, pick up boxes of the cheapest fruit we could find, bought in bulk. One afternoon, someone carried home a crate of some forty pears that had been too long upon either the floor of the orchard or the floor of the warehouse. On the inside they must have been all but rotten: the juices weeping through the skin, the cores turning black to brown and creeping into the white flesh. You could not pick them up by the stalk because the stalk would just pull loose, taking with it the

244

head of the fruit itself. If you looked at those pears long enough, you could almost see them warbling and rocking inside themselves … waving, shimmering, *gurgling*.

A handful of us set to eating three a day in order to avoid the waste of throwing them out, entered a race with the crate before the fruit completely rotted through. All that week we went at them, hardly the nicest of fruits, tickling at the gag reflex. You had to toughen yourself up, get used to the texture, they went down like little green hand grenades, three-quarters biodegraded … all enzyme. Safe inside the gut they exploded, digestive cataclysm, fermented everything. The things melted all they touched … came galloping through with the last of autumn, artillery fire landing with explosions of earth flying upwards on the heels of routed cavalry.

At the local grocery, lengths of carpet came back out to cover up the bananas. In summer, the grocers had put cardboard over the top of the bananas, keep the things cool and stop them ripening too fast … an urban version of the large, green leaves that provide shade on the tree. As the weather cooled, once a mild October became a chill November, the carpet would be laid across to keep off the chill … stop the cold bananas turning deathly grey, that shade bananas take on when they realise they were never supposed to have met such a temperature. On my way home, I'd pass the metal rigs of the gas towers, the balloons floating down through their cages as weeks drew on and nights fell ever earlier. As the winter returned, the domes fell faster and faster, rising up and down every few days, inflating and falling, gas burning fast inside the boilers of all those houses growing colder.

South of the river, the final tenants were set to have compulsory purchase orders ejecting their sorry asses from the Heygate Estate. After four decades of controversy rumbling behind the abandoned site, an Australian developer had cosied up with the council and successfully bought twenty acres of central London real estate, the final price some way below what even footballers were starting to sell for.

Diggers fired up and began pulling down walls ... winter blew, and forty years of previously undisturbed rats went scurrying from the brickwork. Chased out by that mechanical pied piper, they infested each housing terrace, shop and café in a two-mile radius.

7 December – EC4 – Docket #42

I coughed. I coughed once. I coughed twice. Glass in my throat. It wouldn't budge. It sticks in deep, I can't get it out, winter and benzene are canoodling, making themselves at home in my lungs. The street keeps flooding, the people go marching by while I try and die politely … millions of them pass, surely a nurse or doctor among them as I try to cough my guts up but the guts stay flatly down. The city is silent, is isolating me from them, from everyone: I'm alone and coughing. I could die here coughing and not one of them would stop, they've got shopping bags that need loading. Hardship in London, it's like a giant finger buffet, the stuff happens everywhere and people have already had their fill.

The sounds weld together: the chatter and rustling clothes, plastic bags, paper bags, limbs against the wind … it all forms one constant roar of laughter. The laughter grows louder the harder I cough: they think I'm funny, think I'm joking. I cough, I cough again … a bat … there's a bat down there, a vampire with serrated wings. I cough and out my throat it bursts, fluttering away to join the crowds. I hug my bag, the world's coldest hot water bottle. I clutch it to my chest, my chest full of needles, deranged gardeners raking up leaves … nothing makes sense down there. I've lost all control, the virus does what it likes, I haven't strength to stop it and nobody in the city even cares.

Delirium settles in my head, is the only painkiller that soothes the abrasion of the coughing. Three days like this and there's no use resisting. I don't know cold from hot … I've got cold sweats and hot shivers … only the postcodes make sense. I'm still at work, of course I'm still at work. I've heard people talk about sick pay, being paid without working, but frankly, I don't believe it exists. I'm sure there's a sophisticated correlation between sickness and capitalism,

I know I learned it somewhere, but right now I haven't the wit to pin anything down. Coals smoulder in my chest. I haven't much strength for this, the thoughts get the better of me: it's just coughing and pedalling down here … much more of this and I'll have to take a day off work. I speak into the radio … *cough* … all I want to say is '*EC4 going WC2*' but it just comes out as coughing. I'm a wreck, a breakdown, I sound like a cracking table leg, crockery crashing to the floor, I sound like a shelf collapsing in an old shed full of dead people's junk. The controller asks me to repeat myself: '*My word, Two-Two … but you don't sound well.*' I can confirm that much, let out my finest coughing fit by way of a yes.

It's the postcodes I can't get my tongue around … my tongue won't hold still, it's flapping, like a barbunya on the deck. My lungs are barking, are two dogs, angry at each another, ready to fight and with flames choking off the oxygen. The fire gobbles up the atmosphere, letting out an almighty roaring sound … lungs pulling in great quantities of air but all of it coming back out in only *cough-cough-cough!* My legs, my legs are starting to scramble, feet working backwards, pushing away at the air, climbing backwards into the wall. Above me the flames are licking at a poker turning white-hot, suspended over me like a Damocles, real hot. My feet keep scrabbling, scrambling. All I want is to get away, to flee, escape, beat it, get the hell out of my body and leave it to die in peace. The poker's on a thread, the flame licks it … the thread frays, the flame licks it and then the thread breaks. The poker is dropping, falling … is coming right for me, straight down the trachea it hits home, it pierces. There is a hiss, a roar, it bursts, it burns, hits bottom. I knew this would happen. I'm sick.

It was always me who got it. I'd try for my eight hours sleep each night, limited alcohol, didn't smoke, ate well: vegetables, vitamins, organics, no junk. I didn't touch the drugs the other riders went in for … and every time … I got sick. Sickness had no interest in the other couriers, it always came looking for me instead, feasted on a real meal. Those guys existed in a constant state of un-health, hadn't been well for two centuries between them. Their bodies had forgotten how it felt to feel fit and so they weathered everything: a permanent sniffle but fit as far as they knew it. I was a better specimen for a virus to sink teeth into, have some fun with. I tried to figure out where I'd got it: prime suspect was the crackhead in Covent Garden, breathing all over me as he begged change, danced on his toes, so close I could make out the shades in the dirt of his face.

After a couple of days' steady deterioration, I put myself to the task of researching my condition on the internet ... always a mistake. Internet is the most pessimistic doctor going. Online you can contract every malady on earth, discover a few new ones by mixing some of the old ones together, the whole experience never more than a click away from death. That I had bronchitis went without saying ... bronchitis with a hint of pulmonary pneumonia, and that was just for starters. In no time at all my condition deteriorated. I didn't know it, but apparently smallpox hadn't been completely eradicated after all, and my sickness was – of course – wholly consistent with the embarrassing and largely unreported tuberculosis epidemic breaking out in London around about then. Unable to sleep for the sputum at my throat, the stuff frothing pink like candyfloss at the fair ... late one evening I got up, spat into the basin, and suddenly things took a dramatic turn for the worse.

According to the Internet, it turned out this was an oedema: a chamber of my heart had collapsed and died, would beat no more. I crawled under the covers, down the mineshaft ... everything washing in sepia as I peered back above the parapet at the room, floating away in one big coughing fit. Books lift off the shelf, a plant pot goes toppling. Dusty bricks go falling from the wall: I peer out on Steppe, jackals in long grasses, eagles and asps at dawn, the clock hand is spinning ... eventually spins out five days. Tough luck ... this was you. Five days lost: two hundred fifty quid.

The beginning of the end was when black mucous started coming out instead of sputum each morning and night. It was a shade of medieval: slaughtered cells that then turned blood red with a traffic light sequence set in motion. The mucous faded yellow, amber, and finally a green ... a delightful, gently marbled green, so that it was such joy to cough green at last, like coming from the throat ... coughing under control and emerging in a shade of comparative health. My head cleared out, the light came on ... good to go, I was back in business.

18 December – E10 – Docket #43

At the end of each day, I struck out of the city and made my way home, back to the unkempt sanity of a half-derelict house. One thing in London stayed with me all through the year ... another treasure from the marshes, that little band of life that held in the city. It was in a small strip of land, a grassless field full of broken water butts, horse shit and traffic cones ... five minutes from my front door and twenty from the alleged finance capital of the world.

In that corner of the city, a gypsy family had abandoned the road ... taken to a nearby house, and in that muddy, rutted quagmire, beneath a pylon, the family kept four sorry-looking horses. Passing by the field it always stank, less when the weather was cold, but a pong all the same: the stale smell of horsehair, hay and manure. There were times when I gulped it down, breathed it in like medication, as much as was possible. To me that smell seemed like just about the only thing in all London that actually existed honestly, in something resembling its true form ... that existed the same as it had done a thousand years earlier and would exist a thousand years into the future. The cosmetic shops doused papers in perfume, put them into litterbins on the pavement outside, so as to lure the people in by fragrance. The supermarkets with their bakery aroma dropped into the ventilation. I was daily hit by all of those fragrances, and then for twenty seconds, that smell became like an anchor to me. The city stank through and through, and yet those horses seemed to be the only thing that smelt of anything at all.

One evening I rode home with Two-Four, still postponing his photography trip to New York. As we reached the horses, he climbed from his bike, uprooted some tufts of grass, poked them through the fence. Green blades and pale, white ears of grass beckoned at them

… leaning in at large teeth as the animals trudged slow and heavy towards the fence, through the ruts of hard earth, their manes shaken and mouths reaching up. I remember how Two-Four, ordinarily so upbeat, gave a long sigh filled with the fatigue of central London. I felt guilty for the thought, but there was something reassuring, comforting in the moments Two-Four was down … a reminder that it wasn't just me, that it could happen to the best of us. I watched his breath, caught in cold, white light as he spoke, a cloud of mist, its wings spreading to lift away, turning from his mouth the sad words, *'Animals are so much nicer than humans.'*

23 December – E8 – Docket #44

Ten days before Christmas and a friend of a friend from the university called me up. Her name was Georgia, a girl I'd never known so well. To be honest, I'd always been a little put off by the size of her heart. Quaker, more wholesome than oats, she couldn't get over the need to do good. She was living at a house in Hackney, knew it was on my ride home, and with Christmas coming, she invited me to join her for carol singing with a group of friends. Carol singing was low on my list of things to do for Christmas, I hadn't sung a religious thing since primary school, wasn't enthusiastic to start doing so again. But she was insistent, and so kind-hearted that my stubbornness failed me.

I arrived after work, dropped my bag in a corner of the room. It was a large kitchen: wooden floors, an old broken Aga on one side, a large range on the other. On the hob, a pot of wine was mulling, oranges and bark floating at the surface, cinnamon in the air. There were six of them living there, renting from some landlord, paying-off her million-pound mortgage while she lived in Australia instead. In the kitchen I looked around to see entire families: streams of siblings who didn't hate one another, kept close, had voluntarily chosen to spend time together as adults. The kitchen was full: stacked with smiles, chatter and laughter … some elder brothers and sisters who had brought their children too, a toddler up on shoulders, a couple of prams parked to one side. Georgia was handing out carol sheets, gave me a big hug, grinned a rosy-cheeked grin. Tinsel falling from the top of her bob, she hooked an arm round the back of my neck and pulled me in … me, she, and a clutch of carol sheets, all embracing lovingly. '*Well done for coming, you … it's really nice to see you!*' And she kept on smiling as if she really meant it. I smiled back, warmed somehow as she urged me to eat something, handed me a bowl of raw carrots and celery. She scuttled on with her carol sheets, handing them out to the rest of the impromptu choir.

I look around myself: everyone is engaged in conversation, all I can really make out are the accents ... wall-to-wall in perfect elocution, long, rounded vowels and *A*'s the length of the bay windows. Everyone is smiling, they all look so damn happy. I shuffle through to the table at the centre of the kitchen, set with chopping boards covered in cheeses, a variety of shapes wrapped in wax, or sitting in small, wooden trays. Apples have been sliced up thin, there is a bowl of red cabbage, pickled onions, some homemade ceramic filled with redcurrant jam, a glass jar of homemade chutney ... handwritten label scrawled over it and stuck down, tiny illustrations at the corners: '*Marrow chutney - September 2010*'. I still don't understand why the British middle classes enjoy writing labels quite so much ... always plastered to their preserves and sloe gin. My best guess is that it helps them feel in control ... their own way of making sense of the universe.

A young boy with mittens hanging on his sleeves comes to the table beside me, the boy eye-height with the cheese board. He picks up the handle of a cheese knife with its curved blade, and I watch as he goes in for the Stilton, steadying himself with his other hand. Not more than eight years old and already a taste for bloody Stilton. He presses down a little, cuts through the block with an effort that shakes his arm when knife hits board: he flails, knocks over a bowl of radishes. Up into the air they fly, pink cue balls, bouncing to all angles. Pinballing, they shoot across the wooden floor with a hard, rumbling noise, the bowl bouncing down and up on its rattling plastic base. I hear the child let out an exclamation: '*Sorry, Daddy, I knocked over the radishes! I'm sorry.*' And his father turns with a smile, ruffles his son's hair as the boy squats down with a concerned expression. Stooped, the boy starts urgently retrieving radishes from across the floor ... shuffling forwards in his squat, small limbs grasping after the escaping balls of pink.

Nibbling on a wedge of cheese, I watch ... shake away a memory of my own childhood and look down at the carols. There are no jingle bells to be found, no decking halls with holly, not a Rudolph in sight, not for these guys ... none of the cheap, Merry Christmas tat ... they're singing in Latin! *Boar's head ... Lay thee low ... In the bleak midwinter ...* you have to be pretty cheerful about things to get excited about a song called 'Bleak Midwinter'. I'd never heard a single one of them, never even heard *of* a single one of them. A voice interrupts the chatter: calls out, sends out a boom. It's an uninhibited voice, born to be heard, the sort of voice that calls the first meeting after the apocalypse, encourages people to pick themselves up and rebuild. I resented those voices as much as I wouldn't have minded having one for myself.

The room is divided up: men and women, even arranged in order of voice, tenor to bass. We weren't just singing carols, we were practising too, hitting notes ... apparently they'd been rehearsing since November. There was no stopping them, was nothing they would not do in the name of wholesome ... absolute fiends, complete and ruthless junkies of emotional nourishment. We sing our carols: me on the end of the row, two-thirds of my lungs and diaphragm up for it and engaged, the remainder holding back, self-conscious. They all sing so well, so organised and in tune, but still ... I don't get it ... the whole thing seems like a lot of trouble to go to, just to stand around a kitchen and sing at one another. Half an hour of carols later and the same voice booms out again: '*OK, guys ... I think that's enough!*'

I'd had a couple of mugs of mulled wine by then, loosened up, become a bit more sanguine. Was it over already? Fairly painless in the end ... perhaps I'll come back next year even ... tradition not so bad after all. Everyone fetches coats, children are loaded into prams, the destinations are called out: '*We'll go up the road ... we'll hit Wayman Court first ... then the George, the Spurstowe.*'

Jesus! They weren't ... but they weren't going to... surely not? They couldn't have been *that* crazy. Holy crap. They were taking it outside. We were going to *hit* pubs with carol singing, they talked as if it were armed robbery! We were going to open our lungs and do the whole thing in public. Had they no shame?

There was no stopping them … they wouldn't see reason, nobody had told them the body public was done for, Thatcher and the death of the community had passed them right by, been left in the last century. There must have been thirty of us all in all, out on the street and even the bloody children are singing away in Latin, tugging the sleeve of a parent and insisting that we simply must sing 'Boar's Head' at the first opportunity. Everyone is dressed up for the night … a couple of the girls have gone to the trouble of putting batteries in their hoods and fairy lights over their shoulders. Each one of the troop stomps along under so much wool … wool wrapped round necks and heads, shawls, the collars of their jackets and the hem of their boots. They were garishly well-prepared, sheep shivering across the world in order to keep that lot warm. I was loath to admit it but the whole thing came to me as pretty solid evidence for why proles had always needed a few bourgeois to help get things done.

We march off down the road: a mob of good intention, humming and whistling … the drum of sturdy footwear keeping pace. The children totter on with paper lanterns, snatches of conversation coming from their tiny lungs: '*So we can't set off the flying lanterns this year, because they cause fires at recycling places?*' Some of the older children are holding jam jars with candles in, tied by chicken wire on the end of garden canes … the flame illuminates faces with a red glow, casting dark shadows round the nostrils. I bump along, clueless at what right or reason they'd all found to be so upbeat about absolutely everything. Suddenly, someone calls a halt, calls a hush, proceed with caution! We arrive at the first house, the court where they had lived previously. We are called to a whisper as we make our way inside, so that the first sound of our arrival will be the song itself. The courtyard, 1960s social housing, stands around us on all four sides: a few shrubs, balconies hanging above, penitentiary-style. The first female voices open up:

> *'The boar's head in hand bring I, Bedeck'd*
> *with bays and rosemary...'*

The children delight, they beam ... the choir begins to clap out tune, the candles light up faces, the children looking like angels and the adults still looking exactly like children: children with beards, with spectacles, some of them even with grey hair and wrinkles, but they're all children, none of them tainted by life, so full with hope and love. We burst to song:

> *'...Our steward hath provided this, In honour of the King*
> *of Bliss ... Caput apri defero, Reddens laudes Domino!'*

Foot stamping starts up, in tune with the claps, faces glowing once with candlelight and twice with joy. Slowly it starts ... the housing estate stirs, people begin coming out to balconies above. An old lady appears, wrapped in a dressing gown, wringing first at her hands, and then at her shoulders. She embraces herself, looking every bit like she is about to fall into tears ... as if life is suddenly perfect, as if nothing bad has ever happened: the Second World War a distant memory, her husband and friends not dead after all. Doors open in front of us, a man comes out to see what all the fuss is about, stands square-on in the doorway, the exploding drama and gunfire of his television screen behind him in the front room. His face softens as he folds his arms to lean against the doorframe. A young girl rushes to his side, she hides behind a leg, clutching at it as she watches, all starry-eyed and glittering.

They clapped, they shouted thanks as we left ... I hadn't heard *'God bless you'* said so many times since cancer got my grandmother. We walked the streets of Hackney, singing Christmas carols that almost nobody had ever heard before. And yet my word ... what fucking happiness it seemed to bring. A woman came out of her house with a tray of mince pies she'd baked, homemade mincemeat even: the things tasted awful, all orange peel and no fruit but that was besides the point right then, milk of human kindness was boiling over! We walked into pubs, exploding into song, jubilant to the last and the punters absolutely terrified. They thought we were after their wallets, collecting for charity! Either that or religious loons. A voice booms out, out of the choir: '*We're not Christians and we don't want your money!*' The room relaxes, some old men even start to smile, '*A long time since I've seen anything like it.*' A woman grabs up the hand of the man sitting next to her, as if the warmth of the scene made her fall in love a little, in love with that hopeless lug all over again. We shuffle for the door, traipsing the streets, flytipping Christmas cheer ... human spirit dribbling out behind us, rattling like tin cans through the alleys.

Hours later and most of us at least half-drunk, walking back to the house, I find myself next to Georgia. She talks to me about her work: how she's going from one job to the next, '*environmental consultancy*' the title she had given to her own predicament of no idea where the next wages were coming from. Together we walk back down the street, bringing up the rear ... separated a little from the rest of the group. She asks about couriering and how it's going. She doesn't flinch, doesn't stir when I tell her about it ... neither does she make a romance of it, doesn't draw the conclusion of the free spirit that so many others had always jumped to. We talk about our backgrounds, she from the countryside, from Shropshire, bucolic. Me from the Midlands, post-industrial, decline. She asks about my family, my brothers and sisters, the jobs my parents worked. I return each of her questions, send them her way as we get to know one another. I ask about her parents, she looks at me a moment, a gaze that doesn't want to talk about it. I watch wide, innocent eyes, curly hair coming out of her hat with mistletoe sticking in it. She answers

in a deep breath ... swallows hopeless, absent, the only time the life
left her face. She looks round at me, 'My mother's a carer ... my
father died ... last year.'

And I felt a pang so sad, to see her, so full of warmth until you
got a glimpse of the grief she'd suffered. She was doing her best to
survive upbeat, spirit all intact until you made her mention the thing
itself. I wish that at all times we could see the hurt we all suffer, the
pain we rise above ... be made aware how hard it is in those lives
behind the faces that pass us on the streets. That night something
changed in me, I've joked with them since, said that lot cured me
of the class system. With their cheer and their indiscriminate love,
there was no doubting it ... we were on the same side.

Epilogue

It never ends ... the energy takes new forms and you just reach the point at which one story stops. We all went on making our deliveries, clients squeezing the companies on to lower prices that were soon passed on to our diminishing wages. In time, from Westminster, the politicians announced the economy was fixed ... we were said to be living Recovery, even if it seemed not so very different to Recession, or even those boom years we'd apparently enjoyed before it. The wider economy had learned from that old couriering technicality, and self-employed was made the new term for unemployed. The government started paying public benefits to people forced to work for free for private companies making private profits ... they called them jobs all the same and stuck them in the official statistics. People accepted redundancies, lay-offs and 10 per cent pay cuts that, eventually, once enough had piled up, translated into a 0.25 per cent growth in The Economy. Apparently it had been a good trade, and it was as if people believed in the paper and figures to such extent that growth was higher than any ideals that remained. Thinksters talked with increasing fervour about injustice, but precisely, you felt, because they no longer believed the challenges surmountable ... for so many it was as if change had become an identity more than a project or a goal.

None of that seemed so important to me any longer: it was only the umbrella above, the top of a hierarchy people needed for their sense of security. The more brutal it was, the safer they felt, with scarcely a thought that all along it had been theirs to change themselves. As far as I was concerned, it all seemed bizarrely distant for once ... the real world was out on the roads, in the loading bays and amongst the messengers ... the messengers ... but don't let me forget about them. I should tell you what became of the road family I'd once joined.

When the quiet of January really hit, Two-Four left the circuit, took up full-time work making his mirror balls. Mirror Ball Paul was the name of the guy in Islington he'd started working for, and Two-Four laughed that Mirror Ball Paul was the biggest name in international mirror balls, had a near monopoly on the entire world market. Nightclubs and casinos from Singapore to Vegas were having mirror balls assembled … glass pressed into putty … from a basement in north London.

Three-Six, unlucky as ever, ended up in the nick. We all heard how it happened. Some punk nudged his car into him on Shoreditch High Street, another of those thousand-kilo punches. Eight-Seven had been on hand to watch it unfold, though, not so concerned about public order as I'd been, did nothing to stop Three-Six punching the driver straight in the face. Eight-Seven came on the radio after the action, said he was picking up the abandoned dockets, watching Three-Six being loaded by police into the back of a riot van.

Seven-One wasn't much more fortunate … started losing his grip on his mortgage and whatever sense of responsibility it had once given him. The man wasn't one for getting too put out by that sort of detail, and so he simply relinquished his sense of future, went back to life lived one day and night at a time. I remember finding him late spring, a Monday morning beside the half-century-old tea stand near St Leonard's Church. Seven-One was nursing a hot drink, crouched over the Styrofoam as if to catch the escaping warmth. His face was bruised yellow, his eyebrow swollen, burst open and then sewn back together again in black thread. I couldn't see the cracked ribs that stopped him laughing with me, but the story had started with drinks at the pub, acid at a house party, some snuff – indicated with a wiping of the nose – '*So as to keep going like.*' It all ended with a ride home next morning: sleepless, fermenting, stitching a ride as he gripped the metal puck of a skip truck, holding on as the truck pulled him directly into a pothole, Seven-One landing on his face in the road.

A fortnight later he was telling me almost the same story ... the only difference that he'd been riding up the inside of traffic when a door had opened on him, thrust him off the bicycle and into a lamp post. Seven-One was hapless all right, embraced ever more hedonism as his mortgage finally unravelled. Come the end of summer he'd smashed his arms in two, both of them done in falling down a lift shaft as he broke in to open a squat on Saffron Hill. He was left with screws in his bones and scars crawling all round his arms and shoulders, twisting back and forth like fat, purple tapeworms. After that, Seven-One couldn't hold his own weight up on the handlebars. Instead, he found work in Bristol shipyards: driving from site to site, inspecting fire drill protocol. He was all set to leave London the day after Notting Hill Carnival, but still drunk from the night before, police pulling everyone over for breathalysing on the road out of the city. They got Seven-One straight out of the car, a tube in the mouth and a moment later a three-year driving ban ... farewell to the licence that was needed for the Bristol job. I'm sure I'll see Seven-One again, once his arms have healed and he can hold himself upright.

Four carried on his old ways, ogling ladies by day and getting sodomised by night. His knees started playing up more and more as age got into him, and the pain especially bad over the cold of winter. He started trying to save money ... £4,000 to do the training that would get him a job as an attendant on the Underground. He's still saving, but I keep seeing him on the roads ... know he'll never make it.

Six ... Six was half-a-happy ending. He'd always loved my cycle round the world, often told me he'd like to do something similar himself. To be honest, I'd taken his ambitions with a pinch of salt, but as time passed, it seemed Six was genuinely preparing to pedal into Europe and prove me wrong. He kicked his cocaine, kept to himself, saved some money and then saved a little more. He saw out his parole period, got a passport and then bank account, and one evening in May we had a goodbye drink to mark his leaving. A few of us turned up to wish Six so long, sombre partings and solemn words about who knew how long it would be before we saw one another next, whether this night was goodbye forever. Ten days later he was back. The Eurostar had left him in Paris without a word of French, surrounded by rude Parisians and Six having never before set foot outside Barking. Disillusioned, he had decided against cycling anywhere, got a train direct to Amsterdam, where a prostitute talked him into love until his money was gone and he was on the next train back to London. On the circuit we heard the controllers joke: '*He's not Phileas Fogg … he's Phileas Flop!*' Six was in spirits not too bad as a result. He smiled, broad and peaceful, he smiled as he said it to me, '*Y'know what, Two-Two … at least I gave it a go … at least I found out it wasn't for me.*' And he was dead right.

And what of me? I suppose I got better, I'm better now … but it took time for me to be able to say that, to shrug off the idea that the world had to be changed and that the burden of doing so was mine alone. 'Depression is like you're drowning … only you can see everyone around you breathing.' That was what some German wrote once, but it never really came like that to me. For starters I'd never really thought myself depressed … looking around I still can't imagine a more natural way of feeling about much of what goes on in our name. Depression seems not much more than a medical term for paying attention. I only used a word like *depression* to help treat it like an illness, a condition I'd contracted and could one day be rid of again. Writing it that way makes sense, but I suppose that's not really it either. You don't contract depression, just like you never get cured of it. Slowly you realise you're miserable, or numb, or something like it … and then, slowly, one day … you realise you're OK. My troubles were generally of the optimistic variety anyway. We could make so much more of this place … could be so much nicer to one another. I knew how good it all could be if only a few more of us had realised, or else dared to realise, or cared. That was what always got me down … 'One day we'll all die … and what a circus! … that alone should make us love one another, but it doesn't.'

I came to value my writing, I suppose. Regardless of what anyone else made of it, I realised I probably owed my sanity to it, to that and the bicycle. I kept on scribbling even after they'd all rejected my manuscript flat. '*Why do you bother with this whole writing malarkey? … It just doesn't look like it'll come to anything*' was how people phrased it. But asking me why I wrote was the same as asking one of those Steppe dung beetles why they rolled up balls of dusty shit and then bored down underground with the results. Bukowski's poem didn't put it far wrong: we're born into this, the impossibility of being human, and writing the nearest I'd ever found to a sane response. I'll take it over the biomedical options the doctors go meting out at every opportunity.

Instead of my old despondency, I learned to nurture the moments of hope instead, stoked my battery with them. The times when I'd see an adult taking a nap in a park, a side of newspaper for their mattress upon the grass. So too when I found someone peacefully reading a book, a bicycle propped beside the bench where they sat. Those sights would make me believe a little again, came as important reminders of what simple creatures we actually were. A council installed a bicycle pump in a bollard, a fire pit in a new park, and as campaign groups began demanding taxes on financial speculation, there also emerged energy companies that generated only renewables. None of it had ever seemed so much to ask … some politics with a heart for people's lives, a sense that we all deserved something better. All in all I calmed down, checked out … I suppose I had to. I've still got my spirit, but somehow my engines cooled. Two-Nine paid me a nice compliment once, after my return from the world. She'd read my writing, liked the stories, '*You're a great courier,*

Two-Two,' she laughed, scratched her head. *'But I don't know ... you'd be a much better something else!'*

Figuring out what that might have been still felt a taller order. Delivering envelopes and parcels can be invitingly simple amidst the pantomime turning all around. The constant happiness, it's not for me, and sometimes the future shines so unbearably bright. People still think I'm cynical, they always will, but they're wrong – I'm such a terrifying idealist, and I've so much love for all us humans, blemishes and all. One day we'll build something new, and something better, but be sure it's going to take a monumental patience. The keys to the banks, newspapers, the politicians' offices ... they're mostly in the hands of people too smart to be caught believing in change and too comfortable to need to. We'll win them round, in time, and a century later they'll be claiming our struggles as their own, but that's just the way it goes. Either way ... let it be ... that's enough out of me for now. Whatever comes next, down on the roads of London, each of us went about making our own ways through the world. We all got on with life. Or else ... perhaps ... life got on with us.